FAMILY LAW IN PERSPECTIVE

THIRD EDITION

By

WALTER WADLINGTON
James Madison Professor Emeritus
University of Virginia

RAYMOND C. O'BRIEN
Professor of Law
The Catholic University of America

CONCEPTS AND INSIGHTS SERIES®

FOUNDATION PRESS
2012

THOMSON REUTERS™

© 2001, 2007 FOUNDATION PRESS
© 2012 By THOMSON REUTERS/FOUNDATION PRESS

    1 New York Plaza, 34th Floor

    New York, NY 10004

    Phone Toll Free 1–877–888–1330

    Fax 646–424–5201

    foundation–press.com

Printed in the United States of America

ISBN 978–1–60930–045–6

Mat #41179007

"The text is old, the orator too green."
— The Taming of the Shrew, William Shakespeare

WW
Ruth Miller Hardie

— on the occasion of her 100th birthday

ROB
Michael & Dawn Lovelace

— because they are family

INTRODUCTION TO THE THIRD EDITION

The fact that this book is now in its third edition confirms the evolving status of family law. Judicial and legislative developments at the state, national, and international levels have continued unabated, and based on the research that contributed to this edition, the trend will continue. The goal of this book is to offer a perspective, which for the authors, means a vision or discernment into what we consider to be among the most important issues arising in family law at the start of the twenty-first century. Among these issues are the multiplicity of family arrangements in society. There continues to be a rise in nonmarital cohabitation, and in single-parent households. The debate over the validity of same-sex marriage continues, with federal benefits an ultimate goal. But the debate over same-sex marriage heightens the importance attributed to marriage; similar status arrangements such as domestic partnerships and civil unions remain viable. And the rights of children continue to occupy a central focus in state, national, and international perspective. This edition discusses the changes in such issues as custody relocation, imputing income for child support guidelines, foster care and termination of parental rights, and the continuing phenomenon of intercountry adoptions. Both in the issuance of custody and support orders, and in their enforcement, the nation has been assimilated into an international community with all that this implies.

This edition seeks to capture a bit of the changes that have occurred in the laws pertaining to assisted reproductive technology. The establishment of parenthood has evolved significantly. In just one area, posthumous conception, cases seeking to establish the rights of the parties struggle to forge a new consensus out of old statutes, all the while suggesting the need for legislative guidance. This issue of posthumous conception, as well as others, prompt concerns over religious free exercise exemption from options demanded by a secularizing nation. Litigation over abortion, grounds for divorce, and parental rights over children illustrate the debate. Because this book offers a perspective, we hope that it also contributes to an appreciation of what has occurred in the past, thereby providing some perspective on what will surely evolve.

Because this book is intended to be used by American law school students, and is purposefully concise, we have provided a mechanism by which students may discover additional information. The footnotes offer links to cases and Internet reference; there is also a Table of Internet Sites to provide further information. We also recommend DOMESTIC RELATIONS: CASES AND MATERIALS (6th ed. 2007), and a compilation of statutes and short synopsis, FAMILY LAW STATUTES: SELECTED UNIFORM LAWS, FEDERAL STATUTES, STATE STATUTES, AND INTERNATIONAL TREATIES (4th ed. 2011). Both of these books are written by the same authors. As always, we welcome your comments and hope that these materials assist you in any discussion of family law. And we extend our sincere appreciation to Daniel McGraw for his research and editorial assistance.

WALTER WADLINGTON
wjwadlington@gmail.com
RAYMOND C. O'BRIEN
obrien@law.edu

NOTE ON EDITING AND ACKNOWLEDGMENT

Footnotes begin numbering at the start of each chapter. Several cases include only a Westlaw citation due to the fact that no other citation was available at the time the book went to press. In other cases, Westlaw reported that the citation would not be available in the National Reporter system or some other official reporter. In some places, due to space limitations, we have included references to materials in the text, rather than create a footnote. We express our appreciation to the National Conference of Commissioners on Uniform State Laws for permission to reprint the text of selected Uniform Laws.

SUMMARY OF CONTENTS

TABLE OF CONTENTS

FAMILY LAW IN PERSPECTIVE

Chapter 1

Conceptualizing Modern Family Law

I. Defining Family Law

The second decade of the twenty-first century continues trends that were nascent in the final decades of the previous century. For example, nonmarital and premarital contracting between adults, advancements in assisted reproductive technology, genetic and de-facto parenthood, parental custody presumptions, and expanding definitions of what constitutes property for both division and support obligations. These are a few of the many trends that were generated by societal, constitutional, and technological changes that occurred gradually after the end of the Second World War and continue today. Certainly, the evolution of personal communications, media, and demographics accelerated these rapid changes, at least in part. Previously, taken as a base measure, family law consisted of marriage, divorce, annulment, alimony, and child custody. The existing law was state specific, static, and predictable, promoting the objective values of society rather than the subjective wishes of individuals.

Today, family law bears faint resemblance to the hodgepodge of state regulations that constituted the earlier conceptualizations of family relationships. Initially, state regulation was the norm in the United States not only because of the federal system, but also because families were consistently validated by local views of propriety, societal norms pertinent to an individual state. These local views provided a basis for marriage, annulment, divorce, or defined the best interest of a child. Also, local hegemony was aided by federal abstention. From the middle of the nineteenth century there developed a federal exception to family law jurisdiction, a practice that continues today, based partly on a decision by Congress to voluntarily divest the federal courts of power to issue divorce, alimony, or child custody decrees. This abstention power is granted to Congress under Article III of the Constitution.[1] State regulation of family law went unchallenged until plaintiffs–or defendants–sought redress from state prohibitions through recourse to the federal Constitution. One of the earliest cases involved

---

1. Ankenbrandt v. Richards, 504 U.S. 689, 698–700 (1992).

1

polygamy. In *Reynolds v. United States,*[2] the Supreme Court reject-ed an asserted First Amendment argument based on freedom of religion, when a defendant sought redress from a state law crimi-nalizing his polygamous marriage. Instead, the Court upheld the right of the Territory of Utah to define marriage as monogamous. But this constitutional challenge to state family law presaged what would occur nearly one-hundred years later when equal protection, due process, and privacy rights, derived from the federal Constitu-tion, would be the basis of many changes in family law.

As state family laws were challenged under provisions of the federal Constitution, there was a concomitant movement by Con-gress to enact various federal laws that impacted the family. For example, in order to safeguard the integrity of Native American culture and identity, Congress enacted the Indian Child Welfare Act of 1978. To protect and enforce child custody determinations, Congress enacted the Parental Kidnapping Prevention Act in 1980, the International Child Abduction Remedies Act in 1988, and the International Parental Kidnapping Crime Act of 1993. Enforcement of child support was sought through enactment of the Child Sup-port Recovery Act of 1992, protection of the traditional definition of marriage through the Defense of Marriage Act of 1996, protection against abusive relationships was sought with passage of the Vio-lence Against Women Act, and a ban on partial-birth abortion was enacted through the Partial–Birth Abortion Ban Act of 2003. These federal statutes form only part of the panoply of federal laws pertinent to families, laws that have increased in number and scope, evidencing a significant federal presence.[3]

There are reasons why the definition of family law has shifted from being state-specific. The mobility of the nation's population mitigates the prerogatives of community standards. Likewise, infor-mation collection and dissemination has shifted from local to na-tional, and even international. Correspondingly, uniform state laws have been promulgated and recommended to states by focus groups such as the National Conference of Commissioners on Uniform State Laws. Likewise, academic enterprises such as the American Law Institute offer recommendations and perspectives meant for national and international application. If a state adopts a uniform law in whole or in part, a commonality results among the states, and this practice has increased dramatically in the last five decades.

---

2. 98 U.S. 145 (1878).

3. For a comprehensive description, including provisions of various federal, state, uniform, and international stat-utes, *see* WALTER WADLINGTON & RAYMOND

C. O'BRIEN, FAMILY LAW STATUTES: SELECT-ED UNIFORM LAWS, FEDERAL STATUTES, STATE STATUTES, AND INTERNATIONAL TREATIES (4th ed. 2011).

Examples of such uniform laws include the Uniform Marriage and Divorce Act, one of the first uniform acts. When promulgated in the 1970s, the act had a significant impact on states seeking to respond to federal constitutional challenges pertaining to paternity, child custody, marriage, and divorce. Then, the Uniform Adoption Act prompted states to implement national standards pertaining to the adoption of children. Also, the Uniform Parentage Act and then the Uniform Status of Children of Assisted Conception Act sought to keep pace with the rapid technological changes occurring in the area of assisted reproductive technology.

While there are many uniform acts pertaining to family law, two specific acts illustrate the connection between these newcomers to family law and the increasing involvement of federal regulations. One act is the Uniform Child Custody Jurisdiction and Enforcement Act, and the other is the Uniform Interstate Family Support Act. While the former pertains to child custody enforcement, and the latter to child and spousal support, each state has adopted the uniform acts as a prerequisite to receipt of federal assistance for children under the federal Personal Responsibility and Work Opportunity Reconciliation Act of 1996. In order to ensure better state standards for the establishment of paternity and the enforcement of child support obligations by parents, Congress initiated efforts at the federal level, thereby illustrating the preemptive authority of federal control. The preemptive authority of Congress implemented uniform acts, thereby replacing what had heretofore been the norm in family law: individual state control.

A final element in any expanding definition of family law must include recognition of an increasing number of international treaties, either providing for international enforcement of current federal laws, or providing for cooperation in the promotion of a specific international endeavor. For example, the Uniform Child Custody Jurisdiction and Enforcement Act specifically refers to enforcing an order for the return of a child made under an international treaty, the Hague Convention on the Civil Aspects of International Child Abduction. Similarly, international adoptions are referenced in the Uniform Adoption Act; adoption is also referenced in the Hague Convention on Protection of Children and Cooperation in Respect of Intercountry Adoption. Increasingly, Congress discusses initiatives relating to international protection of children, recognition of foreign marriages, international prosecution for violence against women, and enforcement of support obligations.[4] These examples

4. For a compilation of international statutes and treaties, *see* D. MARIANNE BLAIR & MERLE H. WEINER, INTERNATIONAL FAMILY LAW: CONVENTIONS, STATUTES, AND REGULATORY MATERIALS (2003).

are but a few illustrations of the instances of when the definition of family law includes international applications. As with federal statutes and uniform laws, the demographic shifts and expanding communications networks will surely bring more international applications of an expanding definition of family law.

II. Private Ordering

As we have described, the trend in the evolution of family law has been away from community standards and towards national and then international regulations. The enactment of federal, then uniform, then international laws evidenced this. But there is another trend that has gained momentum as family law shifted from local to national and international standards. This is the trend towards private ordering among adults. While difficult to define, private ordering is best evidenced in a phrase used by Associate Justice Brennan in his majority opinion in *Eisenstadt v. Baird,*[5] writing that "if the right of privacy means anything, it is the right of the *individual,* married or single, to be free from unwarranted governmental intrusion ... " Individual liberty, based on the right to privacy enumerated in the 1965 *Griswold* decision, would be the basis of a famous palimony decision from the Supreme Court of California in 1976, the *Marvin* decision. There, the state's highest court announced that two unmarried adults could enter into a valid contract involving sexual intimacy because such a contract met their common expectations. Rejecting any prohibition based on public policy, the court provided for public enforcement of private ordering.[6] More recently, the shift towards private ordering found further support in Associate Justice Kennedy's 2003 decision of *Lawrence v. Texas,*[7] writing that "liberty presumes an autonomy of self that includes freedom of thought, belief, expression, and certain intimate conduct." And there are many other examples of state recognition of privately ordered family relationships.

The substance of private ordering is best illustrated through examples of family arrangements that would have been inconceivable five or six decades ago. Examples include the following: nonmarital contracts, premarital agreements, same sex marriage, defacto parenthood, human embryo transfer, and standby adoption. These are but a few examples, typifying when adults may, through compe-

---

5. 405 U.S. 438, 453 (1972) (emphasis added).

6. *See* Marvin v. Marvin, 18 Cal.3d 660, 557 P.2d 106, 134 Cal.Rptr. 815 (1976).

7. 539 U.S. 558, 562 123 S.Ct. 2472, 2475, 156 L.Ed.2d 508 (2003).

tent and fully informed decisions, order their own affairs to provide status, obligation, and termination with little or no regard to state status interference. While there is little notoriety involving human embryo transfers or standby adoption statutes, media attention has provided extensive coverage to nonmarital cohabitation obligation enforcement. Certainly the prevalence of nonmarital cohabitation provided the impetus to recognizing domestic partnership benefits for nonmarital partners. Eventually, reciprocal beneficiaries evolved, and then civil unions were provided. But same sex marriage, emphasized by significant media attention, illustrates the contest between an established definition of marriage, and the contrasting intent of two adults seeking to change that definition so as to derive all of the benefits of marriage. Perhaps more than any other issue, the litigation and legislation seeking to allow adults to "self order" the traditional definition of marriage illustrates and symbolizes the momentum of private ordering in the conceptualization of modern family law.

III. Assisted Reproductive Technology

Historically, scientific advances, as applied to family law, focused on conception and contraception. Indeed, commentators credit the refinement in technological birth control devices during the 1950s as contributing to a sexual revolution. At a minimum these advances contributed to greater self-ordering. Eventually, scientific advancements progressed, allowing for a more accurate assessment of paternity, and today, even maternity. But as the technology advanced, traditional common law and statutory regulations pertaining to family law have been strained; faced with unique and difficult choices, the law sputters along seeking to avoid ethical dilemmas and provide for the best possible solutions.[8] Increasingly today, state and federal law is seeking to balance the rights of a child—or potential child—against the competing interests of adults seeking to assert paternity, maternity, or ownership.[9] Issues arise in the context of artificial insemination, in vitro fertilization, surrogacy contracts, and nascent efforts to regulate fertility clinics.

Family law disputes occur as persons or couples contest ownership of eggs, sperm or embryos. Because of scientific advances, cryopreservation permits any or all of these human products to be preserved, allowing for conception or birth long into the future.

---

8. *See generally*, HEALTH LAW BIOETHICS (Sandra H. Johnson, Joan H. Krause, Richard S. Saver, and Robin Fretwell Wilson eds, 2009).

9. *See generally* Marsha Garrison, *Law Making for Baby Making: An Interpretive Approach to the Determination of Legal Parentage*, 113 HARV. L. REV. 835 (2000).

Because of cryopreservation, issues arise as to custody rights, inheritance rights, and whether or not the products should be considered as property subject to division upon divorce. In recent years disputes have also arisen in reference to whether a child or children born long after the death of the decedent gamete provider, through a procedure termed posthumous conception, may inherit from the estate of the decedent provider. Most often the dispute arises in the context of whether the child should be able to derive Social Security benefits from the decedent parent, such benefits are statutorily restricted to the minor children of the decedent. Few states have addressed the issue of posthumous conception with a comprehensive statute, but most states have simply deferred the matter to the state's legislature.[10] Courts also look to the state legislatures to address whether the gametes should be considered as property for division, or treated as persons entitled to custody, when divorce or separation occurs. And if conception or birth occurs due to a contractual arrangement initiated by two persons, neither of whom made any genetic contribution to the birth, should these contractual partners be entitled or responsible for parenthood?

Conceptualizing the future of family law must include a careful review of the parameters of assisted reproductive technology. As illustrated with the issue of posthumous conception, there are few statutory guidelines and issues will persist with further technological advances. The laws pertaining to distribution of property at death, testamentary laws, have made significant advances and should provide models for courts and legislatures seeking to address issues of paternity, maternity, division at divorce, and custody during periods of cryopreservation.[11] Likewise, the parameters of gestational agreements must be addressed,[12] and far more needs to be done to monitor facilities assisting with fertility and gamete storage.

IV. The Best Interest of the Child

In 2000, the Supreme Court ruled that parents have a liberty interest under the Fourteenth Amendment in the care, custody, and control of their children.[13] The majority opinion traces the

---

10. *See generally*, Raymond C. O'Brien, *The Momentum of Posthumous Conception: A Model Act*, 25 J. CONTEMP. HEALTH L. & POL'Y 332 (2009).

11. *See, e.g.*, UNIF. PROBATE CODE § 2–120 (2010).

12. *See, e.g.*, UNIF. PARENTAGE ACT 9B U.L.A. 295 et seq. (amended 2002); UNIF. STATUS OF ASSISTED CONCEPTION ACT 9C U.L.A. 363 et seq. (2001); UNIF. PROBATE CODE § 2–121 (2010).

13. Troxel v. Granville, 530 U.S. 57, 120 S.Ct. 2054, 147 L.Ed.2d 49 (2000).

lengthy jurisprudence sustaining the fundamental right of parent to raise his or her child. But the same decision also notes the extensive demographic changes that have occurred in the context of families with children: more than a quarter of all children under eighteen live with a single parent. But there are additional systemic problems that the decision does not address: Large numbers of children remain in foster care while waiting for parents to cooperate with state efforts to reunify the family; increasing numbers of parents wish to relocate with children, change the children's names, or to surrender their children to the state or to another person because they, the parents, are unable to care for them. In addition, there remain many instances of child abuse, neglect, and abandonment.

Increasingly, courts and legislatures seek to provide for the best interest of a child, but remain within the parameters of the constitutional rights of a parent to raise that child. The balance is precipitous, but the demographics and the well-established need to provide permanence for a child have initiated some dramatic innovations that are now part of family law. At the federal level there are a number of innovations. The Adoption and Safe Families Act of 1997 illustrates a shift in government attitudes. Under the terms of the statute, if a child remains in foster care for fifteen of the most recent twenty-two months, the state must file a petition to terminate parental rights. Also, the Parental Kidnapping Prevention Act of 1980 seeks to provide permanence for a child through enforcement of state custody decrees across state lines. And there is a similar provision relating to international protection and enforcement. There is also a federal Income Tax Credit for Adoption Assistance, the objective of which is to promote permanence for a child through adoption.

At the state level several statutes seek to provide for the best interest of the child. Some states have initiated a Safe Haven Law, whereby a newborn infant may be left at a designated location and a presumption arises that the parent has consented to termination of parental rights. The parent may remain anonymous and will suffer no legal consequences. Also, some states statutorily appoint special advocates for children, and child abuse reporting statutes have been enhanced to better monitor the continuing well-being of children. Likewise, some states have enacted statutes to provide expanded consent to medical care for minors, and others have entered into interstate compacts on the placement of children, and a few have standby guardianship statutes. A few states permit open adoption, allowing for a child to retain contact with his or her genetic parents after adoption by another family.[14] Plus, some states promote adoption of special needs children through subsidized adoption statutes. And finally, long-term foster care or permanent foster care statutes and programs seek to provide permanency for a child who is difficult to place because of special needs.

Consistent with the fundamental rights of a parent in his or her child, there are increasing instances of when the government has initiated family law efforts to provide for the best interest of the child. All of these efforts, plus the other elements listed in this chapter, will be discussed in far greater detail as we progress through the remaining chapters of this book.

---

14. *See, e.g.*, N.M. STAT. ANN. § 32A–5–35 (West 2010).

Chapter 2

Marital And Postmarital Contracting

I. The Right to Contract

The ability of adults to enter into enforceable contracts is a premise upon which society is structured. Nonetheless, in matters pertaining to family law, perhaps because the state was often present as a third party, the ability of adults to contract was curtailed in some instances. These instances involved, for example, contracts in which sexual activity was occasioned, or when the contracting adults were in a confidential relationship, or when the best interest of a child was the paramount concern. Prevailing views of public policy limited contracting. For example, prior to the 1970s, couples were prevented from enforcing oral or written contracts involving nonmarital cohabitation arrangements. So too, gender stereotyping casting women as inferior to men in matters of finance and education made contracting between genders precarious to predict. Women were viewed as weaker due to inexperience, hence any contract involving a woman with a man was presumptively suspicious, if not invalid. And even between adults married to one another, the ability of a wife to contract with third parties without the permission of her husband was rare.

In spite of the tenuous viability of many contracts involving family law issues, courts had specific instances when tort law was used to compensate adults for certain contract-sounding claims, such as a breach of promise to marry. These "heart balm" causes of actions were meant to soothe the broken hearts of those abandoned by a suitor after the suitor made extended and reliable promises of a marriage to occur in the future. Tort damages were assigned to the victim based upon "contused feelings, sentimental bruises, blighted affections ... and for the loss of the pecuniary and social advantages which the marriage offered."[1] Concomitantly, court orders were issued specifying the return of engagement rings and other items of significant value given in contemplation of the purported marriage. Premised upon an implied contract of marriage, the return of the ring or valued item was required once the marriage failed to occur. As family law progressed, with the exception of a few holdouts such as North Carolina,[2] states began abolishing these torts by statute.

---

1. Piccininni v. Hajus, 429 A.2d 886, 888 (Conn. 1980).

2. *See, e.g.,* Brown v. Ellis, 678 S.E.2d 222 (N.C. 2009).

During the last decades of the twentieth century the scope of contracting between adults in the context of family law expanded expeditiously. Public policy shifted radically. Hindsight allows us to posit definite factors that contributed to the enhanced capability of adults to enter into enforceable, mutually agreeable, contracts. The first factor is the increasing economic independence of women. In spite of persistent disparity with male counterparts, women have experienced increased employment opportunities, judicial and legislative guarantees of equality, and autonomy in contracting and other related family law issues.

The second factor is globalization. Mass media has lessened regional identities and mores, but there is also greater access to information, extended community involvement, and hence, ratification of divergent points of view and behaviors. Associated with this factor is the mobility of the population in the modern age: the national and international migrations that shape the population. Throughout this book we will discuss illustrations of this, including international custody disputes, international support enforcement, and intercountry adoptions.

And with the greater awareness of options, there developed a third factor: adults establishing functional family arrangements. Heretofore, families were most often grouped according to form: relationships by blood, marriage, or adoption. But increasing numbers of persons began to establish family-style arrangements based on function, that is, families that existed because they functioned as such, without regard to blood, marriage, or adoption. Census statistics testified—and continue to testify—to the growing number of function families, prompting judicial recognition and status.[3] These function families include nonmarital cohabitation by opposite-sex and same-sex adult couples. And in order to provide a modicum of economic protection for the expectations of the individual parties, courts developed theories of implied contract, equitable estoppel, and quantum meruit. This trend to provide protection for the expectations of function families evolved, eventually prompting businesses and communities to provide a measure of status through domestic partnerships, then reciprocal beneficiaries. All functional families originated in the contracting ability of adult parties to self-order their lives and their assets. We will discuss functional families further in Chapter 4, Contractual Alternatives to Marriage, *infra*.

---

3. *See, e.g.*, Marvin v. Marvin, 557 P.2d 106 (Cal. 1976) (validating non-marital contracts between a cohabitating man and woman); Braschi v. Stahl As-socs. Co., 543 N.E.2d 49 (N.Y. 1989) (including same-sex partners within city rent control ordinance as family members).

A fourth factor that contributed to the enhanced ability of adults to enter into family law contracts is the rise of no-fault divorce. By 1969, a legislative innovation enabled either party to obtain a divorce without the necessity of being an innocent spouse. This innovation commenced in California, but has since spread to every state. As a result, either spouse could obtain a divorce on grounds that had nothing to do with the common law fault grounds of adultery, cruelty, or desertion. Instead, an adulterous spouse could petition for a divorce based on a new ground, such as irreconcilable difference or remaining separate and apart for a definite period of time. With this innovation, the number of divorces increased rapidly. In light of the easily attainable divorce, coupled with the financial and educational independence of each adult party, courts and legislatures were more accepting of prenuptial contracts addressing the economic issues arising at death or divorce. This trend is also evident in the acceptance of postmarital contracts. Indeed, acceptance of adult couples private ordering evolved into encouragement, and courts are increasingly dependent on couples to address their own economic situation through mutually agreed upon separation agreements. Once drafted by the attorneys for each of the adults involved in the divorce, legislation makes them presumptively binding. Only unconscionability, duress, or fraud would vitiate such agreements. And courts are willing to use the apparatus of contempt to enforce the self-ordering contracts. Through incorporation but not merger into the court's final decree of divorce, any contract would attain res adjudicata and enforcement through civil contempt. We will discuss no-fault divorce further in Chapter 5, Dissolving a Marriage, *infra*.

A fifth and final factor is the technological advancement within the field of assisted reproductive technology. Once medical technology made it possible for children to be born with sperm or eggs, provided by contractual donors, and gestational surrogacy became a commercial reality, adult contracting related to family law reached another level. Without discussing the ethical and moral implications of contracting to bring about human birth, the fact that such contracts exist and are enforced is an added indication of how far private ordering in family law contracting has evolved. Until now, adult contracting provided for the expectations of the adult parties; now additional parties are involved: Donors, surrogates, and most importantly, children who result from these procedures. Much has been written about assisted reproductive technology, but for our present purposes, it is necessary to establish the progression of contracting between adults as having progressed from courtship to the enforcement of contracts related to legal disputes involving ownership of eggs, sperm, or cryopreserved embryos. In addition, contracting between adults may establish parentage of the non-related child, born with the assistance of a gestational surrogate.[4] Furthermore, prenuptial contracts, postnuptial contracts, nonmarital contracts, surrogacy contracts, and fertility clinic storage contracts are arguably enforceable, subject to the jurisdiction and public policy considerations pertinent to human issue and surrogate participants. Thus, contracting rights of adult parties have evolved significantly.

The issues involved with assisted reproductive technology will be discussed further in Chapter 7, The Parent–Child Relationship, *infra*. These issues, as with the other enumerated factors illustrate the progressive expansion of adults' contracting rights in a family law context. We now need to restrict our inquiry into particular developments that form the basis of current law pertaining to premarital, postmarital, and separation agreement contracting.

II. Premarital Contracts

The objective of every premarital agreement is to provide economic certainty regarding the marital property when the marriage dissolves because of death or divorce. At death, a deceased spouse's property could pass through a valid last will and testament, intestate succession, or through a variety of non-probate transfers. And if the surviving spouse is dissatisfied with any of these means of distribution, the surviving spouse may elect against the applicable distribution scheme and take a statutory amount.[5] Nonetheless, through the use of a valid premarital agreement, either or both of the parties to the marriage may release any claim against the other's estate, either in whole or in part. Such a release provides certainty: The decedent spouse may die knowing that his or her estate plan will not be thwarted by the state's probate scheme, or the surviving spouse's statutory right of election.

Likewise, the premarital agreement provides certainty at divorce. In community property states, all community property is presumptively divided equally between the two spouses, and any separate property is retained by each. In common law states—often referred to as separate property states—upon divorce, courts are expected to divide the assembled marital property according to equitable factors. These factors vary among the states, most recognizing the length of the marriage and anything special performed

---

4. *See, e.g.*, Raftopol v. Ramey, 12 A.3d 783 (Conn. 2011).

5. *See* Raymond C. O'Brien, *Integrating Marital Property Into a Spouse's Elective Share*, 59 CATH. U. L. REV. 617, 626–678 (2010).

during the marriage by either of the spouses, but there is little certainty in application. We will elaborate further on distribution of property upon divorce in Chapter 6, Spousal Financial Considerations In Dissolution and Divorce, *infra*. But with a valid premarital agreement, couples may achieve a degree of certainty in the division of either marital or community property assets, thus providing safely for a child or children from a prior marriage, or efficiently disposing of a family heirloom or treasure.

Viewed from today's heightened desire for certainty in planning estates, and in dividing property during an acrimonious divorce, it seems axiomatic that premarital agreements achieve a status as valid and easily obtainable. Nonetheless, their history regarding recognition and enforcement has been arduous. Initially, many state courts scrutinized premarital agreements in the context of three factors: (1) Was the agreement obtained through fraud, duress, or mistake? (2) Was the agreement unconscionable when executed? (3) Has the situation of the parties changed so dramatically since its execution, so as to make the agreement's enforcement unfair? To a degree, these issues still arise in any discussion of premarital agreements today. But these factors were compounded by issues of gender. Because women were viewed as less informed about finances and bargaining for terms, any agreement that adversely affected a woman was scrutinized more carefully. Also, many courts expressed concern over the validity of any agreement executed by parties in a confidential relationship. How can the parties sufficiently disclose their financial data when they are in a confidential relationship? In other words, how can parties in love, perhaps only weeks or days before their wedding, investigate fully each other's finances? Surely, when people are in love, the hands-on bargaining that usually enters into any valid contract is absent.

In order to overcome the dilemma of determining the effects attendant to any confidential relationship, courts often applied a heightened level of scrutiny to prenuptial agreements: The "parties must exercise the highest degree of good faith, candor and sincerity in all matters bearing on the terms and execution of the proposed agreement, with fairness being the ultimate measure."[6] Courts would apply a heightened scrutiny to factors such as duress (was the future bride pregnant when the agreement was signed?), independent advice (were both parties represented by separate attorneys?), understanding (was the agreement written in a language understood by both parties?), voluntary (did each of the parties

---

6. In re Estate of Hollett, 834 A.2d 348, 351 (N.H. 2003) (citations omitted).

have sufficient time to reflect on the terms and conditions of the agreement?), and sufficient disclosure (did each of the parties possess complete and accurate knowledge of the assets and liabilities of the other party?). Heightened scrutiny prompted costly litigation at divorce or death. In addition, heightened judicial scrutiny lessened the likelihood that the agreement would be enforced, depriving the decedent or divorcing spouse of certainty that is so desirable in the administration of assets. Persons wishing to provide for children from prior marriages upon death, or to safeguard separate assets upon divorce, were unable to assuredly rely upon their prenuptial agreements because of future claims of alleged unfairness.

To better provide for planning certainty, state legislatures began enacting statutes that have the effect of making premarital agreements more reliable and hence, more certain upon application. The first statute, currently adopted by more than half of the states, was proposed by the National Conference of Commissioners on Uniform State Laws. This statute, the Uniform Premarital Agreement Act ("the Act")[7] is a significant departure from the judicial validity tests previously followed. In addition to listing the issues that may be the subject of any premarital agreement, the Act allows for the agreement to be enforceable even though there is vast disparity in the distribution of assets. Thus, disparity is not objectionable as long as, at the time of signing, the adversely affected party had full and fair disclosure, had waived full disclosure, or reasonably could have had sufficient knowledge of all relevant information. The ability to disclaim wealth is part of the new trend towards self-ordering. Restricting scrutiny to the parties' knowledge and any factors contributing to duress, provides greater certainty of enforcement, making it easier for couples to allow for greater disparity in distribution of assets without fear that such disparity will trigger complaints that unfairness resulted from duress or other toxic effects of the confidential relationship. Also, the Act looks only to factors existing at the time of the execution of the prenuptial agreement, and not to changed circumstances existent at divorce or death, which could be many years into the future.[8] This is a factor unique to the Act, and absent for consider-

---

7. UNIF. PREMARITAL AGREEMENT ACT, 9C U.L.A. 39 et seq. (2001). For added commentary, *see* WALTER WADLINGTON & RAYMOND C. O'BRIEN, FAMILY LAW STATUTES: SELECTED UNIFORM LAWS, FEDERAL STATUTES, STATE STATUTES, AND INTERNATIONAL TREATIES 167 (4th ed. 2011).

8. For an example of a court's refusal to consider a change in circumstances between execution of the 1988 agreement and the 2004 divorce, *see* Crews v. Crews, 989 A.2d 1060 (Conn. 2010).

ations as to the validity of postmarital agreements, and not without critics.

One critic, differing from the Uniform Premarital Agreement Act, is the American Law Institute ("ALI"). The ALI suggests that a better approach to determining the fairness of the prenuptial agreement is to assess fairness in the context of three factors: (1) Whether more than ten years have passed since the agreement was signed; (2) Whether a child was born or adopted after execution of the agreement when the couple originally had no children together; or (3) Whether there has been a substantial change in circumstances that neither party anticipated when the agreement was signed.[9] In addition, the ALI proposes using a rebuttable presumption positing that no duress existed and there was informed consent at the time of the execution of the agreement if: (1) signed at least thirty days prior to the marriage; (2) each party was advised to obtain independent counsel and had ample opportunity to do so; and (3) if no independent counsel was obtained by a party, that the agreement could nonetheless be understood by a person of ordinary intelligence with no legal training, regarding rights that may be altered by the premarital agreement, and finally, that the parties may have adverse interests upon divorce or death.

Evidently, states are moving towards the adoption of a statutory approach to premarital agreements. This comports with the increasing mobility of the population, the erosion of gender disparity, and the ability of adults to contract in the area of family law. As discussed previously, in the first part of this chapter, the trend among courts and legislatures to support the enforcement of premarital agreements is secure. Indeed, an increasing number of states support the ability of adults to completely waive spousal support. The only restraints occur when courts are asked to enforce personal demands contained in individual agreements, such as conditions of sexual activity, religious observances, no-children during the marriage clauses, and of course anything that would adversely affect a parent's duty to support a child. The need for certainty in planning for an adult's self-ordered future—in an age of greater economic independence, subsequent marriages, and no-fault divorce—fuels legislation such as the Uniform Premarital Agreement Act and the trend of courts' willingness to enforce what may appear to be, at divorce or death, an unconscionable agreement.

9. *See Principles of the Law of Family Dissolution: Analysis and Recommendations* § 7.05(2) (2002).

III. Postmarital Agreements

Many persons conclude mistakenly that a postmarital agreement is synonymous with a separation agreement, which is an agreement that precedes, and certainly contemplates, divorce. But postmarital agreements are a distinct and separate category of agreements that occur after a valid marriage: The couple freely contemplating a continuing marriage, but circumstances now dictate that they wish to have an agreement between themselves similar to what they could have entered into prior to marriage. In other words, a postmarital agreement is similar to a premarital agreement, except that it occurs after the marriage has occurred between the parties.

A cursory reading of the Uniform Premarital Agreement Act makes evident that the Act applies to premarital agreements, not postmarital ones. Nonetheless, as states are able to adopt what they wish concerning the Act, they are likewise able to make the Act applicable to postmarital agreements if they wish to do so. Obviously, this would simplify the same issues we raised in reference to premarital agreements: What constitutes validity? Should the validity of the agreement be subject to the vagaries of duress, financial disclosure, and unconscionability? And should courts look only to conditions as they existed at the time of the signing of the agreement, or to changing circumstances? In addition, it is arguable that a postmarital agreement, unlike a premarital agreement, lacks consideration to make it a valid contract. Since the marriage has already taken place, nothing further is expected as a result of signing the agreement.[10]

Similar to premarital agreements, postmarital agreements concern contracts between two adults. However, the difference with postmarital agreements is that they occur after marriage, hence they invite considerations based on a confidential relationship occasioned by marriage. Undoubtedly, marriage provides a confidential relationship. "Courts simply should not countenance either party to such a unique human relationship [marriage] dealing with each other at arms' length."[11] Because of the nature of the confidential relationship of marriage, "postnuptial agreements require stricter scrutiny than prenuptial agreements."[12] This means that the agreement must comply with applicable contract principles, the terms of

---

10. *See, e.g.,* Bratton v. Bratton, 136 S.W.3d 595 (Tenn. 2004).

11. Bedrick v. Bedrick, 17 A.3d 17, 27 (Conn. 2011)(quoting Billington v. Billington, 595 A.2d 1377 (Conn. 1991)).

12. *Id.*

the agreement must be fair and equitable at the time of execution, and not unconscionable at the time of dissolution. Thus, courts are revisiting issues with postmarital agreements that have been statutorily addressed by the Uniform Premarital Agreement Act. But the Act is inapplicable unless we can address the issues analogously.

As with premarital agreements, and specifically with the Uniform Premarital Agreement Act, all postmarital agreements must meet the following conditions: (1) They must be voluntary, without any duress, fraud, undue influence, or coercion; (2) each spouse must be given full, fair, and reasonable disclosure of the amount, character, and value of property, held jointly or separately, and any all debts and liabilities must be disclosed. It seems reasonable to conclude the fact of marriage does not automatically satisfy the disclosure requirement since implied knowledge is insufficient. But each case depends on the totality of the circumstances then present. Nonetheless, "[u]nfairness or inequality alone does not render a postnuptial agreement unconscionable; spouses may agree on an unequal distribution of assets at dissolution."[13]

But there is something different about providing for the validity of a postmarital agreement. With the absence of the Uniform Premarital Agreement Act, and its determination that fairness should be determined at the execution of the agreement, not when the dissolution of the marriage occurs, courts seem willing to look to dissolution of the marriage or death to determine unconscionability. For example: "Unforeseen changes in the relationship, such as having a child, loss of employment or moving to another state, may render enforcement of the agreement unconscionable."[14] Such a position is consonant with the position suggested by the American Law Institute in reference to premarital agreements, that, under defined circumstances, unforeseen developments may make an agreement unconscionable and hence unenforceable. But this is a departure from the policy enumerated by the Uniform Premarital Agreement Act.

What is the future of the validity of postmarital agreements? Even though postmarital agreements were void under the common law, they are increasingly acceptable today. But unlike premarital agreements, they do not have the objective factors enacted in the Uniform Premarital Agreement Act. Thus, in states that have not transferred applicability of the Act to postmarital agreements, such agreements remain vulnerable to scrutiny by the courts under many of the factors identified previously. The most significant

---

13. *Id*. at 28.   **14.** *Id*.

departure from the provisions of the Act is the fact that changed circumstances may make the postmarital agreement unconscionable at the death of a spouse or dissolution of the marriage. Depending on the reader's sense of fairness, this uncertainty needs to be addressed by statute. But it appears likely that the need for certainty in estate planning, and the increasing recognition of the self-ordering of adults to make decisions, even ones affecting family law issues, suggest that the position of the Uniform Premarital Agreement Act is the more viable choice.

IV. Separation Agreements

California's legislature was not only the first state to enact no-fault divorce, it also initiated vast changes in the process of divorce itself. As an increasing number of states followed California's lead, the focus in matrimonial courts shifted from establishing fault grounds sufficient to terminate the marriage, to issues surrounding marital property distribution, child custody, visitation, and support. Gradually, courts were drawn into the brambly terrain of answering what constitutes marital property, which parent better serves the best interest of a child, and what constitutes an adequate level of child support and child visitation. Faced with multiple human hurdles, the courts acquired a greater respect for the ability of the parties to work out the details of their divorce themselves, albeit with the assistance of their attorneys. The courts came to respect and expect a separation agreement negotiated between the two adult parties, an agreement that would be given presumptive validity and enforcement as a judgement. There was no concern over the presence of a confidential relationship to cloud the negotiations. And, since the couple's relationship had already turned acrimonious, the separation agreement could not be considered as promoting divorce, hence violative of public policy. Lastly, there is certainly consideration to support the contractual obligations between the divorcing parties, since each party seeks a divorce.

The Uniform Marriage and Divorce Act, promulgated in 1970, offered one of the first summaries of the expectations and format of a modern separation agreement.[15] The Act specified that separation agreements were meant to promote an amicable settlement for divorcing couples, and when reduced to writing, the agreements were to provide for a resolution of all property issues, all support issues, and custody and visitation of any children. And while the agreement cannot adversely affect the rights of the children, any agreement reached by the parties should be binding upon the

---

15. *See* UNIF. MARRIAGE & DIVORCE ACT,
§ 306, 9A U.L.A.159 et seq. (1998).

courts unless the court determines that the agreement is unconscionable. Then, if the agreement is valid and satisfactory, the court shall order the parties to abide by its terms, making the terms of the agreement enforceable as a judgement of the court, that is, enforceable through contempt.

Modification of the separation agreement depends upon the terms of the agreement itself as they apply to matters affecting the adult parties. Since the agreement is a contract between the divorcing parties, they can expressly specify that the agreement is nonmodifiable. If so, and the agreement is incorporated but not merged into the judgement of the court, then the agreement is nonmodifiable. If the couple says nothing in the agreement concerning modifiability, then the court is free to specify any terms regarding future modifications. The separation agreement is presumptively binding upon the court absent proof of duress, fraud, or unconscionability.[16] In addition, while the adult couple may specify terms and conditions applicable to child custody, visitation, and support, the court is not bound by the parents' determinations, but may modify so as to satisfy the best needs of the child.

The acceptance and utilization of separation agreements by modern courts is consistent with the modern trend towards greater self-ordering by adults in executing binding family law contracts. As discussed in the first part of this chapter, the evolution towards greater reliance upon fully informed adults to manage their family law affairs is now reflected in the courts' reliance on separation agreements for division of property, support of adults and children, and for child custody and visitation determinations. The progression towards acceptance of an adult to self-order his or her family law contracts seems rational and unsurprising. The American Law Institute's Principles of the Law of Family Dissolution § 7.02 (2002), offers modern confirmation of the acceptance of the use of privately-ordered separation agreements, suggesting that enforcement should encompass all remedies that the couple set out in the agreement. The future of contracting between adults includes sperm, eggs, embryos, and surrogate births. To what degree may an adult self-order a contract related to birth of a child? We will discuss this more thoroughly in Chapter 7, The Parent–Child Relationship, *infra*. Contracts involving assisted reproductive technology is the next step in the evolution of contracts involving family law matters.

---

16. *See, e.g.*, Sims v. Sims, 685 S.E.2d 869 (Va. Ct. App. 2009) (holding that gross disparity in the division of assets, the wife's infirmities, and wife's poverty made agreement whereby she waived property and support unconscionable).

Chapter 3

Marriage

I. Marriage as an Institution

Much of family law continues to address issues involving a marriage that occurs because couples meet the statutory requirements, or in those that occur when a couple achieves a common law marriage. This chapter addresses the rules involved with entering into marriage, or rules associated with a status providing the equivalency of marriage. The chapter also addresses those instances when no marriage takes place because of void or voidable grounds. But this chapter also involves duties and status inherent in the marital relationship, such as marital property management responsibility, support obligations, crimes and available defenses. Many of the rules and obligations that we will discuss originated with biblical references; often the uniqueness of what we will discuss stems from how different the current law is from what existed only a short time ago. Invariably, we will examine changes in the law that occurred under evolving constitutional decisions related to equal protection, privacy, freedom of association, or liberty interests. Undoubtedly, the rules regarding marriage, once considered immutable, have changed often and the future remains unclear. Admittedly too, because of the state-specific nature of family law, the law varies from state to state.

Increasingly, state family law innovations have been precipitous. In the absence of a Supreme Court decision, which has the effect of nullifying state laws instantly, change often occurs at the local level, on a state-by-state basis. During the 1960s the Supreme Court shaped the family law landscape, with landmark decisions such as *Griswold* (privacy) and *Loving* (equal protection); in the early 1970s the Court in *Eisenstadt* declared that if the right of privacy meant anything, it meant the right of the individual to be free from unwarranted government intrusion. These are seminal decisions that had a national impact. But subsequent decisions from state supreme courts also had monumental impact. Examples include prohibiting prosecution of consensual sodomy between adults (Georgia), recognizing that the definition of marriage could change to include same-sex couples (Hawaii), and that restricting marriage to opposite-sex couples was a denial of equal protection (Massachusetts). Often, in reaction to these decisions, state legislatures enacted legislation reversing or limiting some of the judicial decisions. Examples of legislative action include same-sex marriage laws, partial birth abortion laws, and restrictions on benefits provided to nonmarital cohabitation. Today, contest continues between legislative and judicial initiatives, the issues surrounding family law being among the most volatile in the nation.

Arguably, the importance of marriage has progressively decreased. In a 2007 survey, the U.S. Census Bureau, reported that the median age for a first marriage in the United States was 25.5 for women, and 27.5 for men. In 1960, almost fifty years earlier, the average woman first married at age 20.3, and the average man at 22.8. Likewise, the number of couples who cohabit, but do not marry, increased by more than one-thousand percent from 1960 to 2006. And while the number of divorces in the United States has decreased today, in 1980, ten years after the introduction of no-fault divorce, half of all people who married would eventually divorce.

While the incidence of divorces has decreased, obtaining a divorce is now relatively easy when compared to only a few decades ago, which suggests that marriage is not what it used to be. In response to this assertion, states initiated marriage awareness courses in state high schools and offered couples seeking marriage licenses an economic incentive to go to class to learn about marriage and its unique responsibilities. Three states have enacted an option for couples contemplating marriage called covenant marriage. This option, available in Louisiana, Arkansas, and Arizona, restricts the covenanting spouses to fault grounds as the sole means for obtaining a divorce in the state. In effect, covenant marriage makes it more difficult for couples to get a divorce in the state. Of course, either spouse could travel to another state, obtain a divorce based on no-fault, and return to the covenant state, which must then recognize the divorce under Full Faith and Credit.

Even while some would argue that marriage is a failing institution, businesses and governments have been quick to assemble marriage-like benefits for couples unable to marry, including domestic partnerships, reciprocal beneficiaries, and civil unions. These efforts to mimic marriage attest to the importance of the marital status. And in the extensive litigation and acrimonious legislative debates, the petitions of same-sex couples to marry signal that there is more to the status than simply the attending economic benefits. As we will discuss in this chapter, the shift in public sentiment, the extensive litigation, and the legislative debates over same-sex marriage have caused people to reexamine their perspectives on marriage. Why is this? All benefits other than the name, were available with civil unions, but Vermont, the first state to adopt civil unions, abandoned civil unions and now makes marriage available to both same-sex and opposite-sex couples. What makes marriage so desirable? Why have legislators endured caustic debates and backlash by many politically active constituents to enact same-sex marriage laws? Arguably, the answer lies in a common denominator throughout much of modern family law, the American notion that people should have the right to self-order their own lives. Many same-sex marriage advocates believe that marriage should be an option for all, regardless of the historical definition, simply because it is the right of each individual to choose to enter into marriage.

A recent event illustrates the importance of self-ordering. After the governor of New York signed the bill on June 24, 2011, that legalized same-sex marriage in the state of New York, the New York Times reported two days later that legislators supported the controversial law because, "they were inclined to see the issue as one of personal freedom, consistent with their more libertarian views."[1] And a week later, the Washington Post, when writing about the New York legislation, quoted a Georgetown University historian, Michael Kazin, as opining that "in general, American are more likely to support movements from the left or from the right that talk in terms of rights and individual freedom than talk about collective rights or responsibilities."[2] Assuming that self-ordering by adult individuals is responsible for what may be perceived as changes in marriage, it is possible to conclude that marriage itself is not changing. After all, marriage may still be defined as a man and woman among some, as a status with concomitant benefits by some, and rejected altogether by others. But marriage as an option is very important to a number of people, even if those same people want other options too.

Certainly, when evaluating the institution of marriage, at least some importance must be given to the religious, companionship, and commitment elements. It is impossible to make generalizations about any of these. But for many couples marriage is a sacred bond that can only be dissolved by death; infidelity occasioning adultery, a serious infraction. Religious writings, doctrines, literature, and even love songs testify to the importance of the institution of marriage. Admittedly, marriage can bring about a change in economic status, as there are certain economic consequences and options available regarding the establishment of paternity, taxation,

---

1. Michael Barbaro, *A Persuasive Cuomo, Rich Republicans and a Shifting Political Dynamic*, NY Times, June 26, 2011, at A1.

2. Alec MacGillis, *The Rise of the Zombie Liberals*, Wash. Post, July 3, 2011, at B1.

and inheritance. And for some, marriage offers a partner with whom life may be shared. Lastly, for some couples marriage is a whim, a fantasy. But it remains a potent option in the American panoply of choices, one that has historical roots and many rules.

II. Limitations on Who Can Marry

A. *Void and Voidable*

There is a distinction between divorce and annulment. With divorce a valid marriage has taken place and now a petition seeks to end the marriage. With annulment, the petition asserts that no marriage ever took place. A petition for an annulment is premised upon the assertion that the purported marriage was void or voidable from its inception. Anyone can file a petition asserting that a marriage is void, and it may be filed during or after the purported marriage. Such leeway is allowed because void marriages result from a serious impediment. Examples of a void marriage include if one or both of the spouses were already married, making the second marriage bigamous and void. Or, if the spouses were related within the prohibited degrees of consanguinity or affinity specified in the state's incest statute, the marriage would also be void. Some states declare that same-sex marriages are void, and other states make a marriage with a person under a specified age void too. Once a decree of annulment is issued by the court, the spouses are able to marry again.

Conversely, a voidable annulment petition may only be brought by an aggrieved party during the pendency of the ground. This reflects the less serious nature of a voidable ground. An example would be when an adult marries another who is a minor, but not sufficiently underage so as to make the marriage void. Instances occur when the minor could marry with the permission of a parent or guardian, but the minor never obtains the permission or falsifies the parent's consent. So long as the minor remains a minor, the parent or guardian of the aggrieved party (minor) may petition a court to obtain an annulment of the marriage. But once the minor passes into his or her majority, the cause of action for the voidable annulment is gone. Besides underage, annulment grounds listed in various state statutes include fraud, habitual intoxication, or addiction to drugs. In addition, when the man lacks the physical capacity to consummate the marriage by sexual intercourse, and at the time of the marriage, the other party did not know of the impediment, an annulment may be obtained.[3] In petitioning for either a void or a

---

3.   UNIF. MARRIAGE AND DIVORCE ACT, 9A U.L.A. Pt. 1, 159 et seq. § 208(2) (1998).

voidable annulment, jurisdiction exists at either party's domicile, the state where the purported marriage took place, or any state with personal jurisdiction over the spouses.

Some concessions are made for annulled marriages, perhaps allowing for validity to occur. For instance, the Uniform Marriage and Divorce Act provides for ratification of the marriage, specifying that parties who cohabit after removal of an impediment are lawfully married as of the date of the removal of the impediment. [Section 207] Often, couples who enter into bigamous marriages could benefit from the ratification provision if either of the previously married spouses subsequently obtains a divorce, or the other spouse dies. If the prior bigamous marriage is no longer binding, ratification can sometimes occur or a common law marriage may then form in those states allowing for them.[4] The Uniform Marriage and Divorce Act also provides that children born of a void or voidable marriage are to be considered as marital children, or legitimate. Such a provision is common among the states. And finally, any person who marries another in the good faith belief that he or she was entering into a valid marriage may be a putative spouse, acquiring the rights of a spouse until such time as that person discovers that he or she was never legally married. [Section 209] To acquire the status as a putative spouse, states typically require that the parties have entered into a marriage ceremony, a guarantee of good faith, even though the Uniform Marriage and Divorce Act is silent as to this requirement. The usual putative spouse situation occurs when a man or a woman marries another in the good faith belief that the other party is not married, hence the marriage is valid. Later, the innocent spouse discovers that the marriage is bigamous because the other party never obtained a valid divorce from a prior spouse, or worse, simply wanted more than one spouse. Until the time of discovery, the innocent spouse is a putative spouse because he or she married in good faith. The innocent party must, upon discovery, bring an action to annul the marriage and then he or she can claim the status of putative spouse.

Many states provide economic benefits for a putative spouse similar to what would be available to a divorcing spouse. Hence, between the time of the marriage and when the putative spouse discovers the ground for the annulment, the putative spouse is entitled to a share of all marital property acquired. But at least one state limits the putative spouse to a division of marital property,

---

4. *See, e.g.,* Lindsley v. Lindsley, No.   12349200 (Tenn. Ct. App. Jun. 11, E2008–02525–COA–R3–CV,   2010   WL   2010).

based upon equitable principles. Thus, the spouse would not be able to obtain support without an express provision in the state's statute. Absent express statutory authority, states have not allowed a putative spouse to obtain spousal support.[5] The Uniform Marriage and Divorce Act does not impose this distinction, but instead, applies to putative spouses rights to marital property, maintenance, support, and custody of children. [Section 208(e)]

With the adoption of no-fault divorce the number of petitions for annulments has declined. Some consider the emotional value in establishing that a marriage never took place; perhaps this was the deciding element in choosing an annulment for celebrities like Britney Spears. But with an annulment comes the responsibility of proving the ground, and such litigation is easily avoided when a divorce petition simply alleges that the marriage is irretrievably broken, or there are irreconcilable differences between the parties. And, as described, there may be adverse economic consequences to the petitioning party if a petition for an annulment, as compared to divorce, is filed.

B. Statutory Formalities Required to Enter into Marriage

Because marriage is a status, the state being a third party, any marriage, according to the Uniform Marriage and Divorce Act, "may be contracted, maintained, invalidated, or dissolved only as provided by law." [Section 201] The practical effect of this is that marriage is not like a civil contract entered into by the parties, the terms and conditions of marriage are fluid. With marriage, every state has a list of requirements, some mandatory and some directory. The requirements usually include the following: (1) two persons otherwise able to marry, (2) each of whom provides consent, (3) obtains a marriage license from the proper state authority, (4) has the marriage solemnized by a person empowered by the state to do so, and (5) the marriage is then registered with the state.

In the absence of any of the enumerated statutory requirements, good faith or a sincere desire to marry is insufficient to create a valid marriage. This fact was illustrated in a Florida decision involving a man and woman who had difficulty in finalizing their prenuptial agreement. The negotiations inhibited the man from obtaining the couple's marriage license from the state clerk prior to the wedding. Nonetheless, the man convinced his bride that they should get married without the license, assuring her that everything would be alright. A year later, they did obtain the license, but never solemnized the marriage afterwards. The couple

5. Williams v. Williams, 97 P.3d 1124
(Nev. 2004).

had two children and then, four years after the marriage, the wife filed for divorce. The man then denied that a valid marriage had ever taken place. Even though the state's statute did not expressly require that a marriage license was mandatory for a valid marriage, the state court, in holding that the couple was not validly married without the license, ruled that the statutory requirements overall presuppose that marriages have a license.[6] Since the state had abolished common law marriage, there was no import to the couple holding themselves out as husband and wife. Plus, the couple could not claim to be putative spouses, based on their good faith and sincerity. The court explained that good faith meant obtaining a license and since both parties knew there was no license at the time of the solemnization, they did not possess the good faith required to be putative spouses.

The Florida decision emphasizes the importance attached to licensing requirements, but it is admittedly the minority approach. The majority approach among the state courts is to look to the words of the state's licensing statute. Unless the state's statute makes the license, or by implication any other requirement, mandatory, then the license is considered as directory only and its absence will not void the marriage.[7] Usually, courts require that the state expressly declares some marriages as void, for example, bigamous or incestuous marriages. Therefore, unless the state expressly states that the lack of a license—or any other requirement—makes the marriage void, then the courts should not declare it void based on the unfulfilled requirement.

C. *Intent to Enter into Marriage*

What level of intent is necessary to enter into a valid marriage? What mental capacity must a person have to meet the level of intent? With the life expectancy of men and women in the United States increasing, more couples are marrying later in life, prompting questions as to what constitutes capacity to enter into a valid marriage. Concern over capacity to execute a valid last will and testament has long been litigated, resulting in a widely used test. There, courts look to the time of execution of the last will and testament and hold that, at the time of execution, the testator must: (1) know the objects of bounty, (2) the extent of wealth, (3) the unique nature of executing a will, and (4) be able to interrelate the previous three. But what of a couple being married? Obviously, the intent of either party cannot be adversely affected by fraud,

---

6. Hall v. Maal, 32 So.3d 682 (Fla. Dist. Ct. App. 2010).

7. Rivera v. Rivera, 243 P.3d 1148 (N.M. Ct. App. 2010); *see also In re* Cantarella, 119 Cal.Rptr.3d 829 (Cal. Ct. App. 2011); Matter of Farraj, 72 A.D.3d 1082 (N.Y. App. Div. 2010).

undue influence, or duress.[8] But the level of mental competency necessary to enter into marriage is more difficult to resolve. Again, borrowing from the example of wills and trusts, we can posit a test for the appointment of a conservator: Whether there is clear and convincing evidence that an individual is likely to suffer harm because the person is unable to provide for property management and cannot adequately understand and appreciate the nature and consequences of such inability.[9] May this test be modified and applied to persons about to enter into marriage?

A Nebraska decision involved an older man and woman who had been diagnosed with mild forms of mental disability. They met while living in an assisted living arrangement, and dated prior to expressing a desire to marry. There were sessions with a minister, and the couple discussed with the minister and others the unique nature of marriage and its responsibilities. Then they obtained a license and solemnized the marriage. After the wedding the husband's guardian sought to have the marriage annulled as voidable, due to lack of proper consent at the time of the ceremony. The court applied a three factor test to determine capacity: (1) the parties must understand the nature of marriage, (2) the parties must understand the financial and intimacy elements of marriage, and (3) the parties must understand the potential lifetime commitment involved in marriage. After a lengthy discussion of these three factors, the court concluded that the couple did in fact have a valid marriage and rejected the guardian's petition to have the marriage annulled.[10]

As with fraud, undue influence, and duress, issues of mental competency will be addressed by a jury as a determination based on the unique facts of each case. As long as the jury applies properly the statutory or common law, a determination by a trial court of mental competency is likely to be sustained by an appellate court.

D.   *Confidential and Proxy Marriages*

A confidential marriage is not a common law marriage. The term confidential marriage applies to the mechanism used by the state to restrict public access to the fact that a marriage license has

---

8.   *See, e.g.,* Clark v. Foust–Graham, 615 S.E.2d 398 (N.C. Ct. App. 2005)(annulling a marriage where undue influence exerted upon a party to the marriage made consent voidable); Wolfe v. Wolfe, 389 N.E.2d 1143 (Ill. 1979)(annulling marriage for fraud because spouse concealed her prior marriage from her Roman Catholic husband).

9.   *In re* Maher, 207 A.D.2d 133, 621 N.Y.S.2d 617 (1994).

10.   Edmunds v. Edwards, 287 N.W.2d 420 (Neb. 1980); *see also* Nave v. Nave, 173 S.W.3d 766 (Tenn. Ct. App. 2005)(applying the same three-factor test but holding that the husband lacked the mental capacity necessary to enter into a valid marriage contract).

been issued to two persons about to be married.[11] In seeking a confidential marriage, the couple is seeking privacy and must comply with any applicable state requirements to have a valid marriage.

Proxy marriages are more common. The Uniform Marriage and Divorce Act provides that if one of the parties to the marriage is unable to be present at the solemnization, that person may authorize another person to act as his or her proxy. The person solemnizing the marriage must be satisfied that the proxy has been duly appointed by the absent party, and that the absent party freely consents to the marriage. The judgement of the person solemnizing the marriage may be reviewed by the court if the parties so desire. History reveals many instances of proxy marriages for Europe's royalty. Marie Antoinette's marriage to the future King Louis XVI is one example. But to meet the needs of members of the Armed Forces serving overseas, California enacted a provision for proxy marriage.[12]

E. *Transgendered Persons*

Advances in medical technology have made it possible for persons born physically identified with one gender to reverse that gender identification later in life. The facts of reported cases suggest that a person gradually realizes that he or she is anatomically one gender, but psychologically identifies with the other gender. Through an extensive medical procedure, the transgendered person seeks to realign his or her psychological self with his or her anatomy, gradually assuming the identity of the gender with which he or she identifies. Once completed, states allow for legal documents, including birth certificates, to reflect this change in gender.[13]

Issues arise when a transgendered person seeks to enter into marriage. Since, as a result of the medical procedure and the revised legal documents, a transgendered person may appear as the opposite gender of the intended spouse for purposes of a valid marriage, courts have been increasingly reluctant to validate these marriages. Instead, states that still only allow opposite-sex marriages typically deny validity to transgendered marriages. The rationale evidenced in American courts is similar to that of a 1970 English decision, which held that a postoperative transgendered

---

11. *See, e.g.,* CAL. FAM. CODE §§ 500–536 (West 2004); MICH. COMP. LAWS ANN. §§ 551.201 (West 2005 & Supp. 2009).

12. CAL. FAM. CODE § 420(b) (West 2004 & Supp. 2008).

13. *See, e.g.,* CAL. HEALTH & SAFETY CODE § 103425 (West 1996); LA. REV. STAT. ANN. 40:62 (2001).

person had not proved that her sex had not changed from male to female, her chromosomes were the same even though anatomically she was transformed into another gender. Thus, according to the *Corbett* rationale, she was still a male for purposes of entering into marriage with another male, even though she may look and function as a female.[14] Therefore, the marriage was void because it involved persons of the same-sex. With one exception, American states have followed the same rationale in denying legitimacy to marriages of transgendered persons.[15] Thus, even in spite of anatomical changes, for one reason or another, the person is still the same gender as the person he or she seeks to marry, and therefore the marriage is void and may be annulled by any person at any time.

There are two exceptions to the cases denying validity to transgendered marriages. The first exception is the obvious one: As states increasingly permit same-sex marriage, the void basis of the transgendered marriage is eliminated; since same-sex marriages are valid, transgendered marriages are valid. In the meantime, transgendered persons can enter into state-accepted domestic partnerships, civil unions, and any other benefits established to protect same-sex partnerships. The second exception arises from a 1976 New Jersey decision. In this solitary American appellate decision accepting transgendered marriage, the New Jersey court rejected tests based on chromosomes and the like. Instead, the court held that there could be a shift in gender through a surgical procedure that harmonized a person's gender identification with proper genitalia. Once a person's psychological self matched his or her anatomical self, and the person was able to perform sexually as such, then this person had changed gender for purposes of entering into a valid marriage.[16]

The current decisions involving transgendered persons do not address issues of child custody, spousal support, division of property, or visitation. It seems appropriate that these issues could be addressed, in states denying a valid marriage, under the law appropriate to nonmarital partners.

F. *Same–Sex Marriage*

Same-sex adults have sought to marry long before the idea of same-sex marriage became public. During the 1960s, when privacy

---

14. Corbett v. Corbett, (1970) 2 All E.R. 33 (P).

15. *See, e.g.,* Kantaras v. Kantaras, 884 So.2d 155 (Fla. Dist. Ct. App. 2004)(joining Texas, Ohio, New York, Illinois, and Kansas in voiding transsexual marriages because they are same-sex marriages), *review denied*, 898 So.2d 80 (Fla. 2005).

16. *See* M.T. v. J.T., 355 A.2d 204 (N.J. Super. Ct. App. Div. 1976).

was established in *Griswold*, and equal protection was applied to marriage in *Loving*, same-sex persons applied to county clerks for marriage licenses and were denied. Then, in the early 1970s, during the heyday of individual liberty announced in *Eisenstadt*, same-sex persons continued to seek licenses. Each petition was premised upon the newly-established Constitutional guarantees. Nonetheless, each petition seeking to enter a same-sex marriage was rejected not because of any lack in Constitutional jurisprudence, but because the definition of marriage did not allow for marriage to exist between persons of the same sex. Thus, despite marriage being declared a fundamental right in *Zablocki*, and the panoply of Constitutional guarantees, the heightened scrutiny that could have been afforded same-sex couples seeking marriage was not applied. Instead, access to marriage was denied because historically the definition of marriage did not include persons of the same sex.[17]

The definitional obstacle to same-sex petitions to marry continued until 1993. Then, in a dramatic decision, the Supreme Court of Hawaii decided that the definition of marriage could change, premising its conclusion upon the *Loving* announcement that persons of different races could marry.[18] By removing the definitional bar to same-sex marriage, the court opened the door to the multiple constitutional challenges prohibiting same-sex marriage. Obviously, in light of its 1993 decision, Hawaii became the first state to address the constitutional challenges. In a stream of litigation, challengers utilized the Hawaii Constitution to argue that they, as same-sex adults seeking to marry, had been denied equal protection, guarantees of privacy and freedom of association, and that they had suffered gender discrimination. Successive judges agreed, applying strict scrutiny under the state constitution, and repeatedly held that the state had not met its burden of providing a compelling state interest to deny same-sex marriage. When it appeared that same-sex couples would be accorded the ability to marry, Hawaii mooted the process by amending its constitution to provide that "The legislature shall have the power to reserve marriage to opposite-sex couples." [HAW. CONST. Art. I, § 223 (2008)] When they changed the constitutional definition of marriage, constitutional challenges were eliminated, at least those challenging the state constitution. The constitutional definition of marriage stripped any constitutional argument of viability.

The Hawaiian litigation made clear to all other states seeking to thwart same-sex marriage that they needed to enact constitutional definitions of marriage, defining marriage as being between

---

17. *See, e.g.*, Singer v. Hara, 522 P.2d 1187 (Wash. App. Ct. 1974).

18. Baehr v. Lewin, 852 P.2d 44 (Haw. 1993).

persons of the opposite sex only. Once this definition was firmly established in the state's constitution, constitutional challenge was without effect. The Hawaiian litigation prompted a second effect. That is, to satisfy same-sex advocates, the Hawaii legislature enacted a new status termed reciprocal beneficiaries, which provided economic and status benefits to same-sex persons similar to those enjoyed by married persons. [HAW. REV. STAT. § 572C–4 & 5 (2008)] Recently, Hawaii adopted civil unions, but for many years, reciprocal beneficiaries enjoyed benefits similar to married couples in the state. For information on the current status of reciprocal beneficiaries in the state, see: http://hawaii.gov/health/vital-records/vital-records/reciprocal/index.html.

A majority of the states have ratified constitutional amendments defining marriage as between a man and a woman; offering exact numbers is elusive as the landscape continues to change. Many of the states prohibiting same-sex marriage enacted state statutes or definitional elements in constitutional amendments. But not all states have statutory and constitutional prohibitions against same-sex marriage. While these states have not adopted same-sex marriage, they might do the following: (1) recognize same-sex marriages validly celebrated in other states; (2) recognize similar status arrangements, such as civil unions validly conferred in other states; or (3) recognize status arrangements, such as domestic partnerships validly conferred by other states or businesses. And again, because state law and practice continues to change, any attempt to provide numbers or listing of states is futile. But it is important to know that not only the state's conferral of the status is important, but also the reciprocity the state will allow with other state's determinations. Full Faith and Credit is inoperative, thus making the strong state public policy the deciding factor in what will be given effect from another state.

Initially, reluctant state legislatures enacted statutes permitting same-sex marriage because of coercion from state courts. Massachusetts enacted same-sex marriage legislation in 2004, after the state's supreme court held that the state did not have a rational basis to deny same-sex couples marriage licenses. The Massachusetts' court decision was based on due process and equal protection grounds.[19] The Connecticut Supreme Court (2008) and Iowa Supreme Court (2009) prompted similar responses from each state's legislature. Such decisions precipitate complaints of judicial activism from critics of same-sex marriage. But in 2009, Vermont became the first state to enact same-sex marriage legislation with-

---

19. Goodridge v. Department of Pub. Health, 798 N.E.2d 941 (Mass. 2003).

out judicial prompting. The same-sex statute, which had to over-come the Governor's veto, refers to marriage as between "two people" who do not need to be man and woman. [VT. STAT. ANN. Tit. 15, ch. 1 § 8 (2009)] Other state legislatures adopted similar legislation permitting same-sex marriage: New Hampshire (2009) and New York (2011); the District of Columbia adopted same-sex marriage in 2009, and the California legislature made same-sex marriage valid from June 16, 2008 until November 4, 2008, when the legislation was repealed by a voter referendum. These states did not have constitutional amendments defining marriage as between a man and a woman.

The issue of same-sex marriage is polarizing. While some states recognize the status, others vehemently oppose any recognition. When a same-sex couple validly married in Massachusetts in 2006, they did not anticipate moving to Texas one day. There, they separated and filed for divorce in 2008. Texas has both a statute and a state constitutional amendment restricting marriage to oppo-site-sex couples and bars any recognition of same-sex marriages. Thus, the issue arose as to whether these provisions prohibited a Texas court from granting a divorce to a same-sex couple. The Texas court ruled that Texas courts have no subject matter jurisdic-tion to award a divorce, since to do so would be to recognize the validity of the marriage. The state legislature prohibited state courts from recognizing the marriage, hence the court lacks juris-diction to render a divorce. The only recourse to a same-sex couple would be to petition the court to have the marriage annulled as void.[20] The court rejected any claims that its policy was unconstitu-tional as a denial of equal protection, or that denying the divorce stigmatizes the parties. Instead the decision to deny the divorce promotes the rational basis of the state's public policy to promote households headed by opposite-sex couples.

The federal response to the same-sex marriage debate is fluid. In 1996 Congress enacted and President Clinton signed into law the Defense of Marriage Act. The Act restricts all federal benefits to opposite-sex married couples. Furthermore, under the Act no state, territory, or possession of the United States shall be required to give effect to any public act, record, or judicial proceeding of any other state regarding a relationship between persons of the same sex that is treated as a marriage under the laws of that state, or any right or claim arising from that relationship. [28 U.S.C. § 1738C (2006)] Many benefits associated with federal law are, as a

20. *In re* J.B. and H.B., 326 S.W.3d 654 (Tex. App. 2010); *but see* Christian-sen v. Christiansen, 253 P.3d 153 (Wyo. 2011) (state courts have subject matter jurisdiction to dissolve foreign same-sex marriages).

result of the legislation, unavailable to same-sex couples even though they have been validly married in an increasing number of states. These benefits include Social Security and immigration status as a spouse. Nonetheless, on February 23, 2011, the Attorney General announced that the United States Department of Justice will no longer defend the constitutionality of the Defense of Marriage Act as applied to same-sex couples who are validly married under state law. Nonetheless, the Act remains in effect until repealed by Congress or found unconstitutional in the highest federal court. To date, this has not occurred.

III. Marital Status Alternatives

A. *Civil Unions*

On July 1, 2000, Vermont created civil unions, a status for same-sex couples that sought to provide all of the benefits, protections, and responsibilities granted to spouses in marriage. Specifically, the civil union statute listed twenty-four benefits, protections, and responsibilities that were available to married couples and now would be available to civil unionists. As in Hawaii when it enacted the reciprocal beneficiary status, the new legislation was designed to provide all of the economic benefits of marriage, but to withhold the status of marriage itself. When Vermont enacted its newly named status, civil unions only applied to same-sex partners. And unlike other status arrangements, such as reciprocal beneficiaries and domestic partners, the same-sex couple had to comply with all of the formalities required to enter into marriage–license and solemnization–plus, if they ended the union, they had to go through all of the procedural divorce requirements. Entering and leaving a civil union was a significant undertaking, as similar to marriage as possible without naming it marriage.

Other states eventually adopted civil union legislation and some other states recognized their validity, even though the process was unavailable in that state. For example, Connecticut, prior to adopting same-sex marriage, enacted civil unions. Likewise, prior to adopting same-sex marriage, New Hampshire enacted civil unions. And then New Jersey, prompted by its state supreme court enacted same-sex civil unions, but the state attorney general acknowledged that the state would recognize other state's same-sex marriages and, of course, civil unions and domestic partnerships. As this book goes to press, Illinois, Rhode Island, and Delaware have civil unions, and finally, Hawaii adopted civil unions. The Hawaii bill was signed into law by the governor in February 2011, taking effect on January 1, 2012. This is a unique development, because Hawaii was the state that originated reciprocal beneficiaries.

B. *Domestic Partnerships*

Domestic partnerships initiated with the business community, anxious to keep gay and lesbian workers who could not enter into marriage, but wanted to bring their partners into the benefit packages of the employer.[21] By registering as a domestic partner of an employee, the partner could share in the health care benefits and any other perks that the company offered, such as discounts or companion seats on airlines. To achieve domestic partnership status, the employee registered the partner at the company's personnel office, and if the relationship ended, the employee simply deleted the former partner's name. Compared to marriage or civil unions, the process was and remains very simple. Later, when Hawaii adopted the status of reciprocal beneficiaries, it was an all-inclusive version of domestic partnership. Gradually domestic partnerships were adopted by cities and states, partly in recognition of the changing perception of gay and lesbian persons, but also as a result of the growing political involvement of the gay and lesbian community.

The status of domestic partners is almost exclusively restricted to same-sex partners. Constitutional challenges to this by opposite-sex partners were unsuccessful: The courts and legislatures reasoned that opposite-sex couples had marriage as an option, but same-sex couples did not. Overall, litigation that sought increased benefits for same-sex couples resulted in one of the most extensive domestic partnership statutes in the United States: the California Domestic Partnership Rights and Responsibilities Act of 2003. [CAL. FAM. CODE § 297.5(a) (2008)] By 2005, same-sex couples had the right to register as partners in California, giving them the same state benefits as opposite-sex couples, both during the relationship and afterwards, whether the relationship ends because of separation or death. The Act also allowed California courts and administrative agencies to recognize the validity of similar status arrangements formed in other states, excluding same-sex marriage.

In 2008, the Supreme Court of California ruled that the state's prohibition of same-sex marriage was unconstitutional, holding that sexual orientation was a suspect class and entitled to strict scrutiny. The state could not justify its prohibition with a compelling state interest, and same-sex marriage seemed inevitable in Califor-

---

21. *See* Raymond C. O'Brien, *Domestic Partnership: Recognition and Responsibility*, 32 SAN DIEGO L. REV. 163, 178–181 (1995).

nia.[22] But on November 4, 2008, California voters passed Proposition 8, which amended the state constitution to define marriage as between a man and a woman. As in other states, this effectively ended the validity of future same-sex marriages in California, but as this book goes to print, litigation continues concerning the enforceability of Proposition 8.

Because businesses make domestic partnership available in many cities and localities, they will remain viable in spite of what occurs in California in reference to Proposition 8. It seems logical that domestic partnerships, reciprocal beneficiaries, and civil unions would cease if and when same-sex couples are granted the ability to marry. But often the states do not want to jeopardize the rights of existing relationships, so they leave the status in existence. However, the future of these existing relationships seems uncertain if same-sex marriage is available. Today, much of the litigation focus concerns the effect of the Defense of Marriage Act, a federal act restricting federal benefits to opposite-sex married couples. In addition, in states that have adopted same-sex marriage entitlements, there is an issue of religious liberty, whether religious organizations and persons may refuse to recognize such marriages based on Free Exercise claims. And finally, whether the partnership status deprives landlord-tenant courts from evicting partners from real estate,[23] considerations of taxation status, and whether there is jurisdiction to dissolve the partnerships.

IV. The Husband and Wife Relationship

During the course of a valid marriage or a status conferring upon parties the benefits of marriage, issues arise that are unique to the married couple. The following is a list of some of the most litigious issues involving persons who are married and have no intention of separating or obtaining a divorce. Thus, the issues that arise do so as a result of the special relationship created by the marriage; often the issues are precipitated by a clash between the traditional law or policy and more modern rulings concerning an evolution of status.

A. *Choice of Names*

Once a woman married it was traditional for her to change her birth name to that of her husband. By no means mandatory, the

---

22. In re Marriage Cases, 183 P.3d 384 (Cal. 2008), *invalidated by* Cal. Const. Art. I, § 7.5 ("Proposition 8"). This constitutional amendment, however, was held unconstitutional. See Perry v. Schwarzenegger, 704 F.Supp.2d 921 (N.D. Cal. 2010).

23. Piotrowski v. Little, 911 N.Y.S.2d 583 (N.Y. Civ. Ct. 2010).

change of names by the woman became common practice. The woman, once she married, had to begin the process of changing all of her legal identification—a common law process—that would result in an effective transition into the name of her husband. Subsequently, if divorce should occur, the former spouse had a number of options: She could resume her birth name as a part of the divorce court's final decree of divorce, or she could retain her former husband's surname. She also could resume her birth name according to the common law practice, or she could assume another name altogether.

No state requires one spouse to take the name of the other upon marriage. And either party is free to change his or her name as long as there is no attempt to defraud others. There was one case that restricted the divorcing husband from depriving his former wife of the use of his name subsequent to the divorce. As part of the divorce decree the husband had sought to force the former wife to surrender his name and resume her birth name. But the court ruled that the choice of her name was a choice the former wife could make and the husband had no property right in his name at that point.[24] As long as there was no attempt to defraud, the former spouse was able to retain the name she chose at marriage.

B. *Management of Marital Property*

In 1971, the Supreme Court ruled that gender discrimination violated the Equal Protection Clause of the Fourteenth Amendment.[25] Then, six years later, the Court ruled that each and every gender distinction must be justified under an intermediate level of scrutiny, that is, any gender classification must serve important government interests and must be substantially related to achieving those interests.[26] While the 1960s and the 1970s inaugurated many guarantees under the Constitution, when viewed in the context of these two particular decisions, the 1970s inaugurated a new era in the rights of married women. Prior to this time: (1) married women could not validly execute contracts without the permission or joinder of their husbands; (2) the wife lost all power over her real property during the course of her marriage; (3) the wife lost all power over her personal property, both during her lifetime and at her death she lacked the ability to give it away or bequeath it to others; and (4) all of the wife's personal property as

---

24. Peniston v. Peniston, 511 S.W.2d 675 (Ky. Ct. App. 1974).

25. Reed v. Reed, 404 U.S. 71 (1971).

26. Craig v. Boren, 429 U.S. 190 (1976).

well as the husband's personal property were subject to the husband's creditors. In return, the husband had to provide his wife with necessities: Clothing, food, housing, utilities, and legal and medical expenses during the marriage. In addition, the husband was responsible for the wife's premarital debts and for any torts she committed before or during the marriage. At divorce, the husband was responsible for the wife's support until she died or remarried unless, of course, she committed the marital offense that resulted in the divorce.

During the nineteenth century, the wife's control over property gradually expanded through enactment of various married women's property acts. But the husband continued to occupy the role as manager of all marital or community property. By 1981, surely with the impetus of the gender equality movement, the Supreme Court ruled that a state statute that automatically made the husband the master of the community violated the Equal Protection Clause of the Fourteenth Amendment.[27] Today, management rules regarding marital property embrace a concept of control by economic equals. The concept is embraced in the Model Marital Property Act, formerly known as the Uniform Marital Property Act, which states that: "The fundamental principle that ownership of all of the economic rewards from the personal effort of each spouse during marriage is shared by the spouses in vested, present, and equal interests is the heart of the community property system. It is also the heart of the Uniform Marital Property Act. Common law states have been moving closer and closer to the sharing concept in both divorce and probate legislation, and the Uniform Marital Property Act builds on the direction of that movement."[28] Likewise, "Each spouse shall act in good faith with respect to the other spouse in matters involving marital property or other property of the other spouse. This obligation may not be varied by a marital property agreement." [*Id.* at § 2(a)]

Premarital agreements, and in some cases, postmarital agreements, often specify property management responsibilities, or particularly reference the management options of each spouse. But even in the absence of these agreements, all property acquired during the marriage is treated as either community property or marital property, with title having no effect in the former, but meaning little in either case. In modern marital property management, the operative feature is that neither party may exercise unilateral control over the management, transfer, or joinder of property acquired during marriage. This rule applies at divorce

27. Kirchberg v. Feenstra, 450 U.S. 455 (1981).

28. Unif. Marital Property Act, *Prefatory Note*, (1983).

through distribution of assets or debt, and at death through elective share statutes.

C. Support During Marriage

At common law, only the husband had a duty to support his spouse throughout the marriage; the wife had an obligation of support if the husband was incapable of doing so. Gender equality now requires both spouses to provide support to each other, and states have enacted legislation mandating this: New York, for example, provides the following: "A married person is chargeable with the support of his of her spouse and, if possessed of sufficient means or be able to earn such means, may be required to pay for his or her support a fair and reasonable sum, as the court may determine, having due regard to the circumstances of the respective parties."[29]

The support obligation was known as the necessities doctrine. It mandated that the spouse provide the other spouse with support for clothing, food, medical care, legal care, and any costs associated with the maintenance of the family home. The Model Marital Property Act provides, in a modern version of the doctrine, that: "An obligation incurred by a spouse during marriage, including one attributable to an act or omission during marriage, is presumed to be incurred in the interest of the marriage or the family." [§ 8(a)] Therefore, when a spouse incurs a necessary obligation during marriage, it may be satisfied from marital property or from the separate property of the obligated spouse. [§ 8(b)(i)] Furthermore, if a spouse brings an obligation into the marriage, or incurs an obligation during the marriage attributable to an obligation that incurred prior to the marriage, that obligation may be paid only from property that is not marital property. [§ 8(a)(iii)] But a spouse's debts may not always be paid from marital assets. If the spouse incurs an obligation to benefit a third party without the knowledge or consent of the other spouse, the innocent spouse should not be accountable to have the debt paid from marital assets. There must be some nexus to the debt, other than being married to the person who assumed it.[30] Even the Internal Revenue Service provides immunity from income tax liability for innocent spouses, as long as the spouse makes a timely appeal.[31]

---

29. N.Y. Fam. Ct. Act § 412 (McKinney 1998).

30. *See* Rice v. Rice, 336 S.W.3d 66 (Ky. 2011).

31. *See* Jones v. Commissioner, 642 F.3d 459 (4th Cir. 2011).

State statutes and the Model Marital Property Act refer to marriage as the prerequisite to an obligation of support between the spouses. But the question arises as to whether there would be a duty of support between nonmarital cohabitants. We will discuss this issue in more detail in Chapter 4, *infra*. Certainly, a support obligation would be present for persons in a registered marital status, such as a civil union or domestic partnership, but it seems that the issue of any support obligation imposed on one nonmarital cohabitant towards the other will depend upon any oral or written contracts existing between the parties. While equitable remedies are available, and cases repeatedly illustrate their use, their patchwork applicability makes reliance upon them elusive.

D. Spousal Crimes of Assault, Crimes Against Property, and Testimonial Privilege

Until well into the last quarter of the 20th century, a majority of states permitted marriage to be a defense to any accusation of rape or sodomy alleged by one spouse against the other. That is, spouses had no legal recourse when unwelcome sexual conduct was forced upon them by the other spouse. The rationale was that the obligation of sexual contact inherent in marriage precluded any ability to reject the sexual advances of the other spouse.[32]

Beginning in the 1980s, there was a gradual evolution of thinking that mirrored the evolution in management of marital property. Increasingly spouses were viewed more as equal partners, able to reject the sexual advances of each other. Judicial decisions and state statutes have supported that view, holding that a spouse does not give up his or her right to state protection from the violent acts of rape or aggravated sodomy committed by the other spouse.[33] Protective orders, and the criminal statutes that complement them, give further evidence of the shift in attitudes. Likewise, as we will discuss, *infra*, spousal tort immunity has also diminished.

The possibility of prosecution for sexual assault or rape occurring between spouses prompts consideration of other issues as well. For instance, crimes against property that could be classified as marital property. Is it possible to prosecute a spouse for the theft or destruction of marital property? The answer seems to be yes if it appears that the property in question had been "sequestered" by

---

32. This may have resulted from the dictum of Lord Hale in the 17th century. *See* Commonwealth v. Chretien, 417 N.E.2d 1203 (Mass. 1981), referring to 1 Hale, History of Pleas of the Crown, p. 629.

33. *See, e.g.*, Warren v. State, 336 S.E.2d 221 (Ga. 1985); *see also* Va. Code Ann. § 18.2–61 (2004).

the victim. That is, even though the property is clearly marital or community property, it has been declared by one of the parties as off limits to the other, and if the other spouse takes or destroys it, the act may be prosecuted under any available remedy under the law, the marriage is not an adequate defense.[34]

Is there a testimonial privilege between spouses? May one spouse testify against the other, with or without that spouse's consent? There are two separate privileges to consider. Under the common law, private communications, including conduct, *between spouses* enjoyed an absolute privilege. Either spouse could invoke the privilege. But, conversely, matters relating to criminal law, where a third party is involved, were addressed separately by the courts. In a seminal decision, the Supreme Court ruled that a spouse may testify against the other spouse in spite of the accused spouse's objection, if the testimony will promote the administration of justice.[35] The decision, ostensibly only governing federal courts, was a significant departure from previous holdings, making a clear distinction between types of privilege. The federal decision also implied that if both of the parties have participated in an alleged crime, then the privilege is unavailable and testimony may be obtained. In addition, no privilege attaches if the spouse is a victim of an offence, the spouses have voluntarily separated, or, as *Trammel* indicates, if one spouse voluntarily testifies against the other.

The issue of privilege is not settled among the various states. Some courts permit a spouse to refuse to testify based on public policy reasons,[36] others look to the type of offense, and others look to a variety of factors affecting the administration of justice. But, as the discussion on domestic violence will indicate, *infra*, the issue of privilege between spouses, between those in similar status arrangements, and between intimate nonmarital cohabitants will continue to arise.

E. Domestic Violence

In order to protect potential victims, property, and other household members from abusive conduct occurring in the context of an intimate relationship, legislatures have enacted statutes to allow for courts to issue civil protective orders. The civil remedy of the protective order is pertinent to crimes of domestic violence,

---

34. *See, e.g.*, People v. Wallace, 19 Cal.Rptr.3d 790 (Cal. Ct. App. 2004); State v. Hagedorn, 679 N.W.2d 666 (Iowa 2004).

35. Trammel v. United States, 445 U.S. 40 (1980).

36. *See, e.g.*, Commonwealth v. Valle–Velez, 995 A.2d 1264 (Pa. Super. Ct. 2010).

because of the special context of when there is an intimate relationship between the parties. The exact definition of intimacy is elusive, but courts have allowed intimacy to be proven if the couple is in a mutually close, or dating relationship.[37] Marital intimacy is not a prerequisite, and the intimacy contemplated within the context of domestic violence may occur between opposite-sex and same-sex couples.

The civil protective order issued by a court may provide for many remedies, to include injunctions mandating that the abusers be kept away from the victim, thereby specifying physical separation, electronic separation, and specific injunctions against visiting a child's school, the victim's parents or workplace, and of course the home. Modern applications involve prohibitions against stalking and electronic surveillance, plus orders to restrict access to pets and friends. The process usually commences with the victim seeking an *ex parte* order of protection, followed by a hearing at which the alleged abuser may appear and argue against the issuance of the order. The initial ex parte order, based solely on the testimony of the alleged victim, is only temporary, but may be extended once the alleged victim is allowed to testify. These temporary orders have been held to be reasonable, even though they infringe on the Due Process rights of the alleged abuser. Courts have found them to be reasonable in light of the potential harm to the victim and the opportunity for the alleged abuser to testify in the near future. The later hearing meets Due Process requirements if it is conducted within a reasonable period of time.

At the initial ex parte hearing, most often in the absence of the abuser, the victim must demonstrate that he or she is in fear of the abuser and apprehensive of serious bodily harm. The level of proof required is low, preponderance of the evidence, and courts often are deeply divided on what constitutes fear on the part of the victim.[38] Often the abuser ignores the civil requirements of the protective order, sometimes resulting in increased harm to the victim. When the police have not been completely effective in preventing the abuser from violence, the issue arises as to whether the failure of the police, agents of the state, violates the Due Process Clause of the Fourteenth Amendment. In 2005 the Supreme Court ruled that before state action could invoke a violation of the Due Process Clause, prompting state liability, there would have to be a precise means of enforcement enacted by the state that had been violated

---

37. Evans v. Braun, 12 A.3d 395 (Pa. Super. Ct. 2010).

38. *See, e.g.,* Tons v. Bley, 815 N.E.2d 508 (Ind. Ct. App. 2004)(holding there was an absence of fear, but with a strong dissent); MD. CODE ANN., FAM. LAW § 4–506(c) (West 2008).

by the police. Without this precision, the victim has no property interest that went unprotected by the police; the police did not fail to provide the victim with due process by failing to provide the victim with protection.[39]

As a result of the Supreme Court's decision, civil remedies against the state for failure to provide protection are extremely rare. But all of the states have enacted statutes to criminalize violations of civil protection orders, a remedy that provides some solace. A person with a protective order can ask for police assistance if there is a violation. The police then can charge the violator with either a misdemeanor or a felony offense. Furthermore, to enhance criminal enforcement, many states have mandatory arrest laws. These laws often take the burden from the victim of placing an intimate partner, who nonetheless is an abuser, into jail for violating an aspect of the civil protective order. Since the arrest is mandatory, incarceration follows an infraction of the civil order, thereby seeming to isolate the victim from the process. Nonetheless, commentary varies on the utility of mandatory arrest as the laws can automatically remove the abuser from an income-producing job, a job often needed for the support of children and the victim.

To address the incidents of interstate domestic violence, Congress enacted the Violence Against Women Act. The Act was initially enacted in 1994, but there have been subsequent revisions to provide better services. Among the added features have been enhanced legal assistance for victims, shelters, a national domestic violence hotline, counselors for victims, tracking of perpetrators, and educational programs for police and criminal enforcement personnel.[40] Primarily, the Act addresses criminal remedies under the powers granted to Congress through the Commerce Clause. So too, the National Conference of Commissioners on Uniform State Laws promulgated the Uniform Interstate Enforcement of Domestic Violence Protection Orders Act in 2002, seeking thereby to better enforce the civil orders of protection across state lines.

F. Marital Torts

A tort is a civil wrong committed against another. Under the early common law, as previously discussed, a husband was liable for the torts of his wife as long as they were intentional, against a third party, and were committed in the presence of the husband. Today, the responsibility for tort damages or for any legal defense attend-

---

39. Castle Rock v. Gonzales, 545 U.S. 748 (2005).

40. VIOLENCE AGAINST WOMEN ACT, 18 U.S.C. §§ 2261–2266 (2006).

ant to any claim by a victim would be gender neutral and arise in the context of the doctrine of necessities, discussed *supra.*

Increasingly today courts allow for one spouse to sue another in tort. Many factors have contributed to this. Certainly the evolution of the concept of spouses as marital partners is one, the more prevalent notion of marital independence, prenuptial agreement enforcement, and an overall sense of enforcement of marital misconduct. The Model Marital Property Act, influenced by changes in the law, allows for a spouse to sue another for any breach of the duty of good faith with respect to the other spouse in matters involving marital property or other property that belongs to the other spouse. As long as the suit is brought within three years after acquiring actual knowledge of the facts giving rise to the claim, one spouse may sue another.[41] Thus, Maryland's highest court provides extensive rationale for abandoning spousal tort immunity and allowing spouses to sue one another in tort.[42] The case involved the husband suing the wife for malicious prosecution. The wife had sought a protective order against the husband, then initiated criminal proceedings against him for stalking, harassment, and multiple counts of violation of the order. The husband alleges that the wife did this in retaliation for his petition of divorce served on her shortly beforehand. The court described the doctrine of interspousal tort immunity as it applied to both negligence and intentional torts as a vestige of ancient times that should be abolished.

Other courts speak only to intentional torts. A New Mexico decision stated that interspousal tort immunity existed only to prevent accusations of marital misconduct and elements of private personal relationships from being brought into a courtroom. But as long as the tort litigation does not involve the intimacies related to the marital relationship, the immunity doctrine should be abandoned whenever the nature of the tort is sufficiently outrageous.[43] Likewise, courts are willing to entertain spousal tort suits when the suit involves a post-divorce action, the key element being that the suit no longer involves the intimate marital relationship.[44]

G. Medical Decision–Making

In the absence of a medical directive naming someone to make medical decisions for an individual, the law will choose from a

---

41. UNIF. MARITAL PROPERTY ACT § 15 (1983).

42. Bozman v. Bozman, 830 A.2d 450 (Md. 2003).

43. Papatheofanis v. Allen, 242 P.3d 358 (N.M. Ct. App. 2010), *review granted*, 240 P.3d 1049 (N.M. 2010).

44. Feltmeier v. Feltmeier, 798 N.E.2d 75 (Ill. 2003); Chen v. Fischer, 843 N.E.2d 723 (N.Y. 2005).

statutory hierarchy of persons in seeking decisions concerning medical care for an incapacitated person. When persons are married, medical decisions are most often made by spouses in the absence of such a medical directive. These health care directives are more popular today, perhaps in response to federal legislation mandating that every patient admitted to a hospital be advised of his or her right to sign a directive.[45] In addition, there have been a series of very public medical-decision cases pitting parents of an incapacitated person against the spouse of the incapacitated person in the decision involving the termination of life-support.[46]

There may be an inherent conflict of interest between the surviving spouse and an incapacitated spouse whose death may result in the surviving spouse inheriting through the probate estate, or devices such as life insurance, complete control over wealth. Before the spouse may terminate life support, in the absence of a health care directive, the spouse would either have to prove that the incapacitated spouse made his or her wishes known, or that it is in the best interest of the incapacitated person to have all extraordinary means withdrawn from life support. The level of proof that must be proven changes with the degree of severity of the medical condition.[47] Whatever the level of proof required, the contentious litigation between the spouse and any other interested parties is preventable through proper planning.

Nonmarital cohabitants are especially vulnerable to state statutes that designate persons to make medical decisions. As we will see in the following chapter, proper objective planning is essential in planning lifetime choices, as well as end-of-life decisions.

---

45. Patient Self–Determination Act, Omnibus Budget Reconciliation Act of 1990, Pub. L. No. 101–508, § 4751, 104 Stat. 1388 (codified as amended in scattered sections of 42 U.S.C).

46. *See, e.g.*, Bush v. Schiavo, 885 So.2d 321 (Fla. 2004).

47. *See, e.g.*, Conservatorship of Wendland, 26 Cal.4th 519, 28 P.3d 151 (2001).

Chapter 4

Nonmarital Cohabitation

I. The Issue

There has always been intimate adult nonmarital cohabitation. But some developments concerning nonmarital cohabitation are recent and noteworthy. First, the number of adults cohabiting in a manner similar to marriage, but not wishing to marry, has increased significantly. From the year 1960 until 2006, the number of adult nonmarital cohabitants increased by more than 1,000%.[1] Second, adults who cohabit are persons of the same-sex and the opposite-sex; the benefits associated with nonmarital cohabitation apply to either group of persons. Presumptively, both groups have the opportunity to marry or to enter into a status equivalent to marriage, but nonetheless they choose to remain in a nonmarital living arrangement. Until the advent of same-sex marriage, or any similar status, same-sex couples were restricted to nonmarital living, as they had no choice to do otherwise. Any benefits the same-sex couples enjoyed were derived from the argument that their relationship was functioning as a family and, unless barred by statute, should be able to partake in family benefits.[2] Today, same-sex couples have far more options yet, like their opposite-sex counterparts, many choose to remain unmarried cohabitants.

Without the economic safeguards of marriage, one of the nonmarital cohabitants was vulnerable once the relationship ended because of dissolution or death. Support was freely given, careers abandoned, and services rendered towards the other partner only to lose it all when the relationship ended. In the most celebrated case of Marvin v. Marvin,[3] Lee Marvin, the television and movie star invited a woman named Michelle to live with him. After she moved into his home they cohabited for seven years until he told her to leave and not come back. She had given up her career and any resulting earnings to live with him, and while he had worked and earned a salary, any assets he owned were titled in his name alone. Because they were not married Michelle was not entitled to one-half of the community property, or to any support from Lee to compensate for the career she abandoned to be with him. After

---

1. THE NATIONAL MARRIAGE PROJECT, THE STATE OF OUR UNIONS 2007, 19 (2007).

2. *See, e.g.*, Braschi v. Stahl Associates Co., 543 N.E.2d 49 (N.Y. 1989) (permitting a same-sex couple to qualify for rent control protection as a family).

3. 557 P.2d 106 (Cal. 1976).

their separation, she brought suit against him, seeking to recover the value of what she alleged he promised to do for her: To take care of her the rest of her life. The promise was implied, an oral understanding, but Lee had no recollection of having promised anything of the sort. Should Michelle be able to recover?

Prior to *Marvin*, there were few options for Michelle. The case illustrates the third development concerning cohabitation: The evolution of contract and equitable remedies to protect the expectations of the nonmarital parties. After *Marvin*, with few exceptions, courts have been willing to permit a nonmarital partner to recover against the other based on express or implied contracts. Courts have been willing to provide remedies based on equitable remedies such as unjust enrichment, which requires that there be: (1) a benefit conferred on the defendant nonmarital partner by the plaintiff, (2) awareness by the plaintiff of the benefit being conferred, and (3) acceptance or retention of the benefit by the defendant under circumstances that make it inequitable.[4] The *Marvin* decision, as we will discuss further in section two of this chapter, *infra*, changed the law regarding the enforcement of nonmarital cohabitation contracts.

Equitable remedies to meet the expectations of the nonmarital parties have become more extensive with the passage of time. The U.S. Court of Appeals for the 9th Circuit held that a woman who had been a nonmarital cohabitant with a man for more than thirty years was, in fact, in a "quasi-marital" relationship. This relationship entitled her to half of the man's pension benefits when they separated, similar to what she would have received if they had been married and divorced. Their nonmarital relationship was sufficient to provide her with a qualified domestic relations order (QDRO), which provided her with rights when their relationship dissolved.[5] Also, the Wyoming Supreme Court, recognizing the family-like relationship of nonmarital cohabitants, equally partitioned the house the couple had owned as tenants-in-common. The fact that the man had contributed significantly more than the woman towards the home did not bar the court using the marital presumption of equal contribution, justifying the equal distribution between the nonmarital cohabitants.[6] The willingness of courts to confer economic benefits upon nonmarital cohabitants creates a fourth development. That is, benefits associated with marriage can be

4. Watts v. Watts, 405 N.W.2d 303 (Wis. 1987); *see also* Porter v. Zuromski, 6 A.3d 372 (Md. Ct. Spec. App. 2010) (utilizing unjust enrichment to grant equitable relief).

5. Owens v. Automotive Machinists Pension Trust, 551 F.3d 1138 (9th Cir. 2009).

6. Hofstad v. Christie, 240 P.3d 816 (Wyo. 2010).

extended to death benefits. The benefits are not restricted to dissolution, but may be applied after the death of either party, if to do so would effectuate an express or an implied agreement between the parties.[7] Thus, at the death of either nonmarital cohabitant, the living party may bring an action against the estate to enforce an express or implied agreement. In the case of an implied agreement, where proof is difficult to obtain, the disappointed partner may petition for an equitable remedy, such as unjust enrichment.

A fifth development concerning cohabitation is the evolution in focus from the economic rights of nonmarital partners, to the parental rights of nonmarital partners. At issue is the following: (1) whether states and the courts will recognize the right of a nonmarital couple to adopt children; (2) whether nonmarital persons may be considered as similar to stepparents when they seek to adopt the child of a partner, such a status would facilitate adoption and not terminate the rights of the genetic parent; (3) whether nonmarital cohabitants may serve as foster parents; and (4) whether a genetic parent may relinquish parental rights to his or her nonmarital partner without terminating his or her own parental rights as the genetic parent. In all of these issues, the parenting rights of nonmarital partners have expanded with each decade.

Originally, most of the litigation involved the rights of same-sex couples, who were unable to marry and sought some permanence in establishing families. But today the evolution applies to both same-sex and opposite-sex partners. Most often, courts have interpreted the state statute or the state constitution to rule that couples, same-sex and opposite-sex, have a fundamental right to privacy in their consensual non-commercial relationships. Based on this right, they should be able to self-order their own lives as long as this does not infringe on the rights of others. Because these couples enjoy a fundamental right of privacy, they should not be forced to choose between being parents and having an intimate relationship with an adult partner.[8] In addition, increasingly courts look to the best interest of the child in establishing paternity and maternity. Thus, when a parent wishes to allow his or her nonmarital partner to adopt that parent's genetic child, courts have been willing to allow the non-genetic parent to adopt when not expressly barred by statute. When viewed in this context, it is possible to allow for a step-parent type of adoption, which does not require terminating the rights of the consenting genetic parent. The rationale follows that a rebuttable presumption of parenthood applies

---

7. Byrne v. Laura, 60 Cal.Rptr.2d 908 (Cal. Ct. App. 1997); *see also* In re Estate of Quarg, 938 A.2d 193 (N.J. Super. Ct. 2008).

8. *See, e.g.,* Arkansas Dept. of Human Services v. Cole, No. 10–840, 2011 WL 1319217 (Ark. Apr. 7, 2011).

when a non-genetic partner welcomes a child into the home with the consent of the genetic parent and then proceeds to openly treat the child as his or her own. This is a presumption that should not be rebutted, since termination of the genetic parent's rights would leave the child with at least one less parent and this is not in the best interest of the child.[9] Establishing paternity or maternity in this fashion is the first step in providing support, access to economic and social benefits, inheritance rights, and social security.

Not surprisingly, a sixth development concerning cohabitation is the backlash against extending rights to nonmarital cohabitants. Critics argue that when courts provide economic benefits to non-marital couples that mirror the rights of marital partners, the courts are in effect enacting common law marriage. Since many of the states grappling with the rights of cohabitants have abolished common law marriage, the court is violating separation of powers by providing such economic benefits.[10] Likewise, critics argue that many same-sex couples can enter into marriage, domestic partnerships, and civil unions and that these status arrangements should be utilized. Otherwise, courts are imposing benefits when none were intended by the parties. But for most critics, the overriding concern is that if courts provide benefits to nonmarital cohabitants similar to what would be available to married couples, eventually couples will not bother to obtain a license and solemnize their wedding. They can get the same result by simply living together. Finally, critics argue that enforcing contracts or applying equitable remedies will only embroil the courts in determining the private understanding of the parties, a task that is difficult and violative of privacy. For some states these concerns are sufficient so as to warrant denying any recognition, especially in reference to same-sex couples.[11]

The seventh development involves the panoply of rights and causes of action that are associated with marriage. These rights have gradually and haphazardly been made available to nonmarital partners. Torts, for example. Courts have permitted a cause of action to be brought by a plaintiff against the defendant if the plaintiff has injured a victim and the plaintiff and victim were closely related. Increasingly, courts have begun to allow unmarried cohabitants to bring a cause of action against the defendant for this tort, without the necessity of being married. Rather, the court looks

---

9. *See, e.g.,* Elisa B. v. Superior Court, 117 P.3d 660 (Cal. 2005), *see also* Am. Law Inst., *Principles of the Law of Family Dissolution: Analysis and Recommendations* § 2.03 (recognizing parents by estoppel).

10. *See* Hewitt v. Hewitt, 394 N.E.2d 1204 (Ill. 1979).

11. *See* Va. Code Ann. § 20–45.3 (2008).

to whether the emotional injury suffered by the plaintiff is genuine and substantial and the relationship was of significant duration.[12] Thus, the nonmarital cohabitant can recover for the emotional trauma suffered without being related to the victim through any of the more traditional ways, marriage being the most common. Nonetheless courts deny recovery for loss of consortium when the action is brought by a nonmarital partner against a defendant who has injured the other partner. But, in some instances, a partner may recover under wrongful death statutes.[13] And significantly, courts have been very willing to allow nonmarital cohabitants, same-sex and opposite-sex, to benefit from domestic violence statutes enacted to protect intimate partners.[14] Even in states with stringent statutes forbidding any recognition of rights for same-sex couples, protective orders associated with the protection of intimate partners from domestic violence have been upheld.

The eighth and final development is that increasingly, courts are willing to consider the period of nonmarital cohabitation when assessing the accumulation of marital property. Thus, in those instances when the couple has cohabited for a number of years and then marries, the court is willing to consider the entire time together in the division of marital property, not only the period of time when they were actually married. As an illustration, the Georgia Supreme Court considered opinions of other state courts and held that it was equitable and proper to consider all thirteen years of a relationship in dividing property upon divorce, not just the two years when the couple was actually married. Since nothing in the alimony statute would prohibit a consideration of premarital cohabitation, the court ruled that it had discretion to include all eleven years in making an alimony award.[15] But not all courts agree. A Minnesota court ruled that to consider premarital cohabitation would be to revive common law marriage, a status that had been abolished by the legislature.[16] Minnesota is a state that only enforces written nonmarital agreements, hence the court's conservative approach is representative of the state's public policy.

II. Ascendency of the Status of Nonmarital Cohabitation

Even though there has always been intimate nonmarital cohabitation of adults, the evident shift today has been to provide status

---

12. Graves v. Estabrook, 818 A.2d 1255 (N.H. 2003).

13. *But see* Clark Sand Co. v. Kelly, 60 So.3d 149 (Miss. 2011) (cohabitant was not an interested party entitled to sue under wrongful death).

14. State v. Carswell, 871 N.E.2d 547 (Ohio 2007).

15. Sprouse v. Sprouse, 678 S.E.2d 328 (Ga. 2009).

16. Cummings v. Cummings, 376 N.W.2d 726 (Minn. Ct. App. 1985).

to cohabitation. That is, during the latter part of the last century and continuing today, the trend has been to provide support and parenthood rights during lifetime, and inheritance and probate responsibilities at death. Heretofore, these vestiges of status were reserved exclusively to married couples. What caused the shift in attitude?

History and a few of the more seminal court decisions are illustrative. In the United States, prior to the 1976 Supreme Court of California's decision in *Marvin*, discussed *supra*, nonmarital couples were precluded from enforcing contracts involving intimate relationships. To enforce a contract that involved nonmarital persons living together was violative of public policy. Because the couple was involved in nonmarital intimacies, any enforcement of the promises based on that relationship would be immoral. But when *Marvin* was decided in 1976, the court changed the perspective. First, the court was willing to take judicial notice of the fact that there was a significant number of nonmarital relationships existent in society. In addition, there was an increasing social acceptance of adults cohabiting. The court wrote that the mores of society had changed so radically in regard to cohabitation that it may be concluded that any standard of alleged morality forbidding cohabitation had been apparently abandoned by many. Second, the public policy abhorring enforcement of contracts based on meretricious sexual services is not similar to nonmarital relationships; these relationships have nothing to do with prostitution. To equate nonmarital cohabitation with prostitution does damage to what occurs between nonmarital partners. Furthermore, forbidding damages based on prostitution does not justify denying recovery for an inequitable distribution of property accumulated during a nonmarital relationship.

A third factor that the *Marvin* court considered was the fact that past courts did distinguish between contracts that rested upon a consideration of meretricious sexual services, and contracts in which two adult parties contemplate a relationship together without marriage, but nonetheless still involves a sexual relationship. The court refers to prior court decisions seeking to provide benefits to nonmarital couples as decisions hovering in the somewhat wispy form of the figures of a Chagall painting. Nonetheless, the court points out, these cases did in fact allow for recovery as long as the consideration was not based solely on sexual services. Therefore, the decision in *Marvin* should not be viewed as so radical a departure from prior decisions.

Fourth, the court recognized the well-established public policy that always sought to foster and promote the institution of marriage. But the court concluded that the perpetuation of judicial rules that result in an inequitable distribution of property accumulated during a nonmarital relationship, is neither a just nor an effective way of promoting that marriage policy. And finally, the court announced a fifth factor, holding that nonmarital partners may enforce their reasonable expectations through express agreements, conduct that demonstrates an implied agreement, or any equitable remedy such as a constructive trust or quantum meruit that protects the expectations of the parties.

The *Marvin* decision was as audacious as it was timely. The court was swayed by the increasing number of nonmarital cohabitants, and motivated by the practicality of dividing any accumulated assets equitably between parties able to prove by word or deed that non-sexual expectations could be established. Furthermore, the court bifurcated the institution of marriage from the economic benefits that parties may assemble while cohabiting. The court did not intend to decrease the status of marriage, but only wanted to enforce the written and implied agreements regarding property that the couple had assembled together. Public policy had shifted. What prompted this shift in public attitude that enabled adults to cohabit without marriage, garner increasing public acceptance, as determined by the highest court of a state to craft a rational enforcement policy?

Sociologists might argue that the change in public perceptions resulted from the change in mores following the Second World War. Others would argue it was the introduction of the birth control pill in the late 1950s, giving women an effective means by which to control pregnancies. Most would argue that it was the establishment of a constitutional right to privacy in the Supreme Court's *Griswold* decision in 1965.[17] But, in hindsight, *Griswold* was a relatively conservative decision, permitting married couples to receive medical advice concerning means by which to prevent conception. Its impact, however, was to establish a constitutional right to privacy at the federal level, a right that is still being explored in today's Court, with repercussions in many state constitutions and decisions. Perhaps more importantly, *Griswold* was the basis of *Eisenstadt*, a 1972 decision by the Court that extended the right of privacy to individuals.[18] In *Eisenstadt*, Justice Brennan, writing for the majority, provided a constitutional basis for individuals to have access to birth control devices. But the opinion goes much further, as it provides an argument that the rights of the individual must be the same as the rights of a married person, especially in matters

17. Griswold v. Connecticut, 381 U.S. 479 (1965).

18. Eisenstadt v. Baird, 405 U.S. 438 (1972).

considered fundamental. *Eisenstadt* inaugurated a national acceptance of individual self-ordering, and precipitated many social changes.

Marriage had been alluded to as fundamental in the 1967 *Loving* decision.[19] Then, six years after *Eisenstadt*, the Court again made reference to the fundamental right to marry in Zablocki v. Redhail.[20] Justice Marshall opined in his majority decision that whenever a statute infringes upon the right to enter into marriage, it enters an area in which the Court has held such freedom to be fundamental. Taken as a whole, these cases, and other like them, provide a firm basis upon which to argue that individuals have a right to individual liberty, and a decision to enter into marriage, as an exercise of this liberty, is therefore a fundamental right. But likewise, if a person has a fundamental right to enter into marriage, an ancient institution, another person must have at least some right to enter into a nonmarital contract by which he or she forms a family, providing many of the benefits of marriage. This is the genesis of adult cohabitation status protection.

Same-sex couples, although originally contemplated within the protected status of *Marvin*, were nonetheless treated differently in reference to sexuality and certainly marriage. A few states retained sodomy statutes, effectively criminalizing any form of homosexual sexual activity. Based upon the privacy right enumerated in *Griswold* and *Eisenstadt,* individuals and organizations argued that consenting homosexual adults possessed a right of privacy in the sacred confines of their bedrooms. As such, homosexuals could not be prosecuted for sodomy. And even if prosecution were pursued, the prosecution would be barred under equal protection. The argument was as follows: If privacy protected opposite-sex couples from prosecution, there is no rational reason to treat same-sex couples differently. Same-sex persons could not be prosecuted for sodomy under equal protection. But a 1986 Court decision thwarted this conclusion. In *Bowers*, the defendant's attorneys argued that the Court should rule that the Due Process Clause granted homosexuals the fundamental right to engage in sodomy, but the Court rejected their argument.[21] By rejecting the argument, the Court permitted the state to enforce its sodomy statute against homosexuals, permitting this class of persons to be treated differently from others.

---

19. Loving v. Virginia, 388 U.S. 1 (1967).

20. 434 U.S. 374 (1978).

21. Bowers v. Hardwick, 478 U.S. 186 (1986).

The equal protection argument was not brought before the Court in *Bowers*. The attorneys representing the defendant thought that doing so would have supported the classification of two sets of persons, one opposite-sex and the other same-sex. Instead, by arguing for a fundamental right to engage in sodomy, the attorneys reasoned that since sodomy is the sole means by which persons of the same sex can be intimate with each other—just as intercourse is one of the means by which opposite-sex couples can be intimate—then intimacy is fundamental to family. Intimacy is the link between same sex and opposite-sex couples and due process creates a fundamental right to engage in intimate contact. But the *Bowers* Court saw no connection between sodomy, on the one hand, and family, marriage, procreation and fundamental rights on the other. In 1986, the argument over intimacy was lost.

Bowers was an aberration in the evolution of individual self-ordering between adults that had started with *Griswold* and *Eisenstadt*. Efforts were made to reverse the *Bowers* decision since it had a chilling effect upon any matters concerning homosexuals. For example, one effort occurred in 1996, when the Court in *Romer* used the Equal Protection Clause to invalidate a Colorado state constitutional amendment banning any laws that protected homosexuals. The Court ruled that the law singled out homosexuals and was the product of animosity, thereby depriving a disadvantaged group from the protections of the laws.[22] But the decision did not reverse *Bowers*. It was not until 2003 that *Bowers* was reversed and the Court would adopt the argument attempted in *Bowers*. The case involved a state sodomy statute and the issue was whether the statute could be used to prosecute two consenting adult males who had engaged in intimate sexual contact in a private apartment. The Court ruled that the sodomy statute was unconstitutional as applied to two consenting adults engaging in conduct in the exercise of their liberty interest under the Due Process Clause of the Fourteenth Amendment.[23] The Court expressly overruled *Bowers,* thus positing homosexuals in the same context as opposite-sex partners. In addition, the Court provides a mantra by which individuals may claim liberty in self-ordering their lives: The right to liberty under the Due Process Clause gives adults the full right to engage in private consensual conduct without the intervention of the government. This policy has implications for persons seeking to establish nonmarital families.

When evaluating the future of nonmarital cohabitation status rights, it seems plausible that the individual liberty arguments,

22. Romer v. Evans, 517 U.S. 620 (1996).   **23.** Lawrence v. Texas, 539 U.S. 558 (2003).

having progressed from *Marvin* to *Lawrence,* will have the following consequences: First, there will be no distinction between opposite-sex and same-sex cohabitants when it comes to enforcement of agreements, or the evolution of equitable remedies. Developments regarding same-sex marriage and similar status arrangements will have no effect on the parallel enforcement of cohabitation agreements. Issues may arise concerning whether a common law marriage will evolve in those states allowing them. But similar to statutory marriage there are requirements that must be met. Second, parties will be able to contract regarding economic and parenting roles as long as the agreements do not adversely affect the rights of others. Children and their best interests will be scrutinized carefully. Through an effective agreement, a non-genetic partner may become a parent to a child, thereby achieving de facto parental status with all of the constitutional protections.[24] Furthermore, adults may release or disparage their rights as they can with prenuptial and postnuptial agreements, but only with full disclosure and sufficient reflection. Third, employment benefits cannot be conferred on a non-employee through nonmarital cohabitation agreements, but only through status arrangements such as marriage, domestic partnerships, or civil unions. The parties are able to apportion property, and even provide for support, but benefits derived from status will not apply in all but the most rare circumstances. Fourth, federal law, often dependent upon state classifications regarding marital status and paternity, will remain unsettled as it grapples with whether cohabitant expenses constitute deductions or gifts. Plus there are many issues involving retirements benefits protected under ERISA.[25]

One of the most challenging consequences of nonmarital cohabitation agreements will be the enforcement of gestational contracts conferring parental status. A few states have enacted statutes permitting the establishment of parenthood through a valid gestational agreement. Thus, parenthood may occur through conception, adoption, artificial insemination, and gestational agreements. As long as the agreement is valid in the state, parental status may occur based on the agreement even though the parents did not adopt the child, and have no genetic connection with the child.[26] These gestational agreements are different from donor agreements, these being more common contracts, that stipulate that men who donate sperm and women who donate eggs have no responsibility

---

24. *See, e.g.*, Smith v. Guest, 16 A.3d 920 (Del. 2011).

25. *See, e.g.*, Estate of Shapiro v. U.S., 634 F.3d 1055 (9th Cir. 2011).

26. *See* Raftopol v. Ramey, 12 A.3d 783 (Conn. 2011).

for the child subsequently conceived and born. These agreements, which release the donor from any support obligation, and concomitantly the donor waives all custody and visitation rights, have traditionally been governed by contract law.[27] As with all contracts, agreements made between nonmarital cohabitants, and with third parties, will depend upon clarity and consideration for enforcement in state and federal courts.

III. Enforcement of Agreements

A. *Express Agreements*

Similar to what was discussed regarding premarital and postmarital agreements in Chapter Two, the more express the agreement, the more likely will it be enforced in the event of separation or death. Two states, Minnesota and Texas, require that enforcement of nonmarital contracts depend upon the agreement being in writing, hence express. [*See* MINN. STAT. § 513.075 (2008); TEX. BUS. & COM. CODE ANN. § 26.01 (Vernon 2007).] Unlike premarital agreements, there is no uniform law clarifying the ingredients necessary to bring about a valid express agreement. But it seems reasonable to assume that the agreement, in addition to being written, must be understood by both of the parties, freely entered into without duress and with sufficient reflection. The consideration is typically the mutuality of the agreed-upon services, and the agreement is modifiable or terminable under the same terms and conditions as any other contract.

The agreement should be binding upon the adult parties and, like a valid premarital agreement, should not adversely impact the rights or status of children. At a minimum, the agreement should specify the division of acquired property and the support obligations attendant upon dissolution or death; division of debt should also be an element. Because statutes involving property and support in the context of marriage are obviously inapplicable, the couple may nonetheless incorporate the provisions of these marital statutes into their express agreement through incorporation by reference, deleting any reference to marriage. In addition, because the cohabitation may cease with the death of one of the parties, the agreement should specifically refer to probate law, and specifically reference binding the estate or the decedent party, rights to elective share, and contractual claims on intestate property and nonprobate transfers. Also, both parties should execute health care directives naming the other party as the conservator, guardian, or possessing

---

27. *See, e.g.,* In re Paternity of M.F., 938 N.E.2d 1256 (Ind. Ct. App. 2010).

a durable power of attorney over the incompetent party. A review of the elements listed in Chapter 6, where the division of marital property upon divorce is discussed, would be illustrative of what is needed for completion.

B. Implied Agreements

Unlike express agreements, the enforcement of an implied agreement between the cohabitants begins with whether or not there was any agreement at all. This fact will depend upon factors such as the couple's life together and each party's contribution to that life, together with each party's expectations. Because the agreement is implied, the court must look to the totality of the circumstances to approximate what could have been promised, what was contributed in reliance upon that promise, and how the contribution failed to meet the promises made. Courts have been willing to hold that an implied agreement could occur, even though one of the parties was married to a third party throughout the relationship with the alleged partner. Permanent cohabitation is not a prerequisite to establishment of an agreement, and the enforcement of the promises made. Rather, courts look to the duration of the relationship, purpose, demonstrated intent of the parties, pooling of resources, and services contributed to the relationship.[28]

Court decisions appear to be very accommodating of the implied intent of either nonmarital cohabitant. Decisions seem rampant in which at separation or death, one of the nonmarital cohabitants seeks compensation, relying upon oral promises made by the living separated partner, or by the decedent during the time they cohabited. Courts have generously sought to meet the expectations of the parties. But in cases when implying a promise has been insufficient, the court rules that there is no agreement at all. Recall that the court's ruling in the *Marvin* decision initiated a shift in public policy permitting recovery for nonmarital cohabitants. But the plaintiff in that case, Michelle Marvin, although subsequently awarded $104,000 in rehabilitative support, later had that support amount rescinded and she received nothing from the defendant, Lee Marvin. On remand, the trial court found no express promise made by Lee Marvin to take care of her, and the conduct of the parties did not give rise to an implied contract. Thus, the court of appeals revoked the award of $104,000, holding that there had been no unjust enrichment and no wrongful act on the part of the

---

28. *See* In re Long and Fregeau, 244 P.3d 26 (Wash. Ct. App. 2010); Devaney v. L'Esperance, 949 A.2d 743 (N.J. 2008).

defendant to warrant the award. [Marvin v. Marvin, 176 Cal.Rptr. 555, 559 (Cal. Ct. App. 1981)] Similarly, other courts have refused to enforce an implied agreement, holding that couples who cohabit without the benefit of marriage do so at their own peril.[29] Implied contracts are a dangerous pursuit, something excused by love.

In order to establish greater objectivity in implied agreements, and hence enforceability, the American Law Institute ("ALI") recommends distinct factors for establishment of what the ALI calls "domestic partners." The term should not be confused with the status of domestic partnership, enacted by some states and localities and used by many businesses. For the ALI, domestic partners consist of two persons who: (1) are of the same or the opposite sex; (2) are not married to each other; (3) have shared a primary residence for a significant period of time as a couple; and/or (4) share a household with another unrelated person but act jointly, rather than as individuals, with respect to management of a common household.

Sharing a life together as a couple is crucial to the establishment of the domestic partnership. This status is determined by evaluating the following factors: (1) oral and written statements, (2) financial interdependence, (3) economic contributions made to the relationship by either party, (4) the conduct of the parties supporting their life together, (5) changes in their lives due to the relationship, (6) designation of either party as a beneficiary of an estate planning device, (7) emotional and physical intimacies shared, (8) community reputation, (9) participation in a commitment ceremony of any sort, and (10) procreation, adoption, or assumption of parental duties towards a child.[30]

The status of nonmarital cohabitation is unsettled in spite of the amazing changes that have occurred. It seems reasonable to suggest that a statutory framework of recognition and enforcement be drafted. Something similar to the Uniform Premarital Agreement Acts seems reasonable and appropriate. Individual states would then have an incentive to interrelate benefits attendant to the adults partners and the children that result. Issues such as whether the nonmarital cohabitation agreements should be restricted to two persons, or expanded to more is also a consideration. And federal benefits must be adjusted to meet the expectations of the parties, both in terms of economics and the various means by which parenthood may be achieved in the age of assisted reproductive technology.

29. Nichols v. Funderburk, 883 So.2d 554 (Miss. 2004).

30. Am. Law Insti., *Principles of the Law of Family Dissolution: Analysis and Recommendations* § 6.03 (2002).

Chapter 5

Dissolving a Marriage: Divorce

I. Historical Context

On August 13, 2010, the governor of New York signed into law a bill that made no-fault divorce available in New York State. No longer will New York married spouses be forced to litigate the elements of a fault based divorce, but instead will be able, under the new legislation, to end a marriage which is, in reality, already over and cannot be salvaged. The purpose of no-fault divorce, proponents argued, is to lessen the disputes that can arise between the parties and to mitigate the potential harm to them and to their children caused by contentious litigation. Once the law became effective, the family court was authorized to grant a decree of divorce if one of the spouses swears under oath that the marriage has been irretrievably broken for at least six months. Then, if the economic and child-related issues are settled, the marriage will be ended. These issues include the division of marital property, any support, child support, custody and visitation of minor children, and attorney fees. The agreement reached by the parties concerning these issues will be incorporated into the court's final divorce decree.

New York was the last state to adopt no-fault divorce, a little more than forty years after the first state, California, changed its divorce laws permitting a marriage to be dissolved if one of the spouses could prove that there were irreconcilable differences between the spouses. Today, all of the states have enacted some form of no-fault divorce and many of the states allow for fault-based divorce too. Furthermore, because the awarding of a divorce occurs through a judgment of the court, if there is proper jurisdiction in the awarding state, the decree of divorce is entitled to Full Faith and Credit in any subsequent state. While there is no similar guarantee of recognition of divorces obtained in foreign countries, divorces obtained in foreign courts are entitled to comity, a process that depends upon the participation of the spouses and the equities of the situation.

The dissolution of a marriage in twenty-first century America is very different from the process that existed when America declared independence from England more than two-hundred years ago. During the colonial period divorce in America was extremely rare, as it was in England. But after the revolution, courts, especially in the northern states, permitted divorce under defined circumstances. Marriage could be dissolved if the innocent party demonstrated, with sufficient corroboration, that there existed established grounds to make the marriage untenable. Common law grounds included cruelty, desertion, and the most common ground, adultery. Later, legislatures added additional grounds. These included habitual intoxication, impotency, homosexuality, and imprisonment. "In Hawaii, leprosy was grounds for divorce; in Virginia, if a husband discovered his wife had been a prostitute, he had the right to get out of the marriage. Tennessee quite reasonably provided that if one spouse tried to kill the other spouse 'by poison or any other means showing malice,' the victim was entitled to divorce ... "[1] But even with additional grounds, only an innocent spouse could petition for the divorce, and litigation always ensued to prove that the innocent petitioner sufficiently met the burden of proof. During litigation, the at-fault spouse could raise a series of defenses to the allegations so as to bar the issuance of the divorce decree. Possible defenses include that the plaintiff spouse was equally guilty of a fault (recrimination), or had condoned the fault that is the basis of the suit (condonation), or had connived to trap the other spouse into committing the fault (connivance). Occasionally the courts would deny the petition for the divorce because of evidence that the spouses had colluded to bring about the ground so as to deceive the court and obtain the divorce (collusion). And always, the petition must be filed by the plaintiff within a reasonable period of time following the discovery of the fault ground or else it could be barred by laches.

The grounds upon which a divorce could be obtained were the product of the mores of the time, each needed to relate to something that went to the essence of the marriage. In addition, the ground had to be significant so that there was no hope of reconciliation. As is true today, people and groups argued that if divorce became too available, then the fabric of society would suffer and the result would be moral decay. Thus, grounds were historically restrictive. Some states during the nineteenth century did make an effort to make it easier for spouses to obtain a divorce. These states developed more extensive grounds for divorce, or they had short residency requirements, or judges were more lenient in evaluating the evidence of grounds such as adultery. Also, as is true today, spouses with sufficient assets were able to travel to another state,

---

1.   JOHN LANGBEIN, RENEE LERNER & BRUCE P. SMITH, HISTORY OF THE COMMON LAW 920 (2009), quoting from Lawrence M. Friedman, *A Dead Language: Divorce Law and Practice Before No–Fault*, 86 VA. L. REV. 1497, 1502 (2000).

establish residency there, and obtain a divorce that would have to be recognized in any other state.

Some state legislatures, recognizing the untenable nature of some marriages, would permit a modicum of relief through a device they borrowed from the ecclesiastical courts of England. These ecclesiastical courts, unable to dissolve a marriage that was valid at the start, would permit a limited form of divorce, a divorce *a mensa et thoro*. Even though neither spouse was free to marry again, an *a mensa et thoro* divorce enabled the court to order division of marital property, support for a disadvantaged spouse, and order custody, visitation and support of minor children. In today's states, when they utilize *a mensa et thoro* divorces, they often provide a separate list of criteria for this limited type of divorce, and then another list for a final decree of divorce, what are called divorces *a vinculo matrimonii*. In spite of the use of the term *a mensa et thoro* divorce and judicial division of property and children, the marriage remains intact for purposes of inheritance if one of the parties should die prior to obtaining a final decree. Furthermore, neither party is able to marry again without the subsequent marriage being bigamous.

By the middle of the twentieth century, the Supreme Court of California, following the example established a short time earlier in England, tweaked the existing divorce statutes to create a new and separate ground upon which a final divorce could be granted. The court introduced "comparative rectitude," which permitted California courts to weigh the relative faults of the "guilty" party and award a divorce when certain criteria were met. This practice sounds trivial in light of present circumstances, but at the time it was a major innovation, facilitating many divorces in the state. Shortly thereafter, the California legislature enacted a new divorce ground for "marital dissolution," the new term the legislature invented to replace divorce. The new ground, for purposes of obtaining a final decree of divorce was called "irreconcilable differences."

Irreconcilable differences in California was a true no-fault ground. Under this ground, either party could petition for the divorce, regardless of fault. And because fault was not a consideration, none of the common law defenses applied. Thus, no recrimination, connivance, condonation, or collusion applied. Instead, either of the parties had to affirm that the spouses were irreconcilable and, if the court agreed, it could terminate the marriage. This statutory innovation eliminated lengthy and ribald litigation, forum shopping for a state with easy divorce laws, and obviously, moribund marriages. Irreconcilability could be established by the couple remaining separate and apart for a specified period of time, but there were no sham adultery scenes to prove fault as in the past. The victims were those spouses who wished to remain married, but now, even though there had been no fault committed, the other party could unilaterally dissolve the marriage through a non-fault decree. Also, easier divorce lessened the chances of reconciliation and the effects of this are still being discussed.

Other states were quick to follow California's lead in enacting no-fault divorce. By 1970, the National Conference of Commissioners of Uniform State Laws proposed to make irretrievable breakdown the sole ground for divorce in the United States. A finding of irretrievable breakdown is a determination that there is no reasonable prospect of reconciliation. A couple's marriage was irretrievably broken if there was evidence to support the conclusion that the couple had lived separate and apart for more than one-hundred and eighty days, or that there was serious marital discord adversely affecting the attitude of one or both of the parties toward the marriage. Their proposal was part of a comprehensive revision of each aspect of family law; the proposals were set forth in the Uniform Marriage and Divorce Act.[2] It is insignificant that the UMDA adopted a term for no-fault divorce that was different from that adopted by California. Eventually, other states would utilize their own language, including "insupportable" or "irremediable". The majority of states would adopt standards that did not rely upon a phrase, such as irretrievable. Instead, these states looked to a period of time in which the couple lived separate and part; often there was an established time for couples without minor children and another for couples with minor children. Thus, some states used the period of separation as proof of the irreconcilable ground, other states used a specified period of separation as the ground itself.

In 1974, the House of Delegates of the American Bar Association approved no-fault divorce, but adopted a resolution that there must be a finding of serious marital discord in addition to a period of separation of at least one-hundred and eighty days prior to the commencement of the proceeding. While the Bar Association's guidelines were more stringent than the UMDA proposed code, it illustrated the fact that no-fault divorce had become the law of the land. Eventually, the American Law Institute's *Principles of the Law of Family Dissolution: Analysis and Recommendations*, recommended that fault-based divorce be eliminated completely. Fault,

---

2. WALTER WADLINGTON & RAYMOND C. O'BRIEN, FAMILY LAW STATUTES: SELECTED UNIFORM LAWS, FEDERAL STATUTES, STATE STATUTES, AND INTERNATIONAL TREATIES, 119, 125 (4th ed. 2011).

the ALI argued, was being used as a subterfuge to disproportionately divide marital property and should therefore be abolished. Thus, if a spouse, during a divorce proceeding, could successfully pursue a divorce claim based on a fault ground such as adultery, then the adulterous conduct could be taken into consideration in giving the "innocent" spouse a greater portion of the marital assets as a form of damages. Such a process, the ALI argues, should be reserved to tort law, not to any division of marital assets upon dissolution.

There are two final developments that need to be included in any consideration of the history of divorce. First, a few states enacted statutes permitting a couple, when they married, to restrict any future divorce to fault grounds only. No-fault grounds were not allowed. These state statutes are called "covenant marriage" statutes and the states include Louisiana, Arkansas, and Arizona. Under the terms of covenant marriage statutes a couple, upon applying for a marriage license may elect to form a covenant marriage and, once the election is made, neither of the spouses will be able to petition a court in that state for a divorce based on a no-fault ground. Because fault grounds require an innocent spouse, a corroborated claim of fault, and defenses to the ground, the process to obtain a divorce will be far more protracted than with a no-fault ground. These covenant marriage states are seeking to delay the process of divorce in hopes that, if disharmony should occur, the couple will resolve their difficulties and save their marriage. Nonetheless, either covenant marriage spouse cannot be prevented from traveling to another state and obtaining a no-fault divorce there. Such a divorce would be entitled to Full Faith and Credit in the covenant marriage state, thereby defeating the state's policy and the initial commitment made by the spouses.

The second development shares the same goal as covenant marriage: To assist couples in remaining married. A few states have sought to provide couples with classes on the duties and challenges of marriage prior to entering into marriage. These states offer a discounted marriage license if a couple will attend classes prior to the wedding. And, similarly, a few states have attempted to mandate classes on reconciliation and support obligations when spouses with children petition for divorce. Thus, a final decree of divorce cannot be obtained in the state unless the classes have been completed.[3] Nonetheless, as with couples entering into covenant marriage, either party is free to travel to another state and obtain a

3. *See* Raymond C. O'Brien, *The Reawakening of Marriage*, 102 W. VA. L. REV. 339, 369–379 (1999).

divorce there without the necessity of classes. Again, such a divorce would be entitled to Full Faith and Credit.

II. Divorce Jurisdiction and Full Faith and Credit

The Uniform Marriage and Divorce Act provides that a state court may enter a decree of divorce upon the petition of either party if the court finds that the petitioner was domiciled in the state or was a member of the armed services and stationed in the state for a period of at least ninety days prior to the petition. [§ 302(a)(1)] Once the petition is filed, the other party must be served in the manner provided by the Rules of Civil Practice and have the opportunity to file a verified response. [§ 303(d)] If the requirements enumerated by the UMDA are met, a final decree of divorce may issue from the court and this decree, as a judgment, would be entitled to Full Faith and Credit in every other state. Thus, the elements required by the statute are important, each requiring an explanation.

A. *Domicile*

The primary aspect of domicile for purposes of obtaining a divorce is residency in the state for a specified period of time. While the UMDA specifies that a member of the armed services must be stationed in the state for ninety days prior to filing the petition for divorce, the lack of a specified period of time for non-military petitioners is unusual. State statutes specify residency requirements and courts apply the residency requirement in a strict fashion. If residency is not established, the resulting divorce is subject to challenge. For example, a couple was married and lived in Ohio for ten years, until the husband's job took the family to California. One month after moving to their new home in California, the husband told his wife that he had been unfaithful and she immediately left him, taking the children and herself back to Ohio. She had been absent from the state for one month, but nonetheless filed for divorce in the state that had been her home for at least ten years. The Ohio court ruled that she had not met the residency requirement of the Ohio statute, which required her to have been a resident of the state for six months prior to filing the petition. The wife argued that she had never abandoned her intent to be a resident of Ohio even though she was absent for one month. But the court ruled that her intent, or the fraudulent conduct of the other party, were irrelevant. The state residency statute of six months must be applied strictly and without interpretation. Because she had been absent from the state for a month, she had not met the six months requirement and would have to delay her filing of the petition until such time as she had been a resident for six months.[4]

Divorce is *in rem*, meaning that each spouse carries the marriage with him or her to any state and may, upon filing a petition based upon proper jurisdiction, obtain a valid divorce. The presence of the other party is not necessary to obtain a valid divorce; only jurisdiction and proper notice to the absent spouse is necessary. As we will discuss in reference to marital property and support, *in personam* jurisdiction will be necessary then, but not in reference to divorce. And each state may establish its own procedures establishing residency jurisdiction. Traditionally, federal courts have abstained from exercising jurisdiction "upon the subject of divorce, or for the allowance of alimony, either as an original proceeding in chancery or as an incident to divorce *a vinculo,* or to one from bed and board [*a mensa et thoro*]."[5] Nonetheless, every state action is subject to constitutional restraints. For example, in the context of domicile, a state is limited by the Due Process Clause from imposing a residency requirement that would unduly burden a petitioner. In 1975, the Court affirmed the right of a state to establish domicile for obtaining a divorce, since any state has the right to require a petitioner to have some attachment to the state prior to using its court system. But the ability of the state to restrict access must be balanced against the right to a hearing contained in the Due Process Clause. There cannot be a total or near-total denial of opportunity to be heard in the court of law.[6]

B. Contesting Domicile

Since divorce is an action *in rem*, obtainable by either party in a state in which the petitioner meets the jurisdictional basis and provides notice to the other party, what options are available to the respondent? Obviously, the responding party, upon being notified of the petition for a divorce in another state has the option of initiating a separate petition for divorce, or traveling to the other state to contest the grounds, or to simply "sit-tight" and await the final decree issued by the court. If the basis for the divorce is a no-fault ground, then the options for contest are minimal at best. But failure to provide proper notice is a valid ground for contest then or

---

4. Barth v. Barth, 862 N.E.2d 496 (Ohio 2007).

5. Barber v. Barber, 62 U.S. 582, 584 (1858); *see also* Ankenbrandt v. Richards, 504 U.S. 689, 693 (1992).

6. Sosna v. Iowa, 419 U.S. 393 (1975).

in the future, as is failure to meet the *in rem* residency requirement. But contest is limited and seemingly futile. If the respondent spouse participates in the original hearing, either in person or through an attorney, and at that hearing had the opportunity to challenge the jurisdiction of the court, the respondent will not be afforded the same opportunity to collaterally attack jurisdiction at a subsequent hearing.[7] In effect, due process requires only fairness, and if a party had the chance to challenge the jurisdiction of the court while participating in the proceeding and did not, then the opportunity is lost.

C. *Full Faith and Credit*

If domicile has been properly established, notice was given to the respondent, and the opportunity to contest passed the applicable time frame, a court may issue a divorce decree. The decree, as a judicial proceeding, is entitled to Full Faith and Credit in every other state. [U.S. Const. art. IV, § 1] In effect, one spouse, in an ex parte proceeding, may go to another state, meet that state's statutory requirements, and obtain a divorce that can then be enforced against the spouse left behind. In a celebrated decision, *Williams I*, the Supreme Court ruled that every state had a right to establish its own divorce requirements and may thereby alter the marital status of any resident wishing to utilize the law of the state. If a citizen of that state obtains a valid divorce decree, then that divorce must be afforded Full Faith and Credit in every other state or it would bring "considerable disaster to innocent persons."[8] The only restraint is whether or not the issuing court had proper jurisdiction to issue the divorce decree. The respondent may contest issues such as proper jurisdiction in the issuing state, but this must be done in a timely fashion and, once acknowledged, jurisdiction cannot later be denied.[9]

State residency requirements vary. Nevada has a very short residency period needed to obtain a valid divorce: six weeks. Other states, such as Massachusetts, Washington, and South Dakota require even less time to establish residency. Coupled with a no-fault ground for divorce, a state with a minimal residency requirement can be a destination for a speedy, if not an easy divorce. Once the divorce is obtained and all of the proper formalities are met, the divorce is entitled to Full Faith and Credit in each and every other state of the union. Thus, even though one state may seek to impose

7. Sherrer v. Sherrer, 334 U.S. 343 (1948).

8. Williams v. North Carolina, 317 U.S. 287, 299–301 (1942).

9. Williams v. North Carolina, 325 U.S. 226 (1945).

a two year residency requirement prior to the filing of a petition for divorce, and demand strict corroboration before a marriage may be declared irretrievable, this state must still recognize a foreign state's divorce based on far less strict grounds. The process inherent in Full Faith and Credit appears to violate the sovereignty of other more stringent states, but absent a constitutional amendment, or a federalization of divorce, the states are free to adopt similar standards or to remain as they are.

D. Comity for a Foreign Divorce

The Full Faith and Credit Clause does not apply to decrees issued by foreign countries. Instead, each state may give what is called "comity" to a foreign decree. That is, a state may or may not recognize a foreign decree, depending upon the equities of each situation. For example, if a foreign country issues a bilateral divorce decree, both parties participated, and the ground upon which the divorce was given does not violate state public policy, then the divorce will likely be given comity in the state. But nothing is certain, and this is the risk in choosing a foreign divorce over a divorce in another state; Full Faith and Credit is inapplicable to divorces issued by foreign courts.

In an age when United States citizens are comfortable with international travel, many citizens are born in foreign nations, there are many instances of foreign divorces and petitions for comity once the divorce is obtained. Despite the fact that many foreign divorces occur when the country imposes a residency of only a few days, comity is almost always given when certain factors are present. Most states provide for comity whenever the foreign divorce decree is in accordance with the public policy of the state asked to award comity.[10] While some states have automatic recognition for foreign money judgments, there is no statute granting automatic recognition of a judgment of divorce.[11] For instance, if both of the spouses appear and participate in the divorce proceedings (a bilateral divorce) the court can be fairly certain that both parties had an opportunity to make challenges and the court should not deprive them of their divorce. In one case, Rosenstiel v. Rosenstiel,[12] a New York court was asked to award comity to a Mexican divorce decree. The petitioner argued that the grounds upon which

---

10. *See, e.g.,* Oehl v. Oehl, 272 S.E.2d 441 (Va. 1980).

11. *See* Sanchez v. Palau, 317 S.W.3d 780 (Tex. App. 2010) (interpreting the Uniform Foreign Country Money–Judgement Recognition Act).

12. 209 N.E.2d 709 (1965), *cert. denied,* 384 U.S. 971 (1966), *and cert denied sub nom.* Wood v. Wood, 383 U.S. 943 (1966).

the divorce was awarded were insufficient when compared to New York. Nonetheless, the court granted comity to the bilateral divorce, quipping that: "Nevada gets no closer to the real public policy concern with the marriage than Chihuahua." Thus, the court acknowledged that since it could not deny recognition for a divorce obtained in Nevada, why should it be concerned about a divorce obtained in Chihuahua, Mexico?

III. Fault Grounds

There are three major fault grounds, often referred to as common law fault grounds. As discussed previously, states have adopted additional grounds, and some states have refined the three we will discuss now. So too, some states have abolished fault grounds completely. But more states have retained fault as a basis for obtaining a divorce, often using fault as the basis for awarding more of the marital property to the innocent spouse by taking from the guilty spouse.[13] In the states using fault in the division of property, the common law defenses that may be employed by the perpetrator of the fault may be economically necessary to retain an equal division of the marital assets.

The objective of fault and no-fault grounds is the dissolution of the marriage; the major difference between the two is that litigation can be engendered by fault. In the heyday of fault divorce, the litigation over corroboration and the defenses presented provided incendiary drama in the courtrooms, a spectacle missing from no-fault divorce. Today, the majority of states permit divorce to be obtained upon either fault or no-fault grounds, hence it is important to review the three major fault grounds and then their common law defenses.

A. *Adultery*

More than half of the states retain adultery as a basis for obtaining a divorce *a mensa et thoro* or a divorce *a vinculo*. The gamut of sexual activity qualifying as adultery is extensive, ranging from intercourse, to sodomy, to casual intimacy, and to what appears to be a committed relationship. The Supreme Court of New Hampshire surprised commentators when the court interpreted the state divorce statute to conclude that adultery may only mean intercourse.[14] But such a narrow interpretation is unusual. Regardless of what constitutes adultery, corroboration is necessary. Sel-

---

13. *See, e.g.*, Howard S. v. Lillian S., 928 N.E.2d 399 (N.Y. 2010) (holding that in limited circumstances egregious conduct may be considered as a factor when distributing marital property, but adultery alone is not egregious).

14. In re Blanchflower, 834 A.2d 1010 (N.H. 2003).

dom are there photographs or witnesses to acts of infidelity, prompting courts to require proof of something more than the mere suspicion of adultery. Most often the courts scrutinize the disposition for, and the occasion to, commit adultery. Facts indicating adultery would include a spouse's parked car outside of a partner's darkened home very late at night, revealing photographs of liaisons, or Internet postings with incriminating language or graphic photographs. In an effort to establish adultery, a spouse sought to subpoena retainer agreements, time sheets, and billing information concerning her attorney-husband and the husband's client. The evidence, the wife argued, would support the disposition for and the occasion to commit adultery. But the court refused to require the client to waive the attorney-client privilege and testify as to the details of the attorney-client relationship. There must be something more, a "smoking gun", before the court will order the privilege to be waived. Therefore, the wife presented insufficient evidence.[15]

Judging from the variety of approaches taken by the states, it appears reasonable to conclude that some states that retain adultery as a divorce ground require a heightened level of proof [*see* Michael D. C. v. Wanda L.C., 497 S.E.2d 531 (W. Va. 1997)], while other courts allow for circumstantial evidence to establish the offense, both for purposes of obtaining a divorce and for distribution of marital property. [*See, e.g.*, Brown v. Brown, 665 S.E.2d 174 (S.C. Ct. App. 2008)] Undoubtedly, future decisions will invite considerations of Internet conversations, postings, and pictures. Introduction of evidence concerning these will be impacted by the Electronic Communications Privacy Act of 1986, which imposes civil and criminal penalties upon anyone intercepting communications that have a reasonable expectation of privacy.[16] And persons who try to access emails and social networking accounts of a former spouse may be prosecuted under the Stored Communications Act, and perhaps prosecution is permitted under the Computer Fraud and Abuse Act.[17] One man who installed keylogging software on his former wife's computer was prosecuted. But it is certain that Facebook has replaced the motel room as the place to look for proof of adulterous behavior.

B. *Cruelty*

Cruelty may be defined as conduct that endangers life, limb, or health. It is conduct that creates reasonable apprehension of dan-

---

15. Giammarco v. Giammarco, 959 A.2d 531 (R.I. 2008).

16. *See generally* Jennifer Mitchell, *Sex, Lies, and Spyware: Balancing the Right to Privacy Against the Right to*

Know in the Marital Relationship, 9 J. L. & FAM. STUD. 171 (2007).

17. *See* Miller v. Meyers, 766 F.Supp.2d 919 (W.D. Ark. 2011).

ger, or unnatural and infamous conduct making the marital relationship revolting. But most courts require that cruelty be a course of conduct that adversely affects physical or mental health. This is the essential ingredient. For example, when a wife discovered amorous emails that her husband had sent to another woman, she petitioned the court for a divorce based on extreme cruelty, arguing that finding the emails seriously injured her health and endangered her reason. But the court denied her a divorce based on cruelty, holding that the state's statute required proof of actual or threatened direct bodily injury, and that mental pain did not suffice.[18] Likewise, when the wife of a Baptist church pastor who was also president of the Northeast Mississippi Baptist State Convention, accused him of infidelity, taunted him, yelled at him, and embarrassed him, the conduct did not evidence sufficient cruelty. The court denied a divorce based on cruelty, holding that the wife's conduct was more akin to rudeness than cruelty.[19]

The duration of the marriage rule is often associated with judicial opinions concerning cruelty. That rule is that the longer the marriage, the more extensive the cruelty must be to establish sufficient cause to award a final decree of divorce. This rule demonstrates a degree of tolerance for cruelty in marriage. Nonetheless, the recent trend shows courts are less tolerant of any abusive behavior when finding sufficient cruelty to terminate a marriage. The enactment of domestic violence statutes, and the practice of some states to permit divorce based on constructive desertion, indicate a trend towards greater acceptance in establishing a lower level of cruelty justifying a divorce on that ground. "Verbal and physical abuse may have been tolerated in another era, and our predecessors at bar may have placed the continuity of the marital bond above the well-being of individual participants, but our values are different today."[20]

C. Desertion

For purposes of a divorce, one of the parties must separate from the marital cohabitation without provocation and with the intent to permanently desert his or her spouse. In addition, the party seeking to prove that he or she had been deserted, must also prove that there was no provocation for leaving and that the deserted spouse wanted the deserting one to return. Usually, the

18. In re Guy, 969 A.2d 373 (N.H. 2009).

19. Anderson v. Anderson, 54 So.3d 850 (Miss. Ct. App. 2010), *review granted*, 49 So.3d 1129 (Miss. 2010).

20. Das v. Das, 754 A.2d 441, 461 (Md. Ct. Spec. App. 2000).

state statute addresses the permanency issue by requiring that the desertion last for a specified period of time. Typically, the specified period of time is one year, and most courts allow for intent to be retroactive. That is, a spouse could leave the home without the requisite intent to desert, but then form that intent at a later point in time. These courts permit the requisite one year to begin when the separation occurred, not when the separation and the intent to desert coincided.

Many of the cases today involve constructive desertion. For example, when a husband moved out of the marital bedroom and into a room on a separate floor of their home he refused to engage in sexual relations with his wife. The wife made requests to have sex with him at least three or four times during the years 2003 and 2004, but he refused. Based on this, the court granted the wife's petition for a divorce based on constructive abandonment. The court ruled that the requirements of the statute had been met when the husband refused to fulfill a basic element of marriage for a period of more than one year.[21] The fact that the couple remained in the same home did not prevent the awarding of the divorce. Increasingly, courts look to the fact that the couple ceases to function as a husband and wife in regards to a significant aspect of marital life, not whether the couple remains together in the same physical location.[22]

IV. Defenses to Fault Grounds

The following list of defenses includes all defenses that may be raised in defense against one of the fault grounds.[23] It is important to reiterate that these defenses do not apply to no-fault divorce, but they remain very important in those states that take marital fault into consideration when dividing marital assets or, of course, those states permitting a divorce on a fault ground. Thus, if a divorce can be obtained upon the fault ground of adultery, the action could result in a disproportionate amount of the marital property passing to the innocent spouse unless the adulterer can successfully argue one of the following defenses. In reviewing them it is easy to see how fault divorce precipitates extensive litigation between the parties.

---

21. BM v. MM, 880 N.Y.S.2d 850 (N.Y. Sup. Ct. 2009); *but see* Davis v. Davis, 71 A.D.3d 13 (N.Y. App. Div. 2009) (holding that refusing social interaction with spouse is not constructive abandonment).

22. Ricketts v. Ricketts, 903 A.2d 857 (Md. 2006).

23. *See, e.g.*, GA. CODE ANN. § 19–5–4 (2004 & Supp. 2008) (adopting the defenses of condonation, collusion, connivance, and recrimination).

A. *Recrimination*

Because it is necessary to have an innocent party to petition for a fault divorce, if both parties have committed a marital offense that would qualify as a marital fault, then there is no innocent party to submit the divorce petition. This is the essence of recrimination, both parties are at fault—any marital fault—so there is no innocent party. Because such a defense results in no divorce, the parties remain married, presumably unhappy and looking for alternative means of ending the marriage. Justifications for the defense focused on keeping the couple together, but increasingly courts have rejected using the defense. The practical consequence is that spouses remain in an unhappy relationship. Thus, courts mitigate recrimination by finding some fault greater than others, thus creating an innocent spouse by estimating one fault as less than another. Recall that the California courts began the no-fault development by providing for comparative fault, and state courts with fault systems employ similar strategies.[24]

B. *Connivance*

When the innocent spouse petitions for a divorce based on a fault ground, the party allegedly at fault may defend his or her conduct by asserting that he or she never would have committed the fault without the consent—the connivance—of the other party. Through implication or express facilitation, the fault was occasioned with the knowledge of the innocent party. Thus, the argument is that the party claiming to be innocent facilitated the fault upon which the divorce is premised, and thus is not innocent enough to petition for a divorce.

C. *Condonation*

If a spouse has condoned—or forgiven—the other spouse for the marital fault it may no longer serve as a ground for divorce. Traditionally, condonation could occur when the guilty spouse was an adulterer, cruel, or even habitually drunk, although most of the cases involve adultery. Proving that the misconduct by one of the parties was actually condoned, or forgiven, becomes a factual issue at trial. This is a matter of intent and intent is difficult to prove. Proving that the couple has resumed sexual intimacies after the misconduct was discovered is one way of showing condonation. Perhaps too, there may be a resumption of cohabitation if the parties had separated following the discovery. Nonetheless, if mis-

---

24. *See, e.g.*, Parker v. Parker, 519 So.2d 1232 (Miss. 1988); *but see* Boyatt v. Boyatt, 248 S.W.3d 144 (Tenn. Ct. App. 2007).

conduct resumes—another incident—after the manifestation of condonation, the subsequent conduct may be grounds for a fault divorce initiated by the party who is not so forgiving the second time around.

The public policy underlying condonation is that the marriage is important and the courts should support efforts at reconciliation. Thus, courts have been willing to look to factors such as the length of the marriage, the sharing of domestic duties, and the presence of minor children to infer that condonation has occurred.[25]

D. Collusion

Recall that divorce grounded upon fault demanded that there be an innocent party to bring the action in court; no divorce could be obtained through consent without fault. Thus, when a party at fault wanted to end the marriage, he or she had to enlist the assistance of the innocent spouse to initiate the proceeding. If the innocent spouse was willing, then most often an elaborate scheme was concocted, whereby pictures of the at-fault spouse were taken in an adulterous context involving a disposition for and an occasion to commit adultery. The pictures then formed the basis of the suit for divorce based on adultery. Such conduct was grounded in collusion. Indeed, the entire fault-based system of divorce contained numerous examples of collusive conduct by the married parties. As one New York judge aptly observed, "She is always in a sheer pink robe. It's never blue—always pink. And he is always in shorts when they catch them."[26] If the collusion between the parties was too obvious, the courts could refuse to grant the divorce, based on the perjury of the spouses.

E. Insanity

If a spouse lacked the mental capacity to commit a marital fault, it was an automatic defense to any of the marital faults. In most cases, insanity was pleaded as a defense to adultery or desertion, the argument being that the mental capacity to commit either was missing. But it was also used in connection with cruelty, but at least one court held that for it to be an effective defense, the respondent must prove the same lack of capacity that he or she would have to prove in a criminal court. Specifically, that the

25. *See, e.g.,* Tigert v. Tigert, 595 P.2d 815 (Okla. Civ. App. 1979).

26. This statement by former Justice Meier Steinbrink was reported in the N.Y. Herald Tribune on October 1, 1965, at page four. For additional commentary, see Walter Wadlington, *Divorce Without Fault Without Perjury*, 52 VA. L. REV. 32 (1966).

respondent lacked the mental capacity to appreciate the wrongful-ness of the act.[27]

Insanity may be a ground for obtaining a divorce too. This is not a no-fault ground. With insanity, the petitioner must prove the respondent's insanity, not simply petition for the divorce based on a dissolution ground. To prove the insanity of the respondent, the requirements could include a spouse being involuntarily committed to a mental institution for a specified period of time. But if the divorce is granted, states can also mandate that economic protections be provided for the incompetent person.[28] And interestingly, a court has ruled that a guardian for an incompetent person may file a petition for divorce on the incompetent's behalf.[29] In reviewing the state's statute that permits a guardian to sue or defend on behalf of the incompetent, the court concluded that this means the guardian can initiate a divorce petition without the active participation of the incompetent ward.

F. Laches and Statutes of Limitation

Any petition for divorce based upon a fault ground must occur in a timely fashion. Some states require that the petitioner file within a specified statute of limitations, such as Virginia's requirement that divorces based on adultery or sodomy occur within five years of the offense.[30] Laches, on the other hand, is an equitable restraint, requiring that the divorce must commence within a reasonable time from when the fault occurred.

V. No–Fault Divorce

Every state has a form of no-fault divorce. For many, the only means by which to obtain a divorce is through no-fault. And for one of these latter states, California, for example, evidence of specific acts of misconduct by either of the parties is improper and inadmissible unless otherwise provided by statute.[31] The rapid adoption of no-fault divorce was in response to the litigation, collusion, and inequity fostered under the fault system of divorce. At some point the states concluded that the cost to the spouses and to the state's

---

27. Simpson v. Simpson, 716 S.W.2d 27 (Tenn. 1986).

28. *See, e.g.*, Pennings v. Pennings, 786 A.2d 622 (Me. 2002)(requiring a commitment for seven years); *see also* Va. Code Ann. §§ 20–91(9), 20–93 (2004)(specifying economic protection for the incompetent spouse, but holding that insanity is no defense).

29. Broach v. Broach, 895 N.E.2d 640 (Ohio Ct. App. 2008).

30. Va. Code Ann. § 20–94 (2004).

31. *See* Cal. Fam. Code § 2335 (West 2004 & Supp. 2009).

court system was oppressive when compared to the benefit of keeping spouses together in hopes that they would reconcile.

When enacting no-fault divorce statutes, states adopted one of two approaches. One approach is to permit divorce when the couple has separated for a period of time, and the second approach is when the court is satisfied that the marriage is irretrievably broken or that the spouses are irreconcilable. In a petition based on either ground, there is no longer a need for an innocent spouse to serve as petitioner; either spouse can seek a divorce, even the one most guilty of misconduct.

A. Living Separate and Apart

Most states provide that a divorce may be obtained if the couple lives separate and apart for a period of time. Perhaps this no-fault ground developed from the Uniform Marriage and Divorce Act. The Act, the first modern uniform legislation on family law, permitted divorce solely on a finding that a marriage was irretrievably broken. But later, the Act was amended to require that this fact be corroborated by the couple living separate and apart for 180 days, or that there be evidence of serious marital discord. Today, some states require the separation period to be brief, only sixty days, while others require the separation to be as long as two years. Then too, some states provide that the period may be shorter if there are no minor children, or if the couple consents to the divorce.

To meet the period of living separate and apart, some states allow the couple to occupy the same household as long as they are leading separate lives.[32] The rationale seems similar to courts interpreting the fault ground of desertion. The primary consideration must be the intent of the parties to live separate lives on a permanent basis, not the physical proximity of the parties. Whether the couple has met the burden of living separate lives is a fact-based determination and any reconciliation will reset the clock on their separation period.

B. Breakdown Grounds

It is possible to petition for a divorce based on a fault ground and a no-fault ground at the same time.[33] But if the parties seek a no-fault ground such as irreconcilable differences, the ground will have to be proven. California defines an irreconcilable marriage as

---

32. *See, e.g.,* Ky. Rev. Stat. Ann. § 403.170(1) (West 2008) ("Living apart shall include living under the same roof without sexual cohabitation.").

33. *See, e.g.,* O'Neal v. O'Neal, 17 So.3d 572 (Miss. 2009); Flanagan v. Flanagan, 956 A.2d 829 (Md. Ct. Spec. App. 2008).

one that has substantial reasons for not continuing. And New Hampshire looks to see if there is a likelihood for rehabilitation, or a reasonable possibility of reconciliation, before permitting a divorce based on irreconcilable differences.

When New York adopted its own version of no-fault divorce with the ground of irretrievably broken, a petitioner argued that the allegation in and of itself should suffice; the ground itself should be irrefutable. The new law, argued the petitioner, was to promote an easier process for divorce and this meant an absence of judicial scrutiny. But the court disagreed, holding that the assertion by the petitioner that the marriage was irretrievably broken, was simply a cause of action like any other. As such, the trier of fact must decide if there is factually some hope of reconciliation before permitting a divorce.[34]

VI. Divisible Divorce

A state court has jurisdiction to rule on a divorce petition if the court has jurisdiction over either of the parties to the marriage. Either party carries the subject matter of the marriage with him or her, so either party can petition for divorce without the presence of the other party. As we have discussed in reference to Full Faith and Credit in section two of this chapter, jurisdiction may be obtained by either one of the parties fulfilling the requirements for residency and providing sufficient notice to the other spouse. Once the court has jurisdiction, then any divorce rendered in that state, no matter if the ground and the residency requirements are radically different from those of another state, must be awarded Full Faith and Credit. This only applies to states, not to foreign decrees of divorce.

Under certain circumstances a court may decline to exercise subject matter jurisdiction over the marriage, thereby declining to issue a divorce decree. Such circumstances include when a divorce action is initiated in another state, or when another state may have greater connection to the married couple, as demonstrated through existing petitions for support of a spouse or child, or when there is a custody petition in another state. Courts have a duty to minimize vexatious litigation whenever possible.[35] But if a court decides to accept jurisdiction over the marriage, and then to award a decree dissolving the marriage, this does not mean that the court will have concomitant jurisdiction over the other issues that might be raised by the parties. These issues include: (1) spousal support, (2) child

---

34. Strack v. Strack, 916 N.Y.S.2d 759 (N.Y. Sup. Ct. 2011).

35. *See, e.g.,* Engle v. Superior Court, 294 P.2d 1026 (Cal. Dist. Ct. App. 1956).

support, and (3) child custody and visitation. Thus, if a court has jurisdiction to litigate individual elements of the family dissolution, but not necessarily all of the elements, the process is referred to as divisible divorce. Hypothetically, one of the spouses could leave Virginia and travel to Nevada alone and obtain a divorce entitled to Full Faith and Credit. The other spouse could remain in Virginia and petition the Virginia court for spousal support from the absent spouse by using the Virginia long-arm statute. Likewise, the same Virginia spouse could petition for an order of spousal support or child support. And since the couple had sent the minor child to live with a grandparent in New York, and the child had been there for more than six months, New York would appear to be the home state of the child and therefore have preeminent status to make a custody and visitation order. The family dissolution would be divisible among three different states.

We have established the parameters of divorce jurisdiction, but it is necessary to elaborate on the jurisdictional basis and enforcement of the other three issues we have identified: Spousal support, child support, and custody.

A. *Spousal Support*

Any petition for division of marital property or for an award of spousal support is dependent upon personal jurisdiction over both of the spouses; unlike marriage and divorce, the court must have personal jurisdiction over both of the parties. The Uniform Interstate Family Support Act, adopted in all states as a result of a mandate by Congress, specifies that a state may have jurisdiction over a party if the party is personally served, or submits to jurisdiction, or meets any of the other criteria listed in the Act.[36] Once the court has personal jurisdiction over both of the parties, the court may divide the marital property and provide for support in accordance with the parameters of the state statutes.

Traditionally, real property is subject to the jurisdiction of the state in which it is located. But foreign real property also may be subject to the jurisdiction of another state's courts if the real property is marital property and the owner of the property is subject to the personal jurisdiction of that court. Once the court has personal jurisdiction and makes a support order, the court retains continuing enforcement jurisdiction over the parties even though they may subsequently leave the issuing state. Modification may be

---

36. *See* UNIF. INTERSTATE FAM. SUP. ACT § 201 (amended 2008), 9 U.L.A. Pt. IB 159 et seq. (2001).

made in another state only if that other state has personal jurisdiction over both of the parties.

B.   *Child Support*

As with spousal support, the court must have personal jurisdiction over both of the parents to issue an order of child support. Jurisdiction over the child is not required, only jurisdiction over both of the persons responsible for the support of the child. In addition to the jurisdiction provisions of the Uniform Interstate Family Support Act pertaining to adult spouses, there are corresponding jurisdictional grounds when a child is involved. As can be imagined, the Act seeks to provide a long list of possible grounds for personal jurisdiction over someone responsible for the financial support of a child.

For example, jurisdiction over an individual may be obtained if the individual resides with the child in the state, provides prenatal care or support for the child, the child is placed in the state because of the direction of the individual, the child was conceived through an act of sexual intercourse in the state, or the individual asserts parentage in the state.[37] Because the Act lists many possibilities, it is probable that more than one state will have jurisdiction to order support. If so, and there are competing jurisdictions deciding child support, Section 204 of the Act establishes a procedure by which the order of one state should gain precedence. Thus, there is a preference for the forum state and if an action for child support was initiated there, then this is the state with precedence and its order is subject to enforcement. If the child support order was originally initiated in another state, then the forum state's order may be enforced only if the forum state files an objection within the time allowed by the other state, and the forum state is the home state of the child.

Jurisdiction to modify a child support order may be necessary as the obligors change residency moving from state to state. Modification of an order and enforcement of an order should be viewed differently. Enforcement began with the initial child support order, rendered by the initiating state. Then, even though obligors may move to other states, the order may be enforced through registering the order of the initiating state in that new state. Nonetheless, if a petition is filed to modify the child support order, the order must be registered in the new state and the new state must have new personal jurisdiction over the parties at the time of the modification

---

37.   *Id.* at § 201(3)—(7).

of the order.[38] Thus, where the parties actually reside at the time of the filing of the motion to modify is what counts for determining if the court has proper jurisdiction to modify. Furthermore, the state being asked to modify the initial child support order may not decline to exercise jurisdiction under the premise that jurisdiction remains with the initiating court. When the petition to modify is filed and the court has personal jurisdiction over both of the obligors, the court is required by the Uniform Interstate Family Support Act to rule upon the petition.

C. Child Custody

Child custody and visitation orders depend on specific statutory parameters, not the physical presence of the child, and not the physical presence of the parents or persons acting in a parental capacity. This is distinctive and different from the jurisdictional basis for support. The rules regarding jurisdiction over a child are listed in the Uniform Child Custody Jurisdiction and Enforcement Act ("UCCJEA"), adopted in every state. Furthermore, a valid order of custody may be enforced internationally through the Hague Convention on the Civil Aspects of International Child Abduction. So too, in order to better protect children, Congress has enacted a number of statutes to enforce interstate child custody orders, the Parental Kidnapping Prevention Act ("PKPA") being one of them. The PKPA shares jurisdictional grounds with the UCCJEA.

But the basis of child custody jurisdiction begins with the UCCJEA. The Act prioritizes jurisdiction. First, the Act specifies that a valid custody order begins with home state jurisdiction. This is defined as the state where the child lived with a parent or a person acting as a parent for at least six consecutive months immediately before commencement of a child custody proceeding. If the child is less than six months of age, then where the child has lived since birth with any of the named persons.[39] Second, if there is no home state, then the court will look to which state has a significant connection with the child. The court will never determine jurisdiction based on the physical presence of the child; child custody determinations and support issues are completely different. If a child is found abandoned or is affected by an emergency situation, the Act specifies that any state making an emergency determination of custody would be making a temporary order; the

---

38. *See, e.g.*, Goddard v. Heintzelman, 875 A.2d 1119 (Pa. Super. Ct. 2005).

39. UNIF. CHILD CUSTODY JURISDICTION AND ENFORCEMENT ACT, § 102(7), 9 U.L.A. Pt. IA et seq. (1999).

home state would still have the opportunity of making a valid custody order affecting future enforcement.

Once a state court makes a valid custody determination, only that court has jurisdiction to modify the custody order. The initiating court will lose jurisdiction only if everyone involved, the child, the parents, and all persons acting as parents have moved from the initiating state. But this event can only be determined by the initiating court. If this court makes a determination that it no longer should have exclusive continuing jurisdiction, and the child is still a minor, then a new home state will have to be established to make a new custody order, even though this is a modification of the previous order. The initiating state will have to make inquiry as to whether it still has a significant connection with the child, even though all of the major parties have left the state. With the increasing mobility of parents and children, a continuing and significant connection with the initiating state may be elusive. Courts tend to look to visitation that may continue in the state, or the presence of relatives other than parents in the initiating state. But when addressing the connection needed with the initiating state, it seems that the test should focus on the child's relationship to the state and to a parent's life in that state. If the child continues to have a significant connection with the state, then the initiating state should continue to exercise jurisdiction over custody of the child.[40]

40. *See, e.g.,* In re Forlenza, 140 S.W.3d 373 (Tex. 2004).

Chapter 6

Division of Marital Property at Dissolution

I. Historical Perspective

Prior to the introduction of no-fault divorce the focus of matrimonial litigation was on establishing a valid fault ground warranting divorce, and then contending with the common law defenses to that ground. No-fault divorce, first adopted in 1970, rapidly spread to every state, providing an option to end protracted divorce litigation; this was one of the goals of the new divorce movement. Litigation quickly shifted to issues other than divorce, such as the division of marital property, the nature of marital property, and the purposes and length of spousal support upon dissolution. Unlike economic support for children, which we will discuss in Chapter 8, the division of marital property and spousal support are resolved without the assistance of a mathematical formula. Instead, courts in common law states utilize a list of factors to achieve an equitable distribution, and in community property states the presumption is an equal division of all property that can be classified as community assets. The economic process is rife with litigation.

As we have discussed in previous chapters, American society has changed. We can identify certain developments that have had an impact on the statutory and common law approaches to distribution of marital property and concomitant support obligations. It is important to understand what has occurred so as to respond to present and future issues. First, gender is no longer an appropriate basis upon which to base any support obligation. Prior to state and federal constitutional litigation promoting equal protection, men were responsible for support both during marriage and upon divorce. Only the marital fault of the female spouse could dissipate or eradicate this support obligation. And in almost all situations the female spouse was entitled to support after the marriage dissolved until she died or remarried. It did not matter how long the marriage lasted, the husband was obligated to provide support. The obligation of the husband could not be waived through a valid premarital agreement, since such agreements were contrary to public policy, viewed as promoting divorce or as an abuse of a confidential relationship. But society's evolution towards gender equality eliminated the male-only support obligation in law, if not always in practice.

Establishing gender equality meant recognizing a corresponding obligation of women to support men during marriage, as well as upon divorce, if circumstances warrant. Nonetheless, commentators consistently call attention to the fact that, on average, women and children are severely economically disadvantaged after a divorce.[1] Furthermore, while no-fault divorce made divorce an unilateral option for the husband, there were economic disadvantages to female spouses that resulted from changes in the law governing spousal support and property division.[2] Women were now expected to be self-sufficient, even though in many cases they remained mothers and homemakers. Many argue that current practice has not addressed the gender disparity of divorce, that reimbursement and rehabilitation alimony do not adequately address the economic realities. Nonetheless, the fact remains that modern law reflects the view that the married couple consists of two equal economic partners, creating economic expectations and responsibilities for both. The only remedy for inequity must come from the contractual negotiations initiated by the married couple.

A second development within modern law is the presence of serial marriages; persons sometimes marry multiple times. The challenge of multiple marriages is that a second marriage jeopardizes the obligor's inclination and ability to meet the support requirements of the first family. This is especially true if part of the property settlement and support agreement made to the first family included children. While marriage is not necessarily a condition to the birth of a child, the intent to create a family often results when a child is born. The challenge is to accommodate multiple marriages into the division of marital property and the support of children and former spouses.[3] A third development of this modern age is multiple marital families. As we discussed in Chapter 4, couples of the same and opposite sex are able to enter into express and implied contractual arrangements that are enforceable upon dissolution and death. So too, these obligations impact the ability of obligors to provide for preexisting families. Just as with marriage, the nonmarital family imposes economic obligations that can compete.

A fourth development is the ability of couples to expand or waive support and property title arrangements through valid pre-

1. Lenore Weitzman, The Divorce Revolution: The Unexpected Social and Economic Consequences for Women and Children in America 339 (1985).

2. Marsha Garrison, The Economic of Divorce: Changing Rules, Changing Results in Divorce Reform at the Crossroads 1 (S. Sugarman & H. Kay eds., 1990).

3. J. Thomas Oldham, *Putting Asunder in the 1990s*, 80 Cal. L. Rev. 1091 (1992).

marital, and sometimes, postmarital contracting. We discussed these contractual arrangements in Chapter 2, but the impact of a valid contract is very apparent in cases and materials addressing marital property and support obligations. Courts are willing to enforce complete waivers of property and support under defined circumstances. Once rare, these self-ordered agreements have become routine, especially among older couples seeking to preserve assets for children from prior marriages. Even in states that had not adopted the Uniform Premarital Agreement Act, there is widespread support for premarital agreements.[4] Plus, the public support for self-ordered arrangements reinforces the rights of adults to enter into these arrangements.

A fifth development is the evolution of property. At one time marital property consisted of the family home, an automobile, some personal property items, and perhaps a savings/checking account. Today marital property has expanded to include stock options and frequent flyer miles, for example. In addition, new marital property developments could include the family pets and certainly due to the plague of the credit card age, excessive marital debt. Perhaps the proliferation of marital properties results from the intensive litigation concerning its division upon divorce. Attorneys litigated to include the value of season tickets associated with employment, goodwill, licenses and degrees, Social Security and military disability pay, plus the myriad forms of stock ownership. Litigation has been instrumental in spawning new types of property, but the economy has evolved too.

A sixth development is the new approach of the courts. Today, the overall objective of marital litigation is to allow the spouses to bid each other a fond fiscal farewell as quickly as possible. While older regimes provided extended periods of alimony, resulting in petitions for modification and problematic enforcement of support decrees, the newer approach seeks to meet the couple's needs solely through division of marital assets. Spousal support is the last resort, only when there are insufficient assets. This has been the approach of strict community property states, but common law jurisdictions have been moving in this direction. Today, at divorce, courts assess the need and ability of each of the parties and seek to use the marital property to arrive at an equitable property settlement. If the property is insufficient, then the court will order rehabilitative support, or seek to order reimbursement. If this is insufficient or not practical, then the court could order indefinite support. While support, defined as rehabilitation, reimbursement,

4. *See, e.g.*, Dove v. Dove, 680 S.E.2d 839 (Ga. 2009).

or indefinite, often requires continuing contact with the parties, enforcement is facilitated through the Uniform Interstate Family Support Act.

As we discussed in Chapter 1, family law in America has become more uniform among the states. But at least conceptually, there are two types of jurisdictions: Community property and common law. Of course, the former results from the influence of the Spanish colonists, who settled states such as Texas, Louisiana, New Mexico, and California. Other states were influenced more by the English system of common law. But it is increasingly difficult to characterize either system. There tends to be overlapping and borrowing by one from the other. Some community property states are strict, such as California and New Mexico. But some community property states allow for equitable factors to be considered in distributing property. This is unthinkable among community property purists. Likewise, in some common law states, property is characterized as separate or community, and then the court applies equitable considerations to the community property. As we will discuss, the states in each of the systems borrow from each other.

II. The Two Systems of Property Distribution

A. *Community Property States*

A court in a *strict* community property state would begin the process by dividing property accumulated during the marriage into two categories. One category would be separate property, the other community property.[5] Separate property may be defined as any property acquired by a spouse through gift, devise, bequest, or that was acquired prior to the marriage. Community property consists of the remaining property acquired by the spouses during marriage; community property would be divided equally upon divorce.[6] In addition, couples executing premarital agreements may classify property as community or separate through the agreements.

One of the distinctive features of the community property system is that title does not matter. This means that even though a spouse may earn a salary, have his or her name listed on the title to the home, retirement account, or bank account, the asset is presumptively community property and would be divided equally between the parties regardless of title. In states classified as strict community property states, equitable principles do not affect the

---

5. *See, e.g.,* UNIFORM MARRIAGE AND DIVORCE ACT, § 307 (Alternative B); *see also Principles of the Law of Family Dissolution* §§ 4.03, 4.12 (2002).

6. *See, e.g.,* CAL. FAM. CODE § 2550 (West 2008).

distribution of assets. Indeed, courts apply a presumption of equal distribution at divorce, seeking to divide assets as evenly as possible, and as quickly as possible, considering the circumstances of each case. One court used non-pension community assets to satisfy the community property interest of the non-employee spouse in the employee spouse's pension. If the court had ordered that a qualified domestic relations order ("QDRO") be submitted to preserve the interest of the non-employee until such time as the employee retired, it would have distorted the underlying presumptions of community property. That is, the non-employee spouse's interest would be subject to retirement decisions made by the employee spouse and this was unacceptable to the court.[7] Instead, if possible, in strict community property states, the goal is that each spouse should have dominion over his or her community interest as soon as possible.

Some states, even though they are traditional community property states, permit courts to use equitable factors in dividing community property at divorce. These states are not strict states. This means that instead of a strict system of classification of property, courts are permitted by state statute to use factors such as length of the marriage, hardship endured by one of the parties, and even marital fault in distributing the community property. Note that both the strict community property states and the community property states employing equity allow for courts to consider economic fault. An economic fault occurs when a spouse deliberately destroys community assets, or transfers community assets without receiving full market value. The court will estimate the value of the asset and then credit a share of this amount to the innocent spouse.

Support is rare in a strict community property jurisdiction. The nature of the system is to divide community assets, permitting each spouse to retain his or her separate property, and then to permit the marriage to dissolve and the couple to end any connection. But in some states spousal support may be "just and reasonable" and, if so, will be "based on the standard of living established during the marriage." Factors include: (1) marketable skills, (2) domestic sacrifices of the party seeking the support, (3) contributions the supported spouse made to the career of the other spouse, (4) the duration of the marriage, (5) age and health of the supported party, and (6) the balance of hardships on each party.[8] Any support is meant to rehabilitate or reimburse the supported party, but each

---

7. Ruggles v. Ruggles, 860 P.2d 182 (N.M. 1993).

8. Cal. Fam. Code § 4320 (West 2008).

case must be viewed individually, and in rare situations involving health or incapacity, indefinite support may be warranted.

B. Common Law (Separate Property) States

The vast majority of states are influenced by the English system of law. Under this system, there are two classifications of property, separate and marital property. Most of these states recognize a distinction between these two, as do the majority of community property states. That is, they allow each party to keep his or her separate property and then divide the marital property.[9] But there are two differences with the common law states as compared to strict community property states. First, in a common law state title matters. This means that property titled in the name of one of the parties is presumptively the property of that party. And second, common law states consider equitable factors in the distribution of marital property. Since title matters, courts look to the list of equitable factors provided by the state legislatures to determine who should receive the property upon dissolution. New York lists thirteen factors to consider in dividing property.[10]

As with strict community property states, spousal support is an option when circumstances warrant it. Also, indefinite support—at least until a spouse dies or remarries—is infrequent. Instead, the court seeks to provide support to reimburse a spouse for a special contribution for which an economic benefit was sought, or to rehabilitate a spouse for his or her voluntary contribution to a spouse's family or career. While we will discuss reimbursement and rehabilitation further, *infra*, it is necessary to emphasize that these are temporary measures. The goal of today's distribution of marital property is to allow each of the parties an economic separation as soon as possible.

Increasingly today, states lack a clear distinction between traditional community property and separate property perspectives. We have discussed the reasons behind this blending of perspectives in Chapter 1. Thus, many of the community property states apply the equitable factors of common law states. And many of the common law states make no distinction between separate property and marital property. Instead, they apply equitable factors to *all of the property* owned by the spouses, regardless of how it was acquired or whether it was brought into the marriage separately. Thus, what each of the spouses owns may be relevant in terms of

9. *See, e.g.,* UNIFORM MARRIAGE AND DIVORCE ACT § 307 (Alternative A).

10. N.Y. DOM. REL. LAW § 236(B)(5)(d) (McKinney 1999).

equity, but ownership of any property will not be conclusive when the court divides it according to the equitable factors.

In the past, judicial inquiry focused on what property should be community or marital, and then which should be considered as separate. But today's concerns involve the classification of property, and then how to divide the property, or how to reimburse one party for the property, or finally, how to rehabilitate one party for having contributed to the property. We will address this in section four of this chapter: The Process of Division. But prior to that, we address issues arising concerning how to classify property.

III. Classifications of Marital Property

Modern marriage dissolution statutes view marriage as an economic partnership of equals. The cases evidence a basic premise that, once the marriage is dissolved, the spouses should divide the marital assets or the marital debts, on a strict community property approach, or on the basis of common law equitable principles. If there are sufficient assets to meet the needs and expectations of the parties, then the parties may incorporate the division of assets into a final court decree and move on with the rest of their lives. But the nature of assets has evolved. In the past there was the family home and a savings account. Today, stock options, season tickets to sporting events,[11] and goodwill often are significant assets. And certainly marital debt is the only legacy of many marriages. Federal benefits such as Social Security and military payments also pose difficulties. Couples may contract between themselves to clarify some of the issues, but only in a few cases are marital contracts effective in resolving the disputes between the parties.

What follows is a description of some of the most frequently litigated items of property involved in marital dissolution proceedings. The rationale used may be applied to other similar items of property.

A. *Marital Debt*

Marital debt, like marital property, should be divided equally between the spouses or apportioned equitably, just like marital property in common law states. The issue for the court to decide is what constitutes marital debt and what constitutes separate debt. If a debt is incurred jointly, then a presumption arises that it is a marital debt, and if a debt is incurred by a single spouse, then a

---

11. Wright v. Wright, No. 09–156, 2010 WL 956150 (Ark. Ct. App. Mar. 17, 2010) (holding that if season tickets to college football games or country club memberships have value they should be marital property).

presumption arises that it is a separate debt.[12] Obviously, in classifying the property, the court will look to the joint signatures of the parties, any agreement that evidences their intent, and the purpose or nature of the item purchased. If a court determines that the debt is indeed marital, it will apportion the debt in the same manner as it would apportion a marital asset.

Not all states create a presumption regarding the nature of property and debt. Nonetheless, even without a presumption, courts will look to the purpose of the expense in determining if it is marital or separate. When a spouse incurred large credit card debts to support a child from a prior marriage, and the other spouse did not know of the existence of the credit card, the debt was treated by the court as a separate debt. As such, the debt would not be shared by both of the parties upon divorce, but paid by the credit card spouse individually.[13]

Often, a spouse will declare bankruptcy because of excessive debt incurred individually during marriage. The issue arises as to what effect this will have on the other spouse: Is the other spouse liable for the payment of the debt? In one case a spouse obtained a Chapter 7 discharge of the debts she incurred on her own credit cards for her separate debt. Later, when she and her husband then filed for divorce, the divorce court sought to assign to her one-half of the marital debt accumulated by the couple. She refused to pay, arguing that when she received the Chapter 7 discharge in bankruptcy she had all of her debt discharged. The court disagreed, holding she was still responsible for one-half of the marital debt even though her separate debt had been discharged.[14]

B. Marital Home

Often the marital home is the major asset of the family. As marital property it could be sold or partitioned between the divorcing spouses. But sometimes the home is the domicile of the parenting spouse and minor children. States will permit the parenting spouse and minor children to remain in the marital home as a form of child support.[15] Thus, the rules affecting the equitable division of marital property may be modified by the exigencies of the family situation.

12. Gilliam v. McGrady, 691 S.E.2d 797 (Va. 2010).

13. Rice v. Rice, 336 S.W.3d 66 (Ky. 2011).

14. Horvath v. Horvath, No. 14–09–22, 2010 WL 338209 (Ohio Ct. App. Feb. 1, 2010).

15. *See, e.g.*, CAL. FAM. CODE § 3802 (West 2004).

There are additional facets to the division of the marital home. For example, if the home is treated as the separate property of one of the spouses, that spouse will retain title, but the other spouse should be reimbursed for the value of any separate or marital assets contributed to the home's upkeep during the marriage. And associated with bankruptcy, if a spouse is ordered to pay the mortgage on the former marital home as part of his divorce from a former spouse, was the support payment nondischargeable in bankruptcy as a marital support obligation? In the Bankruptcy Abuse Prevention and Consumer Protection Act of 2005, Congress made nondischargeable all divorce or separation related obligations to a spouse, former spouse, or a child. The issue however, is in determining the intent of the parties or the state court in creating the obligation. It is important to examine the purpose of the obligation in light of the parties' circumstances at the time. This is essential in determining if the mortgage comes under the protection of the federal bankruptcy code and if it is nondischargeable.[16]

C. Pension Benefits

Pensions and retirement benefits form a significant part of marital property today, and yet, parties are often ignorant of the process by which these assets may be divided upon divorce. The following issues arise: (1) whether a non-vested pension may be divided upon dissolution; (2) whether a former spouse should take a lump-sum settlement at dissolution or take a pay-as-you-go payment whenever the employee spouse retires; (3) federal pension requirements mandated by ERISA; (4) whether the non-military spouse of a member of the armed services may take a portion of the disability pay elected by the retired spouse in lieu of a pension amount; (5) whether benefits may be waived; (6) the procedures for filing a valid QDRO; (7) what is the impact of a qualified preretirement annuity upon a QDRO; and (8) whether the spouses may control any or all of these issues through a valid premarital or postmarital agreement.

Even though a pension is not vested, the law is clear: The contract between the employer and the employee represents a property interest that may be considered as marital property.[17] The rationale is that pension benefits are like deferred compensation. At the time of the divorce the non-employee spouse has an interest in the property as represented by the contract. This interest is valuable and should be divisible upon divorce, even though it vests in

---

16. *See, e.g.*, Bean v. Bean, 902 N.E.2d 256 (Ind. Ct. App. 2009).

17. *See, e.g.*, In re Valence, 798 A.2d 35 (N.H. 2002).

the future. Likewise, stock options are a form of deferred compensation and should be treated as property at present, even though they are only an option to take an interest in the future.[18]

In 1974, Congress sought to protect all employee retirement benefits when it enacted the Employee Retirement Income Security Act (ERISA). Since state courts direct the division of marital property at divorce, ERISA is particularly important because the federal legislation preempts state law. But what Congress takes away, it can also give back. With the passage of the Retirement Equity Act of 1984, Congress restored to state courts the power to divide employee pensions upon divorce. Congress chose to allow courts to order a QDRO for the benefit of the non-employee spouse. Once the spouse obtains a valid divorce decree assigning pension benefits between the parties, the QDRO will enforce the payment when the employee spouse retires. It is incumbent upon the parties to file a valid QDRO with the employer in order to qualify for benefits. Failure to file, or a delay in filing, can have adverse consequences. For example, when an Indiana couple divorced, the wife was awarded a specified share of the husband's retirement account, consisting of General Motors stock. The divorce decree did not specify which party was to file the order, so there was a delay in filing the QDRO. After five months the former wife filed the QDRO. But by the time she filed, the value of the stock had declined significantly and the value the stock represented could not satisfy the share of the marital property she had been awarded by the divorce court. The former husband argued that she was only entitled to this reduced share because she should be subject to the stock's decline, but the wife sought to recover the original award, the larger amount. The court ruled that when the decree does not specify who must file the QDRO, then the risk of any loss must be borne by the party best situated to avoid the risk. Thus, since the former wife could have avoided the loss through a timely filing, she must now bear the loss together with the former husband.[19] If she had filed in a timely fashion, she would have avoided the reduced value of the stock.

Consistent with the increasing recognition of nonmarital cohabitation, a few courts have permitted an assignment of pension benefits for couples who, although not married, were in a "quasi-marital" relationship. In one case, the couple had lived together for more than thirty years, raised two children, filed joint income tax returns, and maintained a joint household. In permitting a QDRO when the couple separated, one court ruled that state law controls,

---

18. *See, e.g.*, Shorb v. Shorb, 643 S.E.2d 124 (S.C. Ct. App. 2007).

19. Ehman v. Ehman, 941 N.E.2d 1103 (Ind. Ct. App. 2011).

and if the property acquired by the couple amounted to marital property under state law, then the QDRO was appropriate. Neither the wording of ERISA, nor the Defense of Marriage Act, bars permitting a QDRO when the state court regards the couple as in a quasi-marital relationship and classifies their property as marital property.[20]

D. *Social Security Benefits*

Employees subject to the Social Security tax pay into the federal program throughout employment, presumptively the length of the marriage. As with pension benefits, it seems logical that the non-employee spouse would share in a portion of the benefits amassed when divorce occurs, since that spouse would share in benefits if the couple had remained married. And under defined conditions, the divorced spouse may share in the Social Security benefits owed to the other spouse. But the issue becomes whether private parties may apportion benefits under a private agreement, or whether the parties abide by the provisions of the federal statute.

The law provides that the non-employee divorced spouse may receive a portion of the former spouse's Social Security benefits if the marriage to the employee spouse lasted at least ten years. In addition, any support paid to a non-employee divorced spouse cannot reduce the benefit to the employee divorced spouse. There is also a choice to be made. If the non-employee divorced spouse worked independently so as to have personal benefits, then this spouse must choose between those independent benefits and any benefits sought from the divorced spouse. If the independent benefits are larger than those from the former employee spouse, then the spouse would waive the benefits from the divorced spouse. If the Social Security benefits are an option, then the non-employee divorced spouse may apply for benefits if both of the former spouses are at least 62. In addition, the non-employee former spouse must be single at the time of the application, and remain single to receive any benefits.

Courts are divided as to whether a divorcing couple may negotiate between themselves and offset any future Social Security benefits against existing marital assets.[21] The process would involve the assignment of a value to the future Social Security benefits and

20. Owens v. Automotive Machinists Pension Trust, 551 F.3d 1138 (9th Cir. 2009).

21. *See, e.g.*, Olsen v. Olsen, 169 P.3d 765 (Utah Ct. App. 2007); In re Marriage of Crook, 813 N.E.2d 198 (Ill. 2004).

all of the conditions that attach. Then, based on this value, the court could equitably apportion the existing marital assets so as to disclaim any claim being made in the future. The debate in the courts centers on the import of anti-assignment and anti-alienation provisions of the federal legislation, but until there is a definitive ruling from Congress or the federal judiciary, the debate will continue over the state court's jurisdiction to ratify a divorcing couple's private agreement to apportion future benefits or to apportion those benefits themselves.

E. Military Retirement Benefits

Because benefits paid to a member of the Armed Services are federal benefits, they are not subject to distribution by state divorce courts without explicit federal permission. In 1982, Congress granted permission to state divorce courts to treat disposable military retirement pay as marital property subject to state court disbursement. The Uniformed Services Former Spouse Protection Act (USFSPA) permits non-military divorced spouses to receive payments directly from the government upon receiving a valid decree of divorce. This seemed to settle the issue as to the rights of spouses to take military retirement pay. But what if retirement pay were taken as disability pay? In 1989, the Supreme Court ruled that a non-military divorced spouse did not have the ability to take a share of the former spouse's military retirement pay that had been elected by the spouse to be taken as disability pay.[22] The federal legislation did not permit this. The effect of the decision was to deprive the former spouse of the military member a significant portion of income because the federal legislation did not waive preemption over the military disability pay. Justice Sandra Day O'Connor dissented, arguing for an offset of the amount of the disability pay against other existing marital assets. Many courts, using the rationale of former Justice O'Connor, apply offset indemnity provisions to protect the interests of former spouses.[23]

F. Income Enhancing Licenses and Degrees

In 1982, the Supreme Court of New Jersey addressed the issue of whether a degree or license that enhances the earning capacity of a spouse should be considered as marital property. The court ruled

22. Mansell v. Mansell, 490 U.S. 581 (1989).

23. *See, e.g.,* Megee v. Carmine, 802 N.W.2d 669 (Mich. Ct. App. 2010) (hold- ing that a former service member remains financially responsible to former spouse under original decree if member subsequently elects to take disability

that it should not be considered marital property,[24] and this ruling became the law of the land with one exception, New York.[25] The majority rule rejected the degree or license as marital property and emphasized three things: (1) any degree or license is personal to the holder, (2) the value of any degree or license is too speculative to consider, and (3) the value of the degree would be earned after the marriage, and state statutes restrict equitable distribution to property acquired during the marriage. Needless to say, the highest court in New York, basing its opinion mainly on the state statute mandating the apportionment of *all* property, rejects the New Jersey approach and continues to do so today.[26]

While the majority approach holds that an income-enhancing license is not marital property, it does not deny the right of the non-license holder from being reimbursed for all reasonable expenses contributed towards obtaining the license. Relying on fairness, the majority concludes that if one spouse contributes to an enterprise in the hope that future benefits will accrue, that spouse deserves to be reimbursed if the marriage ends. But while the majority approach recommends reimbursement, it suggests that courts look to the facts of each case to determine if reimbursement is appropriate. For example, if the license was obtained more than ten years prior to the divorce, it is reasonable to assume that the marriage has already benefitted from the enhanced income, and no further reimbursement is necessary. Some states reduce these considerations to statutes.[27]

G. *Goodwill*

Usually, a business is more than an assembly of tangible personal assets. Instead, the business has a reputation, a history of expertise and service known in the community. Is this reputation property? Likewise, in the case of a person of good and admirable notoriety, is the goodwill attached to that person's name or reputation also considered property? When divorce occurs, courts must determine the marital property value of this goodwill. Often the courts distinguish between *enterprise* goodwill and *personal* goodwill, the former attaching to a business or product name, and the latter to personal reputation. While the majority of courts hold that personal goodwill is not marital property to be divided upon divorce, the same courts hold that enterprise goodwill is marital property. The difference between the two approaches lies in the fact

pay); Surratt v. Surratt, 148 S.W.3d 761 (Ark. App. 2004).

24. Mahoney v. Mahoney, 453 A.2d 527 (N.J. 1982).

25. O'Brien v. O'Brien, 489 N.E.2d 712 (N.Y. 1985).

26. *See* Holterman v. Holterman, 814 N.E.2d 765 (N.Y. 2004).

27. *See, e.g.,* CAL. FAM. CODE § 2641 (2009); IND. CODE § 31–15–7–6 (2009).

that courts regard personal goodwill as unique to the individual, a personal attribute that is not divisible.[28]

But even if enterprise goodwill is marital property, it is extremely difficult to value. The majority of courts regard the enterprise as marital property, but experience difficulty determining what portion of the enterprise is the business and what portion is the person running the business. The quest to value the enterprise as marital property provides ample opportunities to double-count, using the manager's goodwill in tandem with that of the business. But courts struggle with a solution to this dilemma, often settling for a solution that ignores the reality that the court is taking the manager's earnings and personal goodwill into the equation.[29] Courts apply different formulas to value goodwill based on: (1) the price a willing buyer would pay for the enterprise, (2) one year average gross income in the profession, or a percentage thereof, and (3) evidence of sales in comparable professions.[30] The lack of state court uniformity in approach suggests that the only fair approach is for the couple to execute a premarital agreement specifying the goodwill formula to be used to value any business then in existence, or that is planned for the marriage.

H. Personal Injury Awards

If a worker suffers a work-related injury, the worker may be entitled to a disability payment or a personal injury award based on that injury. The issue then arises as to whether such an award is personal to the worker and treated as separate property, or whether it is marital property subject to division in the event of a divorce. The majority of courts focus on the nature and purpose of the personal injury award. Thus, whatever portion of the award is meant to compensate for the disability is treated as separate property; likewise, whatever portion is meant to supplement earnings or retirement support is treated as marital property.[31] A few courts have ruled that personal injury awards are marital property simply because they were received during the marriage; some courts rely on state statutes that explicitly exclude personal injury awards from being considered as marital property.

28. *See, e.g.*, De Salle v. Gentry, 818 N.E.2d 40 (Ind. Ct. App. 2004).

29. *See, e.g.*, McReath v. McReath, 789 N.W.2d 89 (Wis. Ct. App. 2010), *aff'd*, 800 N.W.2d 399 (Wis. 2011).

30. *See, e.g.*, Poore v. Poore, 331 S.E.2d 266 (N.C. Ct. App. 1985).

31. *See, e.g.*, Gragg v. Gragg, 12 S.W.3d 412 (Tenn. 2000); Conrad v. Conrad, 612 S.E.2d 772 (W. Va. 2005) (analyzing various state approaches).

IV. The Process of Division and Support

Once the court has amassed the marital property, even if this only includes marital debt, the court, often with the cooperation of an agreement executed by the parties, will divide the marital property and, when circumstances necessitate, order rehabilitation, reimbursement, or more indefinite support for either of the parties consonant with state statutes. As discussed previously, the trend in modern courts is to allow the parties to cease all economic interaction as soon as possible. This is especially true in strict community property states, but true also in common law jurisdictions mirroring marital property on community property standards. Thus, long-term, or indefinite, alimony is extremely rare; any support is linked to rehabilitation or reimbursement. If possible, the goal is to divide existing marital property, offsetting those assets that are preempted by federal statutes, such as Social Security or disability election, and military retirement pay. This is not an option for all states, but it is the hope of all to allow the marital partners, as quickly as possible, to move on with their lives.

A. *The Marital Period*

The vast majority of states, unless the couple contracts otherwise, consider the marital period to begin at the celebration of the marriage and end when either spouse petitions for a divorce.[32] Timing will affect the classification of property, the valuation of assets, including appreciation, and depreciation. Even though the filing of the petition for the divorce does not end the marriage, it does commence a period of separation and perhaps an award of maintenance in connection with a divorce *a mensa et thoro*. A divorce petition also precipitates a separation agreement that officially and contractually ends the period of marital cohabitation.

As discussed earlier, some courts are willing to consider periods of nonmarital cohabitation in amassing marital property. Likewise, at least one court was willing to consider the entire relationship when one couple had been married, then divorced, and then married again.[33] The period of divorce separation was not excluded from consideration. The essential element seems to be fairness in assessing the property acquired by the parties and not simply the precise marital period.

---

32. Thomas Oldham, Divorce, Separation and the Distribution of Property § 13.03 (2005).

33. *See* Kelley v. Kelley, 79 P.3d 428 (Utah Ct. App. 2003).

B. Rehabilitation

When states adopted no-fault divorce, they also adopted a different approach towards marriage. As we discussed earlier in this chapter, influenced by constitutional opinions and legislative enactments, married spouses became viewed as economic partners. Each spouse was able to exercise management, and neither partner was entitled to support at divorce simply because of the marriage itself. Thus, as we have discussed, divorce courts sought to divide the marital property and then allow each of the former spouses to begin anew. But sometimes circumstances make this initial objective untenable.

The Uniform Marriage and Divorce Act ("UMDA"), the nascent attempt at providing uniformity, provided that, upon dissolution, a court may, in addition to dividing marital property, order additional maintenance to a spouse if there is: (1) insufficient marital property to provide for reasonable needs and (2) the other party cannot meet his or her needs independently or is the custodian of a child needing supervision and care in the home. But even then, the maintenance is finite, as the party seeking maintenance can acquire the skills to permit a lifestyle similar to what the couple enjoyed when married. This was the beginning of rehabilitative alimony. The UMDA specified that the court ordering rehabilitation could consider the educational needs of the supported party, the length of the marriage, the age, emotional and physical health of the supported party, and the ability of the supporting spouse to provide rehabilitation support.[34]

Typically, rehabilitative awards occur whenever there are insufficient marital assets to allow each of the spouses to begin a new life equitably. Thus, if one spouse suffered an injury or illness that cannot be addressed with marital property, the other spouse may be ordered to provide support until such time as the incapacitated spouse reaches a level of reasonable self-sufficiency. Likewise, if one spouse is the stay-at-home caretaker of the couple's children, that spouse may, in addition to child support, be entitled to rehabilitative alimony until the children are in school or circumstances allow employment opportunities.[35] And finally, if one spouse made a significant contribution to the career of the other spouse, and marital assets are insufficient to permit a share of the career's gains, then rehabilitation is an option. To illustrate, consider the spouse who served as host/hostess or offered encouragement and support to the other spouse for multiple years of marriage, but

34. UNIF. MARRIAGE AND DIVORCE ACT § 308 (1998).

35. *See, e.g.,* Taylor v. Taylor, 250 S.W.3d 232 (Ark. 2007).

marital assets are limited. The non-career spouse would be entitled to what is necessary to have a career for himself or herself.

At least one state supreme court has ruled that the length of the marriage is not the sole gauge of time limitations available under rehabilitative alimony.[36] Rather, the test for the duration of benefits is what is needed for the supported spouse to work and begin a personal career. And while a medical condition can prompt the need for rehabilitative alimony, courts struggle with a test for terminating the rehabilitative support. Most agree that the support continues until the supported party is able to find stable, full-time employment that fulfills the need for a reasonable lifestyle.[37] Some states, by statute, seek to manage both the period of rehabilitative awards and the assessment of capacity to enter into the workforce. For example, California provides that, prior to awarding a spouse rehabilitative alimony, the court must order the supported spouse to an assessment made by a vocational counselor. And then, if support is ordered, it may only be for a reasonable period of time, generally one-half of the time of the marriage.[38]

C. Reimbursement

When a couple has insufficient marital assets to divide equitably and the marriage is of short duration, the courts often award reimbursement alimony to either party who has made a contribution to the marriage that cannot be "reimbursed" without a specific award by the divorce court. We have discussed an example of this type of alimony when we discussed income-earning degrees and licenses. Even though in all but one of the states the degree is not marital property and cannot be divided, courts are still willing to reimburse the spouse who contributed to the other spouse's degree. Reimbursement includes all reasonable expenses associated with attaining the degree or license. If more than ten years have elapsed since the degree was earned, the court presumes that existing marital property represents what was contributed to earn the degree. Hence, there is no separate order of reimbursement; division of the marital assets makes the parties whole.[39]

Both community property states and separate property states permit reimbursement awards. A California statute provides for reimbursement to separate property (the property belonging to one

---

36. *See* Solem v. Solem, 757 N.W.2d 748 (N.D. 2008).

37. *See, e.g.,* In re Marriage of Erwin, 840 N.E.2d 385 (Ind. Ct. App. 2006).

38. *See* CAL. FAM. CODE § 4320(*l*) (West 2004 & Supp. 2006).

39. *See* CAL. FAM. CODE § 2641(c)(1) (West 2004).

of the two spouses individually) whenever separate property was used to acquire or benefit community property. Examples include down-payments, payments for improvements, or payments to reduce principal on a loan. Nonetheless, reimbursement does not include interest and the parties may, as we have discussed earlier, waive any reimbursement at all.

D.   Indefinite

Rarely, a court will order an indefinite period of spousal support. Usually this is the last resort, occurring whenever the court finds that one of the parties, by reason of age, illness, infirmity, or disability, cannot reasonably be expected to make substantial progress towards becoming self-supporting. This also might occur whenever the respective standards of living of the two parties are unconscionably disparate.[40] While these two factual scenarios are common among many older divorcing couples, they are often difficult to predict. In one case, the husband and wife had been married for more than thirty years, both had college degrees and the husband had a law degree, and together they raised two children who were now grown. The wife worked part time as she raised the children and did so at the time of the divorce, earning around $30,000 a year; the husband works full-time and earns a yearly salary of $136,000 as a circuit court judge. Both parties are in good health. The state trial court awarded the wife monetary support of $1600 a month until she dies, remarries, or cohabits. On appeal, the court sustained the award, ruling that the disparity in their incomes justifies the indefinite alimony award, holding that it is inequitable to saddle one party with reduced earning potential while the other party continues in the advantageous position he reached through their joint efforts.[41]

E.   Modification of Support

Between themselves, divorcing couples may provide for modification or termination of support as they negotiate the terms of their separation agreement. Unless unconscionable, the court will then incorporate but not merge the terms into the court's final decree of divorce. Likewise, distribution of property, once accomplished, cannot be undone. If the couple does not provide otherwise, and if there is an order of support, only a substantial change in circumstances will permit the modification or termination of a support obligation. This provision first occurred in the Uniform

---

40. *See* MD. CODE ANN., FAM. LAW. §§ 11–106(c)(1)–(2) (2011).

41. In re Marriage of Reynard, 801 N.E.2d 591 (Ill. App. Ct. 2003).

Marriage and Divorce Act, section 316, but it has become the standard among the states today.

Death or remarriage is the most common material change of circumstances. Death is fairly obvious, but remarriage always invites considerations about nonmarital cohabitation. To what degree should nonmarital cohabitation operate as a material change in circumstances, so as to justify modification or termination of support? Some states specify that the cohabitation must be for a specified period of time to be material. South Carolina, for example, requires ninety days.[42] But many courts, when considering cohabitation, even in the context of private agreements specifying a certain period of time, interpret the clauses as contemplating changed economic circumstances. Rather than romance or intimacy, the issue is whether the obligee's new relationship is the type of changed circumstance that would render the support obligation unjust,[43] with economic need being the main consideration.

When the obligor dies the payment of support ceases unless provisions are made for the maintenance of a life insurance policy on the obligor, or the parties agree that the estate of the obligor remains liable for support.[44] Incapacity of the obligor is an additional change of circumstance that could be addressed by requiring the obligor to maintain a policy of disability insurance.

F. *Enforcement*

Because divorce is a final judgment it is entitled to interstate enforcement through Full Faith and Credit. Likewise, if an order of support has monetary amounts that are later reduced to judgment, then these too may be enforced via Full Faith and Credit. But an order of support is simply that: An order that is inherently modifiable. Thus, it cannot be enforced through the Constitution but must find enforcement through the Uniform Interstate Family Support Act ("UIFSA"), which has been adopted in all of the states.

The UIFSA is not federal legislation, but rather a uniform act adopted by the states to cure the problem of conflicting support orders issued by multiple courts. Originally promulgated in 1992, all states were required to adopt the UIFSA as a prerequisite to receiving federal grants. This occurred when Congress enacted massive welfare legislation reform in 1996, the Personal Responsi-

---

42. Biggins v. Burdette, 708 S.E.2d 237 (S.C. Ct. App. 2011).

43. Graev v. Graev, 898 N.E.2d 909 (N.Y. 2008).

44. *See, e.g.,* Findley v. Findley, 629 S.E.2d 222 (Ga. 2006); Dohn v. Dohn, 584 S.E.2d 250 (Ga. 2003).

bility and Work Opportunity Reconciliation Act. The UIFSA was significantly revised in 2001, mandating that a court with jurisdiction to initiate a support order be the court with continuing jurisdiction to modify the order. Only if both of the parties, the obligor and the obligee, submit to the personal jurisdiction of another court, could the originating court lose jurisdiction. The Act has been a significant assist in the enforcement of support orders among the various states. When we discuss child support the Act will be discussed further, together with additional federal and uniform legislation that seek to provide for the best interest of the child.

Chapter 7

The Parameters of Procreation

I. Constitutional Underpinnings

The parent-child relationship, once thought to be created solely through the act of intercourse or adoption, can be established today through a much broader range of options. Assisted reproductive technology has advanced significantly. Today, procreation options are available to married and single persons, either during the lifetime of a gamete donor, or even posthumously, after the death of the donor. In tandem, a number of uniform acts and state statutes provide monitoring mechanisms for assisted conception and surrogacy contracts, but much remains to be done in reference to human embryos stored at fertility clinics, rights at death or divorce, and the many ethical issues raised by the procedures. While these issues have supplied multiple topics for articles and books, we will briefly discuss them in the context of procreation, the establishment of a parent-child relationship.

Technology has not progressed alone. Changes in the law regarding procreation were initiated through series of significant constitutional cases. Most commentators would start any analysis with the 1965 *Griswold* decision. The Supreme Court ruled as unconstitutional a longstanding state statute that made it a criminal offense for any person to use any drug, medicinal article, or instrument, to prevent conception.[1] Also, the statute had an abettor provision, making it a criminal offense to abet or counsel another to commit an offense under the statute. The abettors in the *Griswold* proceeding were the Executive Director of the Planned Parenthood League of Connecticut, and a physician who served as the organization's medical director. These named persons had given technical information and advice to married persons concerning means for preventing conception.

Although the decision included both concurring and dissenting opinions, the holding, written by Justice Douglas, was based on what he termed "a marital right of privacy" emanating from various constitutional guarantees under the first ten amendments to the United States Constitution. Specifically, these guarantees were contained in the First, Third, Fourth, Fifth and Ninth Amend-

---

1. Griswold v. Connecticut, 381 U.S. 479 (1965).

ments. The opinion included a statement that would resonate through many subsequent decisions:

> Would we allow the police to search the sacred precincts of marital bedrooms for telltale signs of the use of contraceptives? The very idea is repulsive to the notions of privacy surrounding the marriage relationship.[2]

Griswold ostensibly only affected married couples, but less than a decade later, Justice Brennan expanded the right of privacy previously only granted to married couples to individuals as well. In the *Eisenstadt* decision, which held that a state statute that banned the distribution of contraceptive devices to single individuals was unconstitutional, Justice Brennan wrote that:

> If under *Griswold* the distribution of contraceptives to married persons cannot be prohibited, a ban on distribution to unmarried persons would be equally impermissible. It is true that in *Griswold* the right of privacy in question inhered in the marital relationship. Yet the marital couple is not an independent entity with a mind and heart of its own, but an association of two individuals each with a separate intellectual and emotional makeup. If the right of privacy means anything, it is the right of the *individual*, married or single, to be free from unwarranted governmental intrusion into matters so fundamentally affecting a person as the decision whether to bear or beget a child.[3]

During the next year, 1973, following *Eisenstadt*, the Court would extend the right of privacy to protect a woman's right to obtain an abortion in the *Roe* decision.[4] The woman's right to privacy and an abortion were nonetheless subject to the state's interest in protecting potential life after viability. Thus, a conflict resulted between the woman and the state's right to protect viable life. Then, in 1992, Justice Sandra Day O'Connor would address the viability test raised in *Roe,* writing an opinion that held that states may regulate abortions, but the state may not place a substantial obstacle in the path of a woman's choice to have an abortion.[5] Subsequent decisions refine what was meant by a substantial obstacle A state could not prohibit pregnant minors from obtaining an abortion by requiring absolute parental consent and notification. And wives were not required to notify their husbands of decisions

---

2. *Id.* at 485–486.
3. Eisenstadt v. Baird, 405 U.S. 438, 453 (1972) (emphasis added).
4. Roe v. Wade, 410 U.S. 113 (1973).

5. Planned Parenthood of Southeastern Pennsylvania v. Casey, 505 U.S. 833 (1992).

to have an abortion. By 2006, the Court would rule that abortions were always warranted when the procedure would avert serious and often irreversible damage to the health of a woman.[6]

The constitutional underpinnings shifted in 2007, when the Court ruled that a federal statute limiting partial-birth abortions was constitutional.[7] Seven years earlier, the Court had ruled that a Nebraska partial-birth abortion statute was unconstitutional because it did not provide a health care exception to protect the woman's health.[8] The health care exception was a product of the 1992 *Casey* decision. Recall that this was the decision that held that a woman's right to an abortion may not be unduly burdened. But in 2007, in sustaining Congress' partial-birth abortion ban, Justice Kennedy applied a rational basis test to the statute, holding that the prohibition of intact D & E abortions—a form of partial-birth abortion—was rational. Specifically, the statute did provide for the health of the woman in a rational fashion since, according to the factual findings of Congress, there were alternative procedures available to women and their physicians that were not foreclosed by the statute.

The impact of the 2007 decision on a type of partial-birth abortion rights is currently being discussed, legislated, and litigated.[9] How will the Court's decision impact state legislation and additional federal legislation concerning abortion? There is renewed interest at the state level in restricting the opportunities for abortion through state statutes. State law includes provisions requiring mandatory notification given to women seeking abortions about the risks and consequences of abortion, to restrictions on abortion clinics, and states are seeking to enact better drafted partial-birth abortion statutes.

A woman's right to abortion stemmed from the right to privacy. But there is a tandem discussion to be had on the broader extent of an individual's liberty interest under the Due Process Clause of the Fourteenth Amendment. In its 2003 decision of *Lawrence v. Texas*,[10] the Court held that consensual intimacies between two adults is protected as private conduct. While the import of the decision was to reverse a prior Supreme Court decision permitting state sodomy statutes to criminally prosecute persons of the same sex from intimate conduct, the *Lawrence*

6. Ayotte v. Planned Parenthood of Northern New England, 546 U.S. 320, 326–328 (2006).

7. Gonzales v. Carhart, 550 U.S. 124 (2007).

8. Stenberg v. Carhart, 530 U.S. 914, 930, 937 (2000).

9. *See generally* Reva B. Siegel, *Dignity and the Politics of Protection: Abortion Restrictions Under* Casey/Carhart, 117 YALE L. J. 1694 (2008).

10. 539 U.S. 558 (2003).

impact is far broader. Specifically, for our purposes, what effect will the decision have upon the parameters of procreation?[11] State courts have ruled that individuals have a property interest in their sperm and eggs, and this interest permits these individuals to make decisions with regard to their disposal.[12] Would an individual's rights in regard to sperm, eggs, or embryos find better foundation in arguing for individual liberty, than in classifying the gametes or embryos as property? And at what point can we say that the gametes or embryos have a liberty interest?

Lawrence relies on the spatial distinctiveness of *Griswold* when it discusses the individual liberty of persons engaged in intimate conduct. That is, the facts of the case relate to two adult persons engaged in sexual activity in a private room. But the *Lawrence* decision, with its individual liberty basis, implies greater freedom of person in matters other than sexual conduct. The decision implied a freedom of procreation, of choices in regard to procreation, and to associated freedom from unwarranted governmental regulation. The extent of this freedom is still to be resolved, but we can examine a few areas of interest in what follows.

II. Establishing Paternity and Maternity

Similar to nonmarital cohabitation, the number of single-parent households has increased dramatically. While not all nonmarital cohabitants have children, all single-parent households do, raising the issue of paternity and maternity of the child. What procedure do you follow to determine parentage? Since children born outside of marriage were regarded as illegitimate, if paternity and maternity cannot be established, the child will suffer from a loss of support and inheritance. For states, status is crucial to providing speed and accuracy in fixing support obligations, establishing lines of descent and distribution of estate assets, and promoting the best interest of the child. And federal benefits, such as entitlement to Social Security from a deceased parent, depend upon a state establishment of paternity for inheritance purposes. Throughout the process of establishing paternity and maternity, the balance must be between the state's interest in speed and accuracy and the best interest of the child.

It has been a few decades since the Supreme Court issued a number of decisions that protected the rights of a nonmarital

---

11. *See generally* Katherine M. Franke, *The Domesticated Liberty of Lawrence v. Texas,* 104 COLUM. L. REV. 1399 (2004).

12. *See, e.g.,* Hecht v. Superior Court, 20 Cal.Rptr.2d 275 (Ct. App. 1993); Kurchner v. State Farm Fire & Cas. Co., 858 So.2d 1220 (Fla. Ct. App. 2003).

child.[13] Gradually the states voluntarily initiated longer statutes of limitations to establishment of paternity and maternity, or the states were prodded by federal mandates that required, as a condition for receiving federal grants, longer time frames to establish proof. For example, when Congress enacted the Child Support Enforcement Amendments of 1984, it required states to extend the period of time in which a child can seek to prove paternity and maternity for purposes of support; it is now extended to eighteen years from the time the child is born. And when Congress revised welfare legislation in 1996, it enacted a requirement in the Personal Responsibility and Work Opportunity Reconciliation Act of 1996 that a valid, unrescinded, unchallenged acknowledgment of paternity be treated as equivalent to a judicial establishment of paternity. Such an acknowledgment has all of the presumptive status as being married to the mother of the child.

In addition to federal prodding, uniform legislation offers additional guidelines. The Uniform Interstate Family Support Act, which every state has adopted by federal mandate, provides that all parties must submit to genetic testing to establish paternity when ordered to do so by the court. In addition, this same Family Support Act provides an extensive list of grounds upon which a state may establish jurisdiction over a resident and nonresident individual. For example, the statute allows for personal jurisdiction over a paternity and maternity action if "the individual engaged in sexual intercourse in [the] state and the child may have been conceived by that act of intercourse."[14]

There are often more than one statute of limitations. Different statutes of limitation govern paternity and maternity support obligations while the child is still a minor than when a child seeks to establish heirship for purposes of inheritance. Most often, the state support statutes permit a petition to establish parenthood during minority, but for purposes of inheritance, the claimant may file a petition with the personal representative of the decedent's estate within a reasonable amount of time.[15] Once the putative child learns that he or she could be an heir, the child's guardian, or an adult claimant must submit a petition to establish paternity within a reasonable amount of time. This may occur after the claimant is

---

13. *See, e.g.,* Levy v. Louisiana, 391 U.S. 68 (1968)(allowing a nonmarital child to recover for the wrongful death of the mother); Gomez v. Perez, 409 U.S. 535 (1973) (holding that nonmarital children are entitled to parental support); Mills v. Habluetzel, 456 U.S. 91 (1982) (requiring longer statutes of limitations to process claims); Clark v. Jeter, 486 U.S. 456 (1988) (applying intermediate scrutiny to classifications based on illegitimacy).

14. Unif. Fam. Support Act § 201(a)(6) (as amended 2008).

15. *See, e.g.,* Wingate v. Estate of Ryan, 693 A.2d 457 (N.J. 1997).

no longer a minor. Once properly filed, the claimant must establish presumptive paternity or maternity, or submit to genetic testing. The two have an interesting interplay.

A. *Presumptive Paternity and Maternity*

Presumptions of paternity and maternity originated at common law. If a child was born during an intact marriage, the child was presumed to be the child of the husband and wife. Thus, even though the mother could have conceived the child with a man other than her husband, the law presumed the husband to be the father of the child. States often reduced the common law presumptions to statute, allowing for the presumption to be rebutted only by the husband or wife, and then only in limited circumstances.[16] The presumption of legitimacy derived from the premise that marriage is founded on the historic respect accorded to the relationships that develop within the unitary family. In other words, the presumption was viewed as in the best interest of the family, and thus, the best interest of the child. Admittedly, since the presumption provided a quick solution to the paternity issue, it benefitted the state too. The adverse consequence is that the presumption also limited the rights of a putative genetic father not married to the mother.

To better safeguard the rights of the genetic father and to provide uniformity among the states, the National Conference of Commissioners on Uniform State Laws promulgated the first version of the Uniform Parentage Act in 1973; it was approved by the American Bar Association the following year. The Act has been amended a number of times, and each amendment sought to incorporate technological changes, with most changes occurring in the field of assisted reproductive technology. Like the common law, the Uniform Parentage Act operates under certain presumptions. First, the mother of a child and a man claiming to be the genetic father of a child may sign a paternity acknowledgment. [Sections 301 and 302] Once signed, the acknowledgment conclusively establishes paternity. Second, a man may be adjudicated to be the father of a child. The Act permits a paternity adjudication to be brought by the child, the mother of the child, the man whose paternity is to be adjudicated, a government agency seeking support for the child, an adoption agency, or any representative authorized by law to act for an individual who would otherwise be entitled to maintain a proceeding but who is deceased, incapacitated, or a minor. [Sections 601–603] There is a two year statute of limitations after the birth

---

16. *See, e.g.*, Michael H. v. Gerald D., 491 U.S. 110 (1989); *see also* 1 BLACK-   STONE'S COMMENTARIES 456 (J. Chitty, ed. 1826).

of the child to adjudicate paternity of a child with a presumed father. A proceeding may be brought at any time if the court determines that the mother and the presumed father neither cohabited nor engaged in sexual intercourse with each other during the probable time of conception, and the presumed father never openly held the child out as his own. [Section 607] Obviously, the Act seeks to protect family integrity, which is more deserving of protection if the family has functioned as a family for more than two years.

Under the Act paternity and maternity can be presumed by other means. Other than being married to the mother of the child when the child is born, a man is presumed to be the father of the child if: (1) he and the mother were married to each other and the child is born within 300 days after the marriage between the father and mother was dissolved; (2) he and the mother entered into a putative marriage, which was subsequently declared invalid within 300 days of the birth of the child; (3) after the birth of the child, the man and the mother of the child married, even if the marriage is declared invalid; (4) the man voluntarily placed his name on the child's birth certificate, listed himself as the father of the child, or agreed to support the child as his own; or (5) within the first two years of the child's life the man resided in the same household as the child and openly held the child out as his own. [Section 204] In addition, a man may become the presumed father of the child by adopting the child, consenting to assisted reproduction by a woman that resulted in the birth of a child to her, or by an adjudication confirming the man as the parent of the child born to a gestational mother (surrogate) if the gestational agreement was validated under Article 8 of the Act. [Section 201] We will discuss gestational agreements and surrogacy later in this chapter.

While the majority of cases involve the establishment of paternity, obviously involving a man, a woman may be presumed to be the mother of a child by such obvious events as giving birth to a child, or adoption of a child. Also, a woman may be adjudicated the mother of the child. And through a separate adjudication proceeding, a woman may be confirmed as a parent of a child born to a gestational mother. Again, as we will discuss later in this chapter, the gestational agreement must be validated under Article 8 of the Act. [Section 201]

The presumption of paternity or maternity, once established, may be rebutted only under limited circumstances. This is an important point. Any suit to rebut the presumption must be brought by a contestant found eligible by the state, within the appropriate period of the statute of limitations, and there must be sufficient evidence to rebut the presumption. Thus, simply because a child with a presumptive parent looks like a third party, talks like a third party, and walks like a third party, does not mean that the third party may bring an action to rebut the presumption and assume parental responsibility over the child. Indeed, once paternity is established through acknowledgment or a judicial proceeding, even though genetic evidence may disprove paternity, the genetic tests are irrelevant and inadmissible.[17] And in spite of the attempted uniformity of the Uniform Parentage Act, the states vary in their approach to the presumptions, the parties with standing, the proof necessary to rebut the presumptions, and the length of the statutes of limitation. Federal support guidelines rely upon state determinations of parenthood, so there will be variations in support eligibility from state-to-state.[18]

B. Rebutting the Presumptions

The presumptions of paternity and maternity, as mentioned previously, rely upon the assumption that a husband—or wife—is the better person from whom to take support for the child. So too, the presumptions rely on the nuclear family as preferable for the social and economic protection of the child. If any rebuttal is allowed, the evidence will result from scientific genetic testing procedures. DNA evidence can accurately identify a man as the father of a child within 99% probability, using a minuscule item of evidence to establish paternity. And identification may be made either before or after the death of the man. [Section 509] If the man refuses to submit to genetic testing, he may be established as the father through default. [Section 508] In addition, any man not submitting to testing is subject to contempt proceedings. [Section 622] The Uniform Parentage Act specifies that a court may order a child and other designated individuals to submit to testing if the request is accompanied by a sworn statement alleging the following: (1) sexual contact and a reasonable probability of paternity; or (2) a reasonable probability that the sexual activity that did occur did not result in the birth of the child. There are some restrictions on the far-reaching mandate of testing. Genetic testing may not be ordered for a child in utero, and a support enforcement agency may order genetic testing only if there is no presumed, acknowledged, or adjudicated father. [Section 502]

---

17. *See, e.g.*, Cesar C. v. Alicia L., 800 N.W.2d 249 (Neb. 2011) (holding the acknowledgment must be challenged within 60 days or it is conclusive).

18. *See* Personal Responsibility and Work Opportunity Reconciliation Act, 42 U.S.C. § 666(a)(5)(G) (2006).

Paternity adjudication is not always permitted. A court can deny a petition to adjudicate paternity of a child with a presumed or an acknowledged father, if the court determines that the conduct of the mother, or the presumed or acknowledged father, estops that party from denying parentage. Adjudication may also be denied if it would be inequitable to disprove the father-child relationship because of the child's best interest, that is, the child's reliance upon the putative father. To determine the best interest of a child, the court will look to factors such as the length of time the putative parent was placed on notice that he might not be the child's parent, or the length of time the putative parent has assumed the role of parent to the child. In addition, the age of the child, the availability of the genetic parent to assume a role in the child's life, and the overall equities of proving or disproving paternity. [Section 608] Understandably, based on what has been discussed previously, courts are not willing to allow adjudication to adversely affect a child or the existing support mechanism already in place. This is true, even though such a course will have a deleterious effect upon the rights of the genetic father.

C. *Registering to Establish Paternity*

Thus far, we have discussed pursuing a putative father to establish paternity. But procedures are available to assist a man who has a reasonable belief that he might be the father of a child and therefore wishes to establish paternity over the child. Thus, a man, in the event of sexual intercourse with someone other than his wife, may register with the state registry of paternity. By registering, the man is not establishing a presumption of paternity, and he is not sufficiently aware of the child's existence so as to commence a proceeding to adjudicate his rights to parenthood. Instead, he simply suspects a child may have resulted from an act of intercourse and he wishes to know if this is so. Once he registers he may be notified of a proceeding for adoption, or the termination of parental rights regarding a child that meets the parameters he recites. The Uniform Parentage Act specifies that the man must register prior to, or within thirty days after the birth of a child. [Section 402]

Information contained in the registry is confidential, but may be shared with a similar registry in another state. Failure of the agency or persons associated to maintain confidentiality is a misdemeanor. [Section 413] And any information given to the registry by a putative father is given under penalty of perjury. [Section 411] The state agency may not contact the mother of the child who is the subject of the registration, but may send her a copy of the registration by the putative father. And finally, if a person seeks to terminate parental rights and adopt a child, the person must obtain a certificate verifying that a search was made of the registry of paternity. Furthermore, if the person seeking to terminate parental rights and adopt the child has reason to believe that the conception of the child may have occurred in another state, then that person must also obtain a certificate of search from that state's registry of paternity. [Sections 421 and 422]

III. Children of Assisted Reproduction

Establishing parenthood through means other than sexual intercourse has traditionally been defined as assisted reproduction. Initial applications involved artificial insemination of the wife with sperm from her husband. But procedures have progressed, now involving in vitro fertilization, the storage of sperm, eggs and embryos, and most recently conception occurring posthumously through any of the means mentioned. Increasingly, assisted reproductive technology is employed by same-sex couples seeking to have children; also, single women are commonly inseminated with donor sperm, becoming single mothers. And procedures exist whereby a woman beyond the ability to produce eggs, can have an embryo inserted and then give birth to a child. So too, surrogacy and gestational agreements are popular in states that allow for them. But as evidenced by the Uniform Parentage Act, the gestational agreements require particular elements to be enforceable. We will discuss these further, later in this chapter. And finally, fertility clinics and individual physicians continue to provide services to single persons and couples, including insemination and storage. State and federal regulation of clinics will surely become more aggressive as procedures and options expand. The past decades have seen an upsurge in suits brought against fertility clinics for destruction of gametes and embryos, which in turn have clarified procedures for disbursement of stored products. What follows are additional individual issues that have arisen in the context of assisted reproduction.

A. *Parental Status of Same–Sex Partners*

Under state statutes similar to the Uniform Parentage Act, marriage is often the primary predicate upon which to raise the presumption of parenthood. Until recently, persons of the same sex were denied the status of marriage or similar arrangements such as civil unions or domestic partnerships. Without marriage or similar status, the issue arose as to whether the partner of a person participating in assisted reproduction could share parenthood status over the resulting child or children born to his or her partner during their partnership. Obviously, if the partner were genetically linked to the birth of the child, then parenthood could be established. But is it a sufficient basis of parenthood to consent to a partner's artificial insemination or donation of an egg or sperm? It would be sufficient if the couple were married. But is consent sufficient to establish parenthood when the couple is not married and there is no genetic connection to the child? This is the dilemma faced by many nonmarital couples.

In the absence of marriage or a genetic connection, courts have been willing to establish parenthood through rare statutes, or through conduct resulting in equitable estoppel.[19] One California decision is noteworthy: *Elisa B. v. Superior Court.*[20] The facts of the case involved two women who met in 1993 and began a committed romantic relationship. A few years later they decided to have children together as a part of their relationship, so each of the women was artificially inseminated with donor sperm from the same male donor; nine months later each of the women gave birth, one of the women having twins. Both women shared parenting responsibilities, manifesting in many ways their intent to raise the children as part of their committed relationship, as part of a single family. Nonetheless, by 1999, two years after the first child was born, the women separated. Although the higher wage earner had agreed to support her former partner and her children, she eventually ceased payment, stating that she was not the parent of the children of her partner. But California's highest court disagreed. The court ruled that a child may have two same-sex parents, and that parenthood can come about through conduct. Here, because the mother's partner held the children out as her own with the consent of the mother, she became the presumptive co-parent with the mother.

Cases arise based on their own set of facts, and the court rulings will differ based on the approach taken in that state. But it seems reasonable to predict that nonmarital couples will best preserve parental status by establishing a genetic connection, executing a written agreement establishing parenthood, and by seeking out states that permit adoption by same-sex couples without terminating the parental rights of the other party. A valid adoption is a

---

19. *See, e.g.*, D.C. Code. § 16–909(a–1) (2009) (creating a presumption of parenthood for same-sex partners); C.E.W. v. D.E.W., 845 A.2d 1146 (Me. 2004) (designating partners as de factor parents).

20. 117 P.3d 660 (Cal. 2005); *but see* T.F. v. B.L., 813 N.E.2d 1244 (Mass. 2004) (rejecting same-sex parenthood by contract on public policy grounds).

judgement and entitled to Full Faith and Credit in any state, regardless of the state's public policy regarding same-sex couples.

B. Cryopreservation Agreements

Increasingly, persons and couples utilize the services of cryo-preservation laboratories for assistance with obtaining, and storage of sperm, eggs, and embryos. Issues arise as to who owns the human gametes or embryos preserved at the facility upon death of the person or divorce of the couple. Courts have ruled that there is a property right, rather than a personhood right, in the gametes or embryos, and that the products are subject to the wishes of those persons donating the gametes or embryos.[21] Often, suits arise based on emotional distress when laboratories destroy the gametes or embryos, or involve possible suits by stored non-implanted embryos for wrongful death of a donor. But most often litigation results from lack of agreement concerning disposition of the stored sperm, eggs, or embryos.

Overall, courts tend to defer to a person's or a couple's execut-ed agreement.[22] This contract approach is problematic when the agreement lacks clarity, or there is no agreement at all. In one case, a couple stored frozen embryos with a cryopreservation laboratory a few months before they married. In the agreement that the two adults signed, if their marriage was terminated, the laboratory was to assume all rights and responsibilities to preserve, dispose of, or donate the embryos. The couple remained married only two months and then divorced. When they divorced the husband sought to destroy the embryos in violation of the agreement's terms. The clinic refused to allow him to do so. He argued that, if the embryos were left to the discretion of the laboratory, a future child could result. Unknowingly, he may have sexual relations with this child, and thus he runs the risk of accidental incest. The court rejected his argument, holding that the contract between the two parties takes precedence and controls the disposition of the embryos.[23] Not all courts or commentators agree that stored gametes or embryos should be governed by contractual agreements. In addition to ethical and moral concerns, arguments are made that these human products may be the last chance for some individuals to procreate,

---

21. For a discussion as to whether the gametes or embryos are persons or property, *see* Jessica Berg, *Of Elephants and Embryos: A Proposed Framework for Legal Personhood*, 59 HASTINGS L. J. 369 (2007).

22. *See generally*, John A. Robert-son, *Precommitment Strategies for Dis-*

position of Frozen Embryos, 50 EMORY L. J. 989 (2001).

23. Karmasu v. Karmasu, No. 2008 CA 00231, 2009 WL 3155062 (Ohio Ct. App. Sept. 30, 2009).

and that circumstances change after the agreements were execut-ed.[24] Thus, because of the unique nature of these products, there should be restraints on the terms of the agreements.

C. Surrogacy

Commensurate with technological advances associated with assisted reproduction technology, persons and couples sought to contract with surrogates to provide them with children. The prac-tice dates from biblical times, but interest piqued with the *Baby M* decision.[25] The case involved a married man and woman who contracted with a surrogate woman to bear their child. The couple agreed to pay the surrogate $10,000, and to pay the Infertility Center of New York an additional $7,500. Nonetheless, after the surrogate was artificially inseminated with the husband's sperm and she became pregnant, the surrogate refused to surrender the child to the contracting parents after the infant girl was born. The couple went to court to seek to enforce the terms of their agree-ment and to gain custody over the girl. The trial court agreed with the couple, thereby enforcing the contract that they and the surro-gate had signed. Nonetheless, the state supreme court disagreed, holding that surrogacy contracts violate the law in a number of ways. First, adoption cannot be associated with money transfers. Second, birth parents must demonstrate unfitness prior to termi-nation of parental rights. Third, in adoptions the natural parent has a right to revoke consent, so a surrogate should have the right to revoke consent. The birth mother was entitled to keep the child born through assisted reproduction.

The New Jersey decision created significant discussion over who is the parent of a child when surrogate contracts are involved.[26] The fact that the payment of money was involved was a significant factor, as was the fact that the father of the child—he had used his sperm—was the man who had contracted with the surrogate. Thus, this case is different from those occurring when the contracting parties have no genetic connection with the child that is subse-quently born. But the case established the parameters of future decisions and statutes that affect surrogacy. Courts continue to struggle with payments being made to the surrogate, whether the

---

24. *See, e.g.,* Congregation for the Doctrine of the Faith, Instruction Digni-tas Personae On Certain Bioethical Ques-tions (2008), *available at* http://www.catholicbishops.ie/2008/12/dignitas-personae/; *see also* Helene S. Shapo, *Fro-zen Pre–Embryos and the Right to Change One's Mind,* 12 Duke J. Comp. & Int'l L. 75 (2002).

25. In re Baby M, 537 A.2d 1227 (N.J. 1988).

26. *See* Anita L. Allen, *Privacy, Sur-rogacy, and the* Baby M. *Case,* 76 Geo. L. J. 1759 (1988).

surrogate has a biological connection with the child born, whether the contracting parties have a biological connection with the child, and whether the state in which the child is born has a statute governing surrogacy contracts.

The most recent version of the Uniform Parentage Act,[27] referencing gestational agreements, authorizes a gestational mother to enter into a valid contract together with her husband if she is married. The agreement must be written, not implied, and allows the mother to waive all rights to a child born by means of assisted reproduction; her husband also waives all right to a child. The agreement may be validated by a court prior to the gestational mother becoming pregnant. The couple must petition the court to issue an order stating that the requirements of the statute have been met. The intended parents must also be parties to the written agreement, and no party may limit the right of the mother to make decisions regarding her health or that of the embryos or fetus. Upon good cause shown, and prior to the prospective gestational mother becoming pregnant by assisted reproduction, the prospective gestational mother, her husband, or either of the intended parents may terminate the gestational agreement by giving written notice of termination to all of the other parties.

Payments to the mother, which constituted a significant factor in the *Baby M* decision, must be reasonable, and in addition, the intended parents may provide additional consideration for all reasonable health care expenses. When the child conceived through assisted reproduction is born to the gestational mother, the intended parents must file a petition with the state court confirming that they are the intended parents and the court will order that a birth certificate be issued naming them as the parents of the child.[28] While the Uniform Parentage Act sought to provide some uniformity among the states in regards to surrogacy, the country remains a patchwork of statutes and judicial decisions.[29]

D. *Posthumous Conception*

Under common law, if a child was *born* within three-hundred days of the death of the father, then the child was the child of that

---

27. UNIF. PARENTAGE ACT §§ 801–809 (2002).

28. *See, e.g.,* Raftopol v. Ramey, 12 A.3d 783 (Conn. 2011) (specifying the parameters of a gestational agreement).

29. *See* Darra L. Hofman, *"Mama's Baby, Daddy's Maybe": A State-by-State Survey of Surrogacy Laws and Their*

Disparate Gender Impact, 35 Wm. MITCH-ELL L. REV. 449 (2009); Robert E. Rains, *What the Erie "Surrogate Triplets" Can Teach State Legislatures About the Need to Enact Article 8 of the Uniform Parentage Act of 2000*, 56 CLEV. ST. L. REV. 1 (2008).

father. In other words, that child is treated as having been in existence at the death of the parent, even though born within 300 days later. But what if the child is *conceived* after the death of the father—or the mother—through artificial reproduction. Is this resulting child a child of the deceased father or mother? This is the issue surrounding posthumous conception. Almost uniformly, state courts have ruled that a child conceived posthumously is not a child of the decedent gamete donor. The consequences for the child is a denial of all federal, state, and inheritance benefits associated with the now-deceased gamete provider. Federal statutes have consistently followed state determinations of paternity and maternity before qualifying a resulting child for federal benefits such as Social Security.[30] The result, to date, is that a child conceived posthumously is seldom entitled to state or federal benefits from the decedent gamete provider.

There are rare exceptions. In 2002, the Massachusetts Supreme Court ruled on facts that appear in most of these decisions. A married man was diagnosed with leukemia and, hoping that he and his wife would have children in the future but wary of the treatments, the man had sperm medically withdrawn and cryopreserved. This was in 1993. Shortly after the procedure the husband died and the wife was appointed as the administrator of his estate. Thus, having access to the sperm, she had herself artificially inseminated and gave birth to twin girls in 1995. The husband had been fully insured under Social Security, so the wife applied to the Social Security Administration for dependent child benefits for her daughters. The children's claim was rejected by the federal agency because the children were not entitled to inherit under the Massachusetts intestate statutes; the girls could not be his heirs because they were not alive at his death, even though they were genetically matched. The Commissioner approved the agency's denial of benefits and the wife then appealed to the federal district court. The federal court certified the question to the state court for an interpretation of the state's intestate statutes, which eventually brought the case to the Massachusetts Supreme Court.

The state statute did not expressly require a child to be in existence at the death of a parent in order to inherit from that parent. The drafters of the state statute, which was drafted in the nineteenth century, never contemplated posthumous conception. But this lack of specificity allowed the state's highest court to rule that the children conceived posthumously could inherit if certain parameters were established: (1) the child must establish paternity

---

30. *See* Raymond C. O'Brien, *The Momentum of Posthumous Conception:* *A Model Act*, 25 J. CONTEMP. HEALTH L. & POL'Y 332 (2009).

or maternity with the decedent; (2) there must be proof that the decedent consented to posthumous conception; (3) there must be proof that the decedent intended to support the child conceived posthumously; and (4) the estate of the decedent must be notified within a reasonable amount of time so as to provide for an orderly distribution of decedent's estate.[31] The court wrote that this approach safeguarded the best interests of the child, the administration of estates, and the reproductive rights of a parent. Thus, the girls were able to receive Social Security benefits in Massachusetts, but this is a singular approach.

The federal circuits are presently divided on this issue. The United States Court of Appeals for the Ninth Circuit ruled that federal benefits do not have to rely on state inheritance laws. Once maternity or paternity is established, the child is entitled to federal benefits earned by the decedent parent.[32] The Ninth Circuit based the decision on the establishment of paternity alone. But the Fourth Circuit has refused to ignore the state determination of statutory inheritance rights as the prelude to federal benefit entitlement. Thus, in a case in which a child was born to a woman through artificial insemination of her husband's sperm seven years after his death, the Fourth Circuit ruled that the child is not entitled to federal benefits derived from the putative father. In denying the child any federal benefits, the court relied on the wording of the Social Security Act and held that to rule otherwise would thrust the federal courts into a myriad of other issues, including the status of children born to surrogate mothers, and from those children born through the artificial insemination of sperm from someone other than the mother's husband.[33] The court concluded that the Social Security Act's reliance on state determinations was the correct interpretation, which also exempted federal courts from deciding family law issues.

There are a few statutes that specifically address posthumous conception. For example, the Uniform Parentage Act provides, under Section 707, that: "If an individual who consented in a record to be a parent by assisted reproduction dies before placement of eggs, sperm, or embryos, the deceased individual is not a parent of the resulting child unless the deceased spouse consented in a record that if assisted reproduction were to occur after death,

---

31. Woodward v. Commissioner of Soc. Sec., 760 N.E.2d 257 (Mass. 2002).

32. *See* Gillett–Netting v. Barnhart, 371 F.3d 593 (9th Cir. 2004): *see also* Capato ex rel. B.N.C. v. Commissioner of Soc. Sec., 631 F.3d 626 (3d Cir. 2011).

33. Schafer v. Astrue, 641 F.3d 49 (4th Cir. 2011); *see also* Beeler v. Astrue, 651 F.3d 954 (8th Cir. 2011).

the deceased individual would be a parent of the child." Please note that the statute refers to spouses, hence to married couples. The Uniform Probate Code does not involve spouses, but instead provides that, under section 2–121 (h), an individual is a parent of a gestational child who is conceived after the individual's death if the following occurs: (1) the child is in utero not later than 36 months after the individual's death, or (2) born not later than 45 months after the individual's death. The statute treats the child as being in gestation at the death of the individual. A few states, California the most notable, have enacted statutes similar to the Uniform Probate Code. It is interesting that the statutes mirror the outlines of the *Woodward* decision, discussed previously.

Chapter 8

Parental Duties Owed to Children

I. The Best Interest of the Child

In 2000, Justice Sandra Day O'Connor reaffirmed the fundamental liberty interest of parents in the care, custody, and control
of their children. The Court ruled that the presumption in favor of
parental judgement and discretion in the raising of children does
not begin with what is in the best interest of the child, and
reiterated the list of former constitutional cases supporting parental rights over children.[1] Consistently, courts have held that so long
as a parent adequately cares for his or her children, there is no
reason for the state to inject itself into the private realm of the
family, or to further question the ability of that parent to make the
best decisions concerning the rearing of that parent's children. In
other words, it is presumed that a fit parent will act in the best
interest of his or her child; the court must accord some special
weight to a parent's determination of what is best for his or her
child. This is mandated by the Due Process Clause of the Constitution.

Balanced against the rights of the parent to raise a child are
the child's rights to life, liberty, and the pursuit of happiness. The
struggle of the courts and the legislatures has been to balance these
often competing interests without egregiously harming either party.
What follows is a brief list of issues illustrating conflict between
what a parent presumes to be in the best interest of the child and
what a child, or a person advocating for a child, perceives to be in
the child's best interest.

A. Emancipation

By law, parents are tasked with the financial support, health
care, education, and supervision of a child during the child's minority. Because of this responsibility, the law allows a parent the right
to discipline a child, and to regulate such things as what the child
wears, where the child goes to school, whether the child has
religious training, what the child eats, and the type of medical care
a child receives. The parent is entitled to the child's services and to
any financial earnings paid to the minor. Only upon attaining the
age of majority, or by becoming emancipated, does this arrange-

---

1. Troxel v. Granville, 530 U.S. 57
(2000).

ment cease. Some states provide for emancipation by statute. California, for example, provides that a minor may become emancipated if married, on active duty in the armed forces, or obtains a judicial decree of emancipation. To obtain the judicial decree of emancipation the minor must: (1) be at least fourteen years of age, (2) willingly live apart from his or her parents by mutual consent, (3) successfully manage his or her own financial affairs, and (4) derive no income from criminal activity.[2]

Disputes between parents and their children often precipitate attempts at emancipation. Conflicts over discipline, lifestyle choices, schooling, or home environment most often cause minors to seek emancipation. And the reverse is likely true. Adult parents may wish to divorce their children, but other than through safe-haven statutes,[3] which are applicable only to infants, a parent is obligated to provide financial support and care to a minor child. Emancipation may occur if a child enters into a valid marriage, or under the common law becoming a parent also emancipated a child. So too, states often allow a child a partial emancipation when the state permits a minor to obtain an abortion with the permission from a court through judicial bypass legislation. And some states allow for a minor to consent to medical treatment for himself or herself if the treatment relates to venereal disease, drug abuse, or medical conditions related to pregnancy. Some statutes allow a minor to refuse extraordinary means of life-support. For the minor's consent to be valid, the unemancipated minor must be of sufficient intelligence to understand and appreciate the consequences of the proposed surgical or medical treatment or procedures to be performed.[4] Increasingly, as we will discuss, courts are more willing to allow a mature minor medical options over the objections of the minor's parent regarding choices relating to appearance, and a positive public perception among the minor's peers.

In all but very rare circumstances, emancipation ends a parent's duty to financially support a child. In all states, a parent has an enforceable obligation to support a minor child, or in some cases, a dependent child. Often, when parents divorce, the duty of child support may be voluntarily extended by either parent in an agreement that is incorporated into the court's divorce decree. Nonetheless, if the child's conduct demonstrates emancipation from the

---

2. *See* Emancipation of Minors Law, Cal. Fam. Code § 7120 (West 2004).

3. *See, e.g.,* Fla. Stat. Ann. §§ 383.50–51 (West 2002 & Supp. 2006).

4. *See* Ark. Code Ann. § 20–9–602(7) (West 2009).

parent's reasonable control, the parent is no longer required to provide financial support.[5]

B.   *Children In Need of Supervision (CINS)*

When a child seeks to end the supervisory control of the parent over his or her conduct, the child often runs away, abandoning the physical and emotional support of the family home. When the child is discovered and forced to return to the supervision of the parents, the child will argue that he or she has a constitutional right to freedoms such as privacy, due process, freedom of association, and that he or she is capable of living alone as an adult. The child will argue that he or she is victimized by an arbitrary age of majority and it is a denial of equal protection to restrict the freedom allowed to an adult. Often, commensurate with running away, the child commits a crime. School truancy, vagrancy, theft, drug abuse, and prostitution are common offenses. Even if there are no criminal infractions, children remain subject to parental control, and their parents can ask the assistance of the state juvenile courts to classify their children as being in need of supervision. Any constitutional rights asserted by the child are not denied, only delayed until they reach the age of majority.[6] Until adulthood, a child is subject to parental authority and a violation of this authority makes the child one in need of supervision.

When a child is in need of supervision, the child becomes subject to the supervision of the judicial system. No allegations are made as to the conduct of either parent, only that the child is beyond parental control and, as such, requires services to assist the parent in gaining control, and to remedy whatever harm the child has done. When a child is in need of supervision, the conduct of the individual parent is not the focus, but rather, the conduct of the child.[7] As such, there is usually no connection with this classification of abuse or neglect of the child by the parent, but there are always exceptions.

C.   *Standby Guardianship*

When a child has more than one parent, the child's welfare is safeguarded if one of the parents becomes incapacitated. The other parent may assume parental duties when the circumstances dictate.

---

5. *See, e.g.,* In re Baumgartner, 930 N.E.2d 1024 (Ill. 2010) (holding that child's prison incarceration terminates parent's financial support obligation).

6. *See generally* BARBARA BENNETT WOODHOUSE, HIDDEN IN PLAIN SIGHT: THE TRAGEDY OF CHILDREN'S RIGHTS FROM BEN FRANKLIN TO LIONEL TATE (2008).

7. *See, e.g.,* N.L. v. Indiana Dep't of Child Serv., 919 N.E.2d 102, 105 (Ind. 2010) ("A CHINS adjudication focuses on the condition of the child.")

But in the case of a single-parent household, a child's well-being is possibly endangered if the parent becomes unable to provide care and supervision. An abrupt finding of incapacity could result in the child becoming dependent and placed with relatives, foster care, or institutional care. This arrangement may conflict with the wishes of the parent. Thus, in a fashion similar to a springing durable power of attorney, the state may provide a mechanism by which a standby guardian could be appointed to care for the child in the event of the incapacity of the parent. Maryland's statute is illustrative.[8]

Maryland's standby guardianship statute permits a designated person, upon the incapacity of a minor's parent or, prior to the actual incapacity, to exercise express authority over the person and property of a child. Each person with parental rights over the child must join in a petition for appointment of the guardian, and the petition must state the following: (1) the duties of the guardian, (2) whether the duties become effective upon incapacity or death of the parent, and (3) that there is a sufficient risk that the petitioner will become incapacitated or die, as applicable, within two years of the filing of the petition. Then, if the court agrees that the best interest of the minor will be promoted by the appointment of the guardian, the court may decree the appointment, and specify when it will become effective.

The state statute also permits the designation of a guardian through a written declaration, signed by both of the parents, if applicable, two disinterested witnesses, and the nominated guardian. In addition to providing a model designation form, the state statute permits the appointment of an alternate guardian, and specifies that the appointment may be revoked at any time. Likewise, the guardian may renounce the appointment at any time by notifying the parent in writing, executing a written renunciation, or by filing a renunciation with the court that issued the decree. When incapacity is to be determined, it is to be established by the parent in writing, or if the parent is unable to comprehend the information, by an attending physician to a reasonable degree of medical certainty.

D. Medical Decisions by and for Children

Because parents are presumed to act in the best interest of their children, their permission is needed prior to their child receiving medical treatment. There are certain exceptions for abortion, as discussed previously, but overall, the parent's discretion

---

8. *See* MD. CODE ANN., EST. & TRUSTS §§ 13–901 et seq. (West 2001).

regarding a child's medical treatment is part of the bundle of rights the parent enjoys, commensurate with a parent's fundamental right to raise the child. Obviously, if there is a threat to the life of the child, or if there is evidence of what may be classified as cruelty or neglect by the parents that would justify state intervention, the state may intervene. But otherwise, the state may not intervene. As one early decision stated: "We have not yet adopted as a public policy the Spartan rule that children belong, not to their parents, but to the state."[9]

Free Exercise of Religion claims buttress the rights of parents. That is, when a child needs inoculations against common childhood illnesses prior to entering school, parents often assert that their right to freely practice their religious beliefs exempts them from being forced to accede to the inoculation of their children. Likewise, when a child's medical condition progressively worsens due to illnesses such as appendicitis, a parent may assert a Free Exercise right to refuse medical treatment. The parent may practice a religion that firmly believes that God cures, not doctors. Using a balancing test, courts have consistently overruled a parent's right of refusal of treatment when balanced against the right of the state to prevent disease, or to protect the life of a child.[10]

But the most difficult cases are those that, although not life-threatening, significantly affect the quality of life of a child. For example, one case involved attempts at the corrective surgery of a harelip and cleft palate of a fourteen year old boy. Another case described whether a parent's objection could be overruled so as to allow corrective surgery for a fifteen year old boy whose face was grossly disfigured due to neurofibromatosis, also known as elephant man's disease. One side of his face was twice as large as the other because of a large malignant growth. The boy had dropped out of school because of the taunting he received from his peers. As a result the boy was functionally illiterate, though of normal intelligence. The parent of the boy refused to give permission for surgery, based on religious grounds. Nonetheless, in a judicial decision that evolved through the entire New York court process, the court overruled the mother's refusal and ordered that the operation could be performed. The court's opinion stated that it would not allow the parent's objection to "stand in the way of attaining through corrective surgery whatever chance he may have for a normal happy existence, which . . . is difficult of attainment under the most propitious circumstances, but will unquestionably be impossible if

9. In re Tuttendario, 21 Pa. D. 561, 563 (Pa. Quar. Sess. 1912).

10. *See, e.g.,* Douglas County v. Anaya, 694 N.W.2d 601 (Neb.), *cert denied,* 546 U.S. 826 (2005).

the disfigurement is not corrected."[11] In so ruling, the New York court adopted "the quality of life for the child" as an additional ground that may be used to overrule parental prerogatives.

Increasingly today, the issue is whether minors, particularly mature minors, should have greater autonomy in making their own medical decisions. A few state statutes permit minors to make medical decisions on their own if they are of sufficient intelligence to comprehend and appreciate the medical consequences of the proposed surgical or medical treatments. For example, there are provisions in the Arkansas and California codes specifying that an unemancipated minor may consent to medical treatment for himself or herself if the minor is of sufficient intelligence to understand and appreciate the consequences of the proposed surgical or medical treatment or procedures.[12] California is more permissive, allowing minors fifteen years and older to make decisions regarding medical care, or allowing a minor who is an alleged victim of incest, child abuse, rape, or needs treatment for an infectious disease or for drug or alcohol abuse to give consent. But California does not allow a minor to consent to sterilization.

In 1989, the Supreme Court of Illinois applied the mature minor approach to a minor seeking to terminate life support treatments.[13] The case involved a minor who was receiving blood treatments for leukemia. The minor wanted to discontinue treatment, which would effectively end her life. In ruling that she had the right to end her treatment, the court traced the many ways in which the autonomy of a minor has expanded, including the Arkansas and California statutes. But, the court emphasized, it was necessary to determine if the minor was mature enough to make the decision. If not, then the court could rely upon the parent's authority, or assume authority over the child herself. Ironically, the trial court in the case found the child to be medically neglected because of the mother's opposition to the blood treatment from the start. Ruling that the mother was neglectful, the court had ordered the treatments and now found itself in the position of allowing the minor to discontinue the treatments and end her life.

II. Parental Financial Support

Parents have a duty to financially support their children; children, in return, have an obligation to obey their parents. The

---

11. In re Sampson, 317 N.Y.S.2d 641, 657 (N.Y. Fam. Ct. 1970).

12. *See* ARK. CODE ANN. § 20–9–602(7) (2009); CAL. FAM. CODE § 6924(b) (West 2004 and Supp. 2006).

13. In re E.G., 549 N.E.2d 322 (Ill. 1989).

extent of the duty to support a child is somewhat similar to the necessities doctrine as applied to support obligation between spouses; the parent is expected to provide food, shelter, clothing, medical, education, and legal support for so long as the child is a minor or, if special circumstances warrant, sometimes longer. And, like with spouses, the amount of support will be commensurate with the standard of living of the family. It is unlikely that courts will interfere with an intact family's choices in regard to support of a child, since the privacy of a functioning, intact family is thought to be beyond state supervision. Nonetheless, if a parent's lack of support results in effects that could be viewed as neglect or abuse under state statutes, then states will intervene to rectify any deficiencies.

When child support is ordered in connection with the establishment of paternity or maternity, or when the parents are divorced, then the state exercises a more supervisory role. Child support guidelines are used to establish adequate support for the child. Every state has provided for the support of the child through a process that begins with these guidelines. During the 1980s, federal legislation mandated that every state establish child support guidelines: The federal regulations specify that the guidelines must take into consideration all earnings and income of the absent parent, both parents must share the costs of raising the child, since support is not the sole responsibility of one parent. Unlike spousal support, child support begins with these guidelines as a presumptive base. Federal regulations require that judges file written findings as to why the guidelines, as applied to any case, would be unjust or inappropriate. In effect, the guidelines may be rebutted, but there must be written reasons why they are rebutted.[14] Possible reasons include a child's special medical or educational needs, or the fact that a child has a separate means of support from, for example, a trust.

While all states have guidelines, the majority of states use the income-shares model. This model provides a rebuttable amount of child support, always based on what the child would have received if the parents had lived together.[15] The amount of support is determined by a statutory formula, which is computed from the following: (1) the income of both of the parents is amassed, including, as we will discuss, many different types of income. Then, (2) an obligation is computed based on the combined income of the par-

---

14. *See, e.g.*, Kauth v. Bartlett, 746 N.W.2d 747 (S.D. 2008) (imputed income can rebut the presumption of the guidelines).

15. For a review of states, *see* Linda D. Elrod & Robert G. Spector, *A Review of the Year in Family Law*, 42 Fam. L. Q. 713 (2009).

ents. This obligation represents an estimated amount of what would have been spent on the child or children if the parents had stayed together. In establishing the estimated amount, the legislatures use surveys on household expenditures on children, but critics argue that the data does not adequately acknowledge the differences among various households. There are many commentaries on why the estimated obligation is faulty, but revision comes slowly. Then, (3) support is added to the estimated amount to account for specific actual expenditures, and for any extraordinary medical expenses. And finally, (4) the total obligation of what the child needs for financial support is then apportioned between the parents based on the income of each. In other words, each parent is assigned a percentage of the total obligation based on each parent's income. The non-custodial parent then pays the amount specified to the custodial parent for the support of the child, and the custodial parent retains the amount owed and presumptively applies it to the financial support of the resident child. On the surface, the child support guidelines appear to simplify the process. But specific issues arise that should be addressed separately.

A. Imputed Income

A Florida decision illustrates what is meant by imputed income. A man and a woman were married and each graduated from law school and passed the New York state bar examination in 1986. The wife had also passed the New Jersey state bar examination and practiced law for six years before moving with the husband and the children to Florida. Once the family arrived in Florida, both the husband and wife took the Florida state bar examination and he passed but she did not. As a new member of the state bar, he then opened a law practice and she worked as his paralegal and raised the children. Sadly, the couple divorced in 2007. The state's divorce court ruled that, with one year's rehabilitation support, she should be able to take and pass the Florida state bar examination. Once a member of the bar, she should be able to earn sufficient money to support herself in a manner that she enjoyed while married, so she was entitled to only a short rehabilitation. Thus, the divorce court imputed to the wife the earnings of an attorney based on her past experiences and education. Nonetheless, the appeals court ruled that there was insufficient substantial evidence that the wife could retake and pass the Florida bar and practice law. Imputing income to the wife was inappropriate under the particular circumstances.[16]

16. Shafer v. Shafer, 45 So.3d 494 (Fla. Dist. Ct. App. 2010).

Most often, courts are not allowed to impute income for purposes of spousal support, but statutes do permit imputation for child support. Indeed, state statutes are very inclusive when computing income for inclusion under the guidelines. For example, child support guidelines in the District of Columbia define gross income as income from any source, including military housing and meal allowances.[17] Likewise, the Minnesota child support statute provides that if a parent is voluntarily unemployed, support must be based on a determination of potential income.[18]

B. Income Used for Calculation

States begin with their statutory guidelines, which will provide specific and more general items as to what is meant by income to the obligor. Courts have interpreted state statutes to include such items as lottery winnings, personal injury awards, all retirement income, bonus payments, separate property such as inheritance,[19] and even Social Security Disability benefits paid directly to the children of the obligor, even though the benefits were paid as compensation for the obligor's disability.[20] So too, courts will take into consideration the financial benefits that may attach to an obligor's new spouse or cohabitant. While the courts are unable to use the personal income of the spouse or cohabitant, it can take into consideration the fact that the obligor is no longer paying the mortgage or other household items individually. Hence, because of the financial contributions made by a third party, the obligor has additional income available for the children.

When the income of either party exceeds the upper parameters of the guidelines, courts may nonetheless use the guidelines as a base amount. Then, having a base, the court may interpret the purpose behind the guidelines to allow the child to have what the child would have enjoyed had the parents stayed together with the child. Thus, an infant, with admittedly minimal needs, nonetheless could have a child support amount established at thousands of dollars for each month. The rationale is that, had the parents stayed together, the infant would have had the best of everything, including food, shelter, medical care, staff, and travel. Indeed, courts have permitted the establishment of educational trust funds, rainy-day funds, and special funds for when the obligor's high-income days may end. Even though the support may be paid after

17. Brown v. Hines–Williams, 2 A.3d 1077 (D.C. 2010).

18. Welsh v. Welsh, 775 N.W.2d 364 (Minn. Ct. App. 2009).

19. In re P.C.S., 320 S.W.3d 525 (Tex. App. 2010).

20. Arkansas Office of Child Support Enforcement v. Hearst, No. 09–135, 2009 WL 4403240 (Ark. Dec. 3, 2009).

the child is no longer a minor, the courts allow collection because the support is being collected while the child is still a minor. The rationale is that the support counts when collected, not when it is used. But not all courts agree. Some courts permit support to be collected from the parents to meet the child's current needs, not needs that occur after the child reaches majority.[21]

Often, the parents voluntarily enter into an agreement that includes child support. Their agreement is then incorporated into the court's decree of divorce, or into an adjudication of paternity. These private agreements are permissible, but the agreement may not disadvantage a child's entitlement to support. Thus, the parents may agree to increase child support from the stipulated amount provided in the guidelines, but they may never decrease the amount. Most common among the agreements is a stipulation that the parents agree to support the child's educational efforts post-majority.

C.   Modification of Award

Modification of child support awards may occur whenever the obligor's income increases or decreases involuntarily. This is the rule, but there must be a substantial change in income. Among the most common petitions for modification include the remarriage of the custodian parent. Even though courts have been willing to consider the economic benefits of a remarriage, to warrant a modification there must be a substantial change in the economic circumstances. So too, an increase in the earning of a parent can precipitate a petition to modify the support award. But many courts require that the earning increase by a particular percentage to justify the substantial change in circumstances. Kentucky, for example, requires at least a 15% increase or decrease in the amount of support owed under the guidelines to justify a modification.[22]

If the obligor's income decreases, the issue arises as to whether the decrease was voluntary or involuntary. In the majority of cases, courts hold that modification of the initial award of child support will not be permitted if the change in financial circumstances is due to the fault, voluntary waste, or dissipation of the obligor's talents or assets. But there are exceptions. In one case, a father was a university English professor at the time of his divorce and concomitant child support order. Thereafter, one year after the divorce, the father petitioned the court for a downward modification of his child

21. *See, e.g.*, In re Marriage of Wilson, 223 P.3d 815 (Kan. Ct. App. 2010), *but see* In re Paternity of Tukker M.O., 544 N.W.2d 417 (Wis. 1996).

22. Dudgeon v. Dudgeon, 318 S.W.3d 106 (Ky. Ct. App. 2010).

support payment, basing his petition on his reduced income. The reduction resulted since he had quit his university professorship so that he could go to law school. The father petitioned the court to reduce his child support payment and the trial court denied the petition. But the appeals court reversed, ruling that there are circumstances when an obligor may reduce his or her income voluntarily and be granted a downward modification of support. Going to law school, the appeals court ruled, was reasonable and justifiable under the circumstances, hence the father's petition to modify the child support payment was granted.[23]

When an obligor is incarcerated, the issue arises as to whether this is a voluntary or involuntary act justifying modification of existing child support payments. Most of the cases involve an obligor who was not incarcerated at the time the support order was issued. But if the obligor is incarcerated at the time of the support decree, the court, in calculating support under the guidelines, may take into consideration what the obligor earned prior to the incarceration, the time to be served in prison, and the probability of employment after imprisonment. If these imputed earnings are considered, there will be a dramatic increase in the support payment under the guidelines. If the guidelines only included prison income, the guidelines would produce a minimum award. Whenever incarceration occurs after the child support order has been established, courts are divided as to whether the incarceration is a substantial reason to modify the award. If the court views the incarceration as voluntary, the child support order remains the same and the support may be taken from non-employment related assets.

Successive families pose a factor in petitions to modify child support awards. Previously, we have discussed the impact of a new spouse or nonmarital cohabitant upon an existing child support obligation. But what is the impact of subsequent children upon existing child support obligations? How should the court compute child support when there are multiple children born to the obligor? The approach varies. Some courts employ the child support guidelines to arrive at a support obligation for the second family, the most recent child, and then apply the guidelines again to compute support for the first family. Other courts use the second family as a material change of circumstances to modify the existing support award ordered for the first family. And what should be done when there are stepparents? Many states statutes require stepparents to

---

23. Adams v. Adams, 2010 Ark.App.
441 (Ark. Ct. App. 2010).

provide financial support for stepchildren, even though they had no duty to do so at common law. Many courts find there is no duty owed by a stepparent to a stepchild.[24] Should the presence of a stepparent permit a petition by a parent for modification of child support? The issue is complicated and there is no federal uniformity. The federal legislation enforcing orders of support permits a state, having proper jurisdiction over the parties, to issue its own support order, and that state has continuing jurisdiction to modify. Federal legislation provides enforcement of the duty, but not establishment of the duty.

D. Termination of Financial Support

Unless a child is dependent, either under the terms of the state statute, or because of a serious disability, the obligation of a parent to provide support ceases when the child reaches the age of majority. Payments of support after the child reaches majority are permitted occasionally because the parents voluntarily agree, but court orders mandating post-majority support are exceptional. South Carolina had a statute that allowed a court to order post-majority support whenever the court found there were exceptional circumstances. But, when challenged, the South Carolina Supreme Court ruled that the statute was unconstitutional, holding that there is no rational reason justifying post-majority support for children of divorced parents, when the court cannot order other parents to do the same. [25]

Support for a child may not be terminated or modified due to any parent-child estrangement. To illustrate, in a Wyoming decision, a father had been ordered to pay child support until the child turned twenty years-of-age. But when the child turned eighteen, the father petitioned the court to terminate child support because the child was now an adult, had changed his name to that of the remarried mother, and there had been no visitation between the father and the child during the last eight years. The Wyoming Supreme Court rejected the petition for termination of support, holding that visitation and support are separate, and that a parent's financial responsibility towards the child persists even when the relationship is strained.[26] Other courts might not rule in the same fashion. When a parent pays support for a child, that parent has a reasonable expectation to be obeyed by the child. If the child refuses reasonable control over behavior, and the child is older,

24. *See, e.g.*, Thacker v. Thacker, 311 S.W.3d 402 (Mo. Ct. App. 2010).

25. Webb v. Sowell, 692 S.E.2d 543 (S.C. 2010).

26. Steele v. Neeman, 206 P.3d 384 (Wyo. 2009).

many courts would rule that the child has made himself or herself emancipated and no longer qualifies for support.

Children with special needs due to physical or mental disabilities, are often classified as dependent and state statutes specify that they are entitled to support post-majority. But the support depends on state statutes and often the child will prefer not to have parental support so as to qualify, as emancipated, for state medical assistance. Again, the support obligation will depend upon the state statute.[27] At common law, support ended at majority, hence parents are not responsible for a disabled child's expenses after the child reaches the age of majority.[28]

III. Enforcement of Child Support Obligations

Increasingly, enforcement of child support obligations have progressed from private, to state, then to federal remedies. The process commences with proof of paternity and maternity, and then personal jurisdiction over the parties must be established. As discussed previously, a court is unlikely to intervene in the support levels of an intact resident family; civil and criminal prosecution for abuse or neglect of children will enforce support obligations by proscribing injurious conduct. In addition, a parent cannot abandon or surrender a child, except in the limited circumstances provided by Safe Haven laws.[29] Thus, until a parent dies, or has his or her parental rights terminated, or the child reaches the age of majority, there is a support obligation entitled to enforcement.

Almost all support issues arise in connection with divorce or nonmarital births. State efforts to impose, and then to collect child support payments, were often minimal or ineffective. Lack of enforcement resulted in single parents and increasing levels of poverty among children, resulting in health issues, lack of educational opportunities, and criminal activity. When states were ineffective, federal involvement soon followed.

Federal involvement started in earnest when, in 1975, Congress created the Office of Child Support Enforcement to supervise the new federal requirement that every state establish a child support enforcement agency. The Office began to monitor state procedures for establishing paternity and obtaining support from parents. To prompt better state efforts at collection, the Office had

---

27. *See, e.g.,* ARIZ. REV. STAT. ANN. § 25–320(E) (2009) (listing factors to determine whether support past the age of majority is necessary); MO. REV. STAT. § 452.340 (2009) (stating relevant child support factors).

28. *See, e.g.,* In re Doney and Risley, 201 P.3d 770 (Kan. Ct. App. 2009).

29. *See, e.g.,* FLA. STAT. ANN. §§ 383.50–51 (West 2002 & Supp. 2006).

the power to give grants, or to withhold funds, to better manage state efforts in an incentive program of grants. For the first time, states were allowed to withhold the wages of obligor parents. The Federal Consumer Credit Protection Act limits withholding to fifty-percent of disposable earnings for a noncustodial parent who is not supporting another family.

Parents who qualify for welfare benefits are entitled to Aid for Dependent Children (AFDC), a program that permits the states, not the individual parent, to pursue support claims. In 1996, Congress revised the AFDC program and enacted the Personal Responsibility and Work Opportunity Act of 1996. The new federal legislation was a radical departure from the system under AFDC, a system that provided parents with specified amounts of support for children, the more children, the more support.[30] The states were responsible for any enforcement efforts against parents, but the support continued unabated. The new approach, enacted in 1996, replaced the support given to parents under AFDC with block grants, providing for Temporary Assistance for Needy Families (TANF) grants. These new grants came with many demands imposed upon the states. No longer could states continue to provide support for children for an unlimited amount of time; five years became a recipient's maximum amount of support. In addition, states were required to impose greater collection mechanisms, encourage parents to enter the workforce, and states were also rewarded with additional grants if they demonstrated success at collection of child support from parents.[31]

The Personal Responsibility and Work Opportunity Reconciliation Act of 1996 enhanced collection of child support through various efforts. Income could be withheld, a national list of parents in arrears was created, new people hired by an employer must be reported to a national directory for identification in the Federal Case Registry of Child Support Orders, and each child must be identified at birth through a Social Security number. So too, federal and state tax refunds may be seized, there was centralized data collection, professional and recreational licenses may be withheld, passports may be confiscated, adverse credit reports may be made to credit bureaus, automobiles may be seized, and of course individuals may go to jail for contempt if support payments are delinquent.[32]

---

30. For criticism of the new federal approach, *see, e.g.,* Jill Elaine Hasday, *Parenthood Divided: A Legal History of the Bifurcated Law of Parental Relations*, 90 GEO. L. J. 299 (2002).

31. *See generally* Laura W. Morgan, *Child Support Fifty Years Later*, 42 FAM. L. Q. 365 (2008).

Additional federal legislation exists to enhance collection of child support. The Child Support Recovery Act of 1992 criminalizes nonpayment of child support as a federal offense. Willful intent to evade payment may result in a fine or imprisonment. Likewise, Congress enacted legislation to enforce interstate child support obligations. The purpose of the Act is to promote stability of the order of support across state lines with a similar status to what would be given to a judgement under Full Faith and Credit. And finally, the Uniform Interstate Family Support Act, adopted in each state under federal mandate, permits enforcement of child support orders issued by foreign countries as long as the Act's conditions are met. The statute provides extensive provisions pertinent to jurisdiction, modification, registration, contest, and enforcement of child support orders from foreign courts.

32. *See* Elizabeth G. Patterson, *Civil Contempt and the Indigent Child Support Obligor: The Silent Return of Debtor's Prison*, 18 CORNELL J. L. & PUB. POL'Y 95 (2008).

Chapter 9

Custody of Children

The legal framework of child custody involves many subsidiary issues. Most people think of custody in the context of two genetic parents competing for physical custody of their child or children after obtaining a valid divorce. But even in the context of this simplistic scenario, there are issues of sole or joint legal custody, sole or joint physical custody, visitation arrangements, possible attempts at future geographical relocation, supervised visitation, and litigation over parental alienation. The process becomes more complicated if one of the parents is not a genetic parent, but instead serves as a de facto parent, a non-genetic partner, or a stepparent. With the proliferation of nonmarital cohabitation, and possibilities available under assisted reproductive technology, persons able to seek and assert parental rights have increased significantly. What are the rights of each parent, when do these rights commence, and when do they end?

Jurisdiction to make a custody determination is divisible from divorce and support. But once custody is validly established, how may the custody order be enforced from one jurisdiction to another? And if the order needs to be modified, how and where must this be accomplished? We have addressed these issues previously in Chapter 5, when we discussed divisible divorce. But it bears repeating that any dispute over custody must commence with proper jurisdiction. This involves a consideration of the Uniform Child Custody Jurisdiction and Enforcement Act, adopted in every state. In addition, there is a federal concern over custody, evidenced by such statutes as the Parental Kidnapping Prevention Act, and the International Child Abduction Remedies Act, and the International Parental Kidnapping Crime Act of 1993. These federal enactments also emphasize the international aspect of child custody. Thus, the enactment of the International Child Abduction Remedies Act in 1988 implemented the Hague Convention on the Civil Aspects of International Child Abductions by the United States Congress. The wide scope and range of custody issues today confirm the assertion that we are not in Kansas anymore.

Custody laws are complicated by the fact that individuals identified as parents enjoy a fundamental right to the care, custody, and control of their children. We will discuss this parental presumption in greater detail in Chapter 10, in connection with termination of parental rights. Grounded in the Fourteenth Amendment of the Constitution, the parent is presumed to be the best person to make decisions regarding his or her child. Because this right is fundamental, it can be rebutted only with clear and convincing evidence, or what is often termed "extraordinary circumstances." Thus, in any custody or visitation dispute between a parent and a non-parent, the parent's presumptive rights will overrule any claim by the non-parent unless the parental right may be rebutted by clear and convincing evidence. Parental status is essential in seeking custody or visitation. In an age of surrogacy contracts, paternity and maternity through estoppel, de facto parenthood, and nonmarital contracts between persons of the same and opposite sex, parenthood is no longer determined solely by biology. Parenthood may come about through many means, but these added means increase the opportunities for preliminary litigation.

Between established parents, there are no presumptions and the test becomes simply what is in the best interest of the child. Approaches to establishing what is in the best interest of the child vary among the states, but any gender preferences, racial classifications, or conjectures have been expressly made inapplicable. For persons who are not parents, in any petition seeking custody over the objection of a parent, the parental presumption must be rebutted prior to considering the best interest of the child. But if there are no parents seeking custody, a custody determination is based solely on the best interest of the child.

As we will discuss further in Chapter 10, the state often seeks custody of a child for a limited period of time, or as part of a petition to terminate parental rights. If the state is successful in terminating parental rights, the child will be placed for adoption. In this context of state versus parent, the parental presumption applies. Thus, the state must establish, by a preponderance of the evidence, the right to temporarily remove the child from the parents. Then, the state must establish by clear and convincing evidence the right to retain custody of the child for longer periods. Permanent removal, or involuntary termination of parental rights, requires at least clear and convincing evidence of parental unfitness.

When viewed from the perspective of parental presumptions, disputes by third parties, and possible state intervention, custody and visitation litigation can be very complicated. Therefore, we have divided the material into four legal constructs: (1) parent versus parent; (2) parent versus non-parent; (3) parent versus state; and (4) non-parent versus state. In discussing these four constructs, recall that parents have a constitutional advantage over non-parents, with the best interest of the child being subsumed in the parental presumption to make decisions for the child. In practice, this means that a court is constitutionally forbidden to begin any analysis involving a parent and a non-parent by asking what is in the best interest of the child. The parent is presumed to know what is in the best interest of the child, and only with clear and convincing evidence to the contrary can you rebut this presumption. Thus, in the second and third constructs the parental presumption applies.

While the four legal constructs are not perfect, they do provide an analytical framework by which we can measure levels of proof needed, the participants, judicial opinions and statutes, and constitutional parameters. The constructs make it easier to arrive at a conclusion with some level of predictability. Once a custody decision is reached, that decision may be modified later by a court with proper jurisdiction, but then only upon a showing of a significant change in circumstances.

I. Four Constructs for Evaluating Custody Determinations

A. *Parent Versus Parent*

Parenthood is the first objective in any custody dispute. Parents are entitled to a presumption of custody and visitation rights for any child or children, and standing to petition for modification of any order affecting the child. As discussed in Chapter 7, establishing parenthood may occur through multiple means. The Uniform Parentage Act is an excellent reference to the various methods by which parenthood may be established.[1] The methods are:

(1) Woman gives birth to a child unless she and her husband sign a valid gestational agreement to the contrary;

(2) Woman or man is adjudicated as the parent of a child born to gestational mother who has signed a valid gestational agreement;

(3) Man or woman are adjudicated the parents of a child;

(4) Man or woman adopts a child;

(5) Man is the presumptive father of a child if any of the following occurs: (a) he and the mother are married to each other and the child is born during the marriage; or (b) he and the mother were married to each other and a child is

---

1. *See* UNIF. PARENTAGE ACT, 9B U.L.A. 295 et seq. (amended 2002).

born to the woman within 300 days after the marriage is terminated; or (c) before a child is born, the man and the mother enter into an invalid marriage and the child is born during that marriage or within 300 days afterwards; or (d) after a child is born the man and the mother of the child marry each other and the man voluntarily asserts his parentage on the child's birth certificate, or he filed his assertion of paternity in a record promising he would support the child;

(6) Man lived with the child and openly held the child out as his own for the first two years of the child's life;

(7) Man consented to assisted reproduction by a woman that resulted in the birth of a child.

Any of these presumptions of paternity or maternity may be rebutted by a civil adjudication, maintained by a person with standing, within the permissible statute of limitations. Persons with standing include the following: The child, the mother or the presumed father, a support enforcement agency, an adoption agency, the legal representative of a person with standing who is deceased, incapacitated or a minor, or an intended parent. An intended parent is a person who has entered into a valid gestational agreement with a gestational mother acting as a surrogate. The increasing opportunities associated with assisted reproduction provide additional opportunities for parentage. They are discussed in more detail in Chapter 7.

The status of marriage is determined by the individual states; we discussed the requirements and options concerning marriage in Chapter 3. If a valid marriage has been formed in a state, the presumptive rights of marriage concerning parentage may accrue to persons entering into civil unions, domestic partnerships, and reciprocal beneficiaries. The laws of the individual state will apply when parentage is an issue, regardless of whether the relationship is considered a valid marriage in another state. But note that the Uniform Marriage Act refers to marriage, hence nonmarital cohabitation will not suffice because this is not marriage. Undoubtedly litigation, if not statutory interpretation or modification, will address this presumptive status of paternity and maternity in the future.

Increasingly, courts are willing to expand the definition of parenthood beyond the presumptive status list enacted by the Uniform Parentage Act. These courts allow unrelated persons–nonmarital persons—to become parents through validly executed gestational agreements. Under state laws, a person becomes a parent only by conception, adoption, or compliance with artificial insemination statutes. But a few states allow for parental status to occur through a validly executed gestational agreement; we discussed the requirements for these in Chapter 7. One Connecticut case involved two men who were originally partners, and then married in Massachusetts. At the time, Massachusetts was one of the few states allowing same-sex marriages. Subsequently, they executed an agreement with a woman who agreed to be a gestational carrier for them. She was implanted with embryos formed from donor eggs and the sperm from one of the men; she later gave birth to twins. The man who had donated the sperm was obviously the genetic father, but the issue became whether his same-sex marriage partner was a parent, since there was no genetic connection between him and the twins. And, at the time, he did not come within the parameter of the state statute conferring parental status. The court ruled that the statute allowing gestational agreements to be valid in the state and conferred parenthood on the unrelated man. Thus, once the man signed the valid gestational agreement he became an "intended parent," irrespective of that intended parent's genetic relationship to the child.[2]

So too, some states allow persons to become "de facto parents," irrespective of genetic relationship, holding that these persons stand in loco parentis to the children. Despite the lack of a genetic connection with the child, the courts find that a parent-child bond may exist if a significant emotional bond is present, the genetic parent has actively promoted the parental role of the other party, and the unrelated person has actively participated in establishing a parental bond with the child.[3] Indeed, some states have, by statute, included the status of de facto parents within the state's definition of parent. Delaware is one of those states, and the state supreme court has allowed a de facto parent, previously denied parental status, to renew her petition for custody under the new status.[4] Some courts have shown restraint in allowing a foster parent to become a de facto parent, holding that to allow foster parents this status undermines the goals of family reunification. Nonetheless, if the child and the foster parent share a parent-child relationship prior to the petitioner becoming the child's foster parent, the court has been willing to allow the foster parent to become a de facto parent of the child.[5]

2. Raftopol v. Ramey, 12 A.3d 783 (Conn. 2011).

3. *See, e.g.,* Kulstad v. Maniaci, 244 P.3d 722 (Mont. 2010).

4. Smith v. Guest, 16 A.3d 920 (Del. 2011) (applying DEL. CODE ANN. tit. 13, § 8–201 (2011)).

5. *See, e. g.,* In re Parentage of L.B., 122 P.3d 161 (Wash. 2005), *cert. denied*

Whenever both parties obtain parental status, courts determine custody based on the best interest of the child alone; no parental presumption is involved. The test for determining custody is simple: What is in the best interest of the child? Originally, to determine what was in the best interest of the child, the European courts held that the father had the right to have custody of his children because he could best provide for them. The father's custody was in the best interest of the child since the father could afford to feed, house, and clothe them. Then, Europe reversed its tender years preference for the father, and instead expressed a preference for the mother if the child was less than seven years-of-age. This reversal was based on the mother's grief over the loss of her young children. Eventually, American courts adopted this maternal preference called the "tender years presumption." But by the 1970s, courts ruled that the tender years maternal presumption was unconstitutional gender discrimination, and this remains the law today.

Gradually, courts explored alternative approaches by which to settle custody disputes between parents. But the courts are nonetheless mindful that having a presumption decreases litigation. Although desirable, any presumption can foster stereotypes. West Virginia created a primary caretaker presumption in 1981, but the legislature abolished it in 2002, finding that it was a substitute for the tender years presumption. Later, the state legislature enacted a list of eight objectives, the purpose of which was to award custody based on a parenting plan allocating parental responsibilities.[6] The West Virginia approach, popular among the states and based on the approach recommended by the American Law Institute's Principles Governing the Allocation of Custodial and Decision–Making Responsibilities for Children, is premised upon the cooperation of the parents. The goal of the parenting plan approach is to require the parents to talk about custody, visitation, and how they will work within the confines of the plan now, and later if future modification is necessary. Once the parents arrive at a plan, the plan becomes enforceable through the judicial process unless the plan is injurious to the children. If the parents fail to agree on a parenting plan, then custody is decided by the court, based on the caretaking responsibilities each of the parents assumed prior to the separation and divorce.

sub nom. Britain v. Carvin, 547 U.S. 1143 (2006); ALI, *Principles of the Law of Family Dissolution: Analysis and Recommendations* 107–108 (2000) (defining de facto parents and distinguishing them from parents by estoppel).

6. *See* W. Va. Code Ann. § 48–9–206 (LexisNexis 2004); *see also* ALI, *Principles of the Law of Family Dissolution: Analysis and Recommendations* §§ 2.06, 2.08 (2002).

In the absence of an allocation approach, such as the one adopted by West Virginia, states will decided upon custody based on factors that seek to identify what is in the best interest of the child. For example, California provides a list of considerations: (1) the health and safety of the child; (2) any history of abuse by a parent against any child, the other parent, or any person with whom the parent had an ongoing intimate relationship; (3) the quality of time the child spent with each parent; and (4) any abuse of alcohol or drugs by a parent.[7] Another approach is offered by the Uniform Marriage and Divorce Act: (1) the wishes of the parents; (2) the wishes of the child;[8] (3) interaction between the child and the parent, child's siblings, any other person with whom the child's best interest would be significantly served; (4) the child's adjustment to his or her home, school, or community; and (5) the mental and physical health of all parties involved.[9]

Most often, courts will award sole physical custody to one parent, with a right of visitation to the other parent. The parents will share joint legal custody, and rarely, courts award sole legal custody to one of the parents. In very rare situations, courts may award joint physical custody to both of the parties,[10] utilizing the concept of "bird nesting" to describe joint physical custody.[11] The California code defines joint physical custody as the following: "Each of the parents shall have significant periods of physical custody. Joint physical custody shall be shared by the parents in such a way as to assure a child of frequent and continuing contact with both parents ... "[12] The court must make a written order explaining its reasons for ordering any arrangement, and there is a presumption of joint physical custody if both parents express a desire to have a joint custody award. Consistently, courts hold that joint physical custody will only be ordered if both parents cooperate and view their custody as a joint effort.

B. *Parent Versus Non–Parent*

Unlike between two parents, when a non-parent seeks custody of a child over the objection of the parent, the non-parent must rebut the fundamental right of the parent over his or her child.

---

7. Cal. Fam. Code § 3011 (West 2004).

8. *See, e.g.*, Foshee v. Foshee, 247 P.3d 1162 (Okla. 2010) (holding that a child's preference is still just a preference, not binding on the court).

9. Unif. Marriage & Divorce Act, 9A U.L.A. § 402 (1998).

10. *See, e.g.*, Durning v. Balent/Kurdilla, 19 A.3d 1125 (Pa. Super. Ct. 2011) (rejecting joint physical custody because facts rarely support its application).

11. *See* Michael T. Flannery, *Is "Bird Nesting" In the Best Interest of Children?*, 57 SMU. L. Rev. 295 (2004).

12. Cal. Fam. Code § 3004 (West 2004).

Thus, the non-parent will have to demonstrate parental unfitness by clear and convincing evidence; this is often described in the cases as compelling reasons, or extraordinary circumstances. Most often, the parents have, through their own conduct, brought about the extraordinary circumstances justifying rebuttal. For example, the parent could have emotionally or physically abandoned the child, allowing for a third party to develop emotional bonds with the child, disruption of which would severely harm the child. But the circumstances involved must be extraordinary. One Washington decision illustrates the test involved. The father had allowed his child to live with his mother, the child's grandmother, after the child experienced difficulties in his school. Some time later, the father had some disagreements with his mother and their relationship became strained, even though she was taking care of his son in another state. The boy remained with his grandmother for nearly five years, and then the grandmother petitioned for custody. The Washington Supreme Court overruled a trial court decision that had granted the grandmother's petition, holding that any petition by a non-parent must demonstrate that the parent is unsuitable, not simply that it would be in the best interest of the child to be with the non-parent.[13] Obviously, the court did not regard the circumstances as extraordinary.

There are additional cases where courts rebut the parental presumption, and all involve some form of clear and convincing evidence of parental unfitness.[14] Once the parental presumption is rebutted, then the court permits a consideration of what is in the best interest of the child. Often the presumption is rebutted by a parent allowing a non-parent to specifically occupy the role of a de facto parent. We have discussed de facto parents previously. For example, two nonmarital persons agree that one of them should give birth to a child, or adopt a child, and that they would raise the child together. Later, the genetic or adoptive parent separates from the partner, and the partner would then petition as a de facto parent of the child for purposes of custody. Sometimes, a parent may allow a set of circumstances to occur that make removal from custody of the parent detrimental to the child. Under these circumstances, estoppel would apply. This is one way to establish the clear and convincing evidence necessary in the Washington grandmother decision just described.

---

13. In re Custody of S.C.D–L, 243 P.3d 918 (Wash. 2010).

14. *See, e.g.*, In re Reese and Henderson, 227 P.3d 900 (Colo. App. 2010) (holding that finding that a non-parent is the psychological parent to the child is not sufficient clear and convincing evidence to rebut the parental presumption).

Generally, the award of child custody to a non-parent over the objections of a fit parent remains a formidable task. California, by statute, provides that an award of custody to a non-parent may be made only if the court specifically finds that awarding the child to the parent would be detrimental to the child and then, second, that the award of custody to a non-parent is in the best interest of the child.[15] While this statute seems to be a mere codification of the due process requirement granting to parents a presumptive right, the level of detriment to rebut the parent's presumption is the real issue in statutory interpretation and judicial decisions. Any clarification lies in the facts of the individual cases. Overall, courts appear willing to allow rebuttal of the parental presumption because of a significant psychological parent-child relationship that has been allowed to develop. In addition, the parent-child relationship is disintegrating, or there is some other factor present, such as a parent's unwillingness to accept committed parental responsibility.

C. Parent Versus State

In Chapter 10 we will discuss termination of parental rights. When we do, we will explain in greater detail the procedure by which a parent loses custody of his or her child to the state. As with the construct of a parent versus a non-parent, the parent's right to the care, custody, and control of his or her child is protected by the Due Process Clause of the Fourteenth Amendment. This right is a fundamental one. But, as we have discussed in reference to abortion, child endangerment, and rebuttal of paternity presumptions, the parent's rights are not absolute. The state serves as a guardian for any and all children. In most situations, the state accedes to parental authority. Examples include such issues as medical decisionmaking, reasonable parental discipline, and deference to the parent when a child seeks emancipation. But courts have increasingly allowed children to bring tort suits against parents, especially when there is willful and intentional conduct on the part of the parent towards the child.[16] And most evident, under federal mandates states have become increasingly vigilant in collecting child support from parents. These issues are discussed more completely in other chapters.

Child custody is another issue where the state has become increasingly vigilant vis-a-vis the parent. The state's involvement with the parent and the child commences whenever the parent

---

15. CAL. FAM. CODE § 3041 (West 2004).

16. *See, e.g.,* Newman v. Cole, 872 S.2d 138 (Ala. 2003).

abuses, neglects, surrenders or abandons the child. We will discuss each of these issues in more detail in Chapter 10, when we discuss termination of parental rights. But usually, prior to termination, the state takes custody of the child while the state offers reasonable services to the parent to correct poor parental conduct. The process most often begins with a report from a neighbor or a teacher that the child has been harmed or neglected. Every state has mandatory reporting statutes that obligate specified persons to report suspicions of child abuse. Once the report has been made, the state may remove the child from the custody of the parent if a preponderance of the evidence supports the abuse allegation. Most often, the child is placed with relatives, or if none is available, then to foster care or institutional care.

The fact that the child may be removed from the custody of the parent on such a slight standard of proof as preponderance of the evidence indicates that the state takes abuse and neglect allegations very seriously. It is permissible to delay the parent's due process rights, as these rights are outweighed by the right of the child to safety. Nonetheless, the parent is entitled to a hearing within a reasonable amount of time. At that hearing, the state must prove by clear and convincing evidence that the parent is responsible for the abuse or neglect of the child. Then, the state must provide a plan to address the conduct and reunify the family. The plan usually includes the state providing reasonable support to the parent, support that may include legal assistance, counseling, vocational training, or housing. If the parent does not cooperate with the state's reasonable efforts, then the parent will lose his or her parental rights in an involuntary petition. Once the parent's rights are terminated, the child may be placed for adoption.

When Congress enacted the Adoption Assistance and Child Welfare Act of 1980, the states had to provide mandatory, but reasonable, services to a parent who lost custody of his or her child. Few exceptions are granted. The legislation did not specify how much time the parent had to correct the injurious conduct in order to regain custody. Correspondingly, the number of children in foster care increased significantly, and Congress became increasingly concerned that too many children were not in permanent placements. To address this, Congress enacted the Adoption and Safe Families Act of 1997, which placed a time limit on the parents' response to reasonable state efforts at reunification of the family. The new federal legislation limits the parental presumption with a time requirement. If the child has been in foster care for fifteen of the last twenty-two months, the state may file a petition for termination of parental rights.

Increasingly, there is evidence that states, perhaps because of federal efforts, have heightened concerns about the best interest of a child. For example, Virginia and other states have established Court–Appointed Special Advocate Programs.[17] The Virginia program provides services to children who are: (1) the alleged victims of abuse or neglect, or (2) in need of services or supervision, as determined by the juvenile and domestic relations district court judge. Program advocates are volunteers who need not be attorneys, but are appointed to investigate allegations, monitor cases, assist any appointed guardian ad litem, and file reports pertaining to the child. This program does not provide legal representation. Rather, it is a community approach to better assess and respond to the conditions that resulted in the temporary removal of a child from the custody of a parent. As such, it evidences greater concern for the child's welfare and safety.

D. *Non–Parent Versus State*

Custody disputes between a non-parent and the state consider only the best interest of the child; since there is no parent, there is no parental presumption. Most often, the non-parent is someone who has gained custody of the child through state intervention, when the child was removed because of a parental problem. Now, the state wishes to remove the child from the custody of the non-parent, and the non-parent objects. However, if a removed child is placed with relatives or with foster parents, these non-parents do not gain any presumptive rights that allow them to keep the child over the objections of the state.

In 1977, the Supreme Court of the United States rejected constitutional claims by foster parents.[18] The child was placed with foster parents, also known as non-parents, while the parents were provided with reasonable services to correct the causes precipitating removal of the child. The state may, in some instances, periodically remove the child from one foster home and move the child to another. This is done to prevent emotional bonds from forming between child and foster parent. In *Smith*, one set of foster parents resisted removal of the child that had been placed in their home for more than one year. They argued that a psychological bond did form between the child and the foster parents, and this entitled

---

17. *See* VA. CODE ANN. §§ 9.1–151 et seq. (2006); *see also*, Shireen Y. Husain, *A Voice for the Voiceless: A Child's Right to Legal Representation in Dependency Proceedings*, 79 GEO. WASH. L. REV. 232 (2010).

18. Smith v. Organization of Foster Families for Equal. & Reform, 431 U.S. 816 (1977).

them to a parental presumption under the Due Process Clause. The Court rejected this argument, holding that foster parents do not constitute a family. Furthermore, removal of the child is responsive to the state's goal of family reunification, thereby preserving the rights of the parents. In a concurring opinion, Justice Stewart wrote that the goal of foster care is not to provide a permanent substitute for the natural parent, but to create a temporary shelter until the child can be reunited with the family.

The rights of foster parents have not expanded since the *Smith* decision. Thus, foster parents cannot claim a Due Process right to the child, based on the child's presence in their home while the state provides services to the parents. The only recourse available to the foster parents is to seek de facto parent status prior to the establishment of the foster care placement, or to achieve this same status, after the foster care placement ends.[19]

II. Considerations in the Child's Best Interest

Previously in this chapter we discussed considerations in the best interests of a child; specifically, we listed best interest factors in the California family code, and then in the Uniform Marriage and Divorce Act. As we stated then, many states have adopted the approach of the American Law Institute, which directs courts to enforce the agreed upon parenting plan, unless it could harm the child. However, if the parents fail to agree on a plan, then the court should allocate custody based on the caretaking responsibilities that existed prior to the divorce.[20] There are certain factors that should not be considered: This is the import of the Uniform Marriage and Divorce Act provision: "The court shall not consider conduct of a proposed custodian that does not affect his [or her] relationship to the child." What are these forbidden considerations?

A. *Racial Classifications*

In 1978, Congress enacted the Indian Child Welfare Act.[21] This unique Act is an exception to the Multiethnic Placement Act of 1994, which prohibited race-based matching policies in reference to child placement and adoption. As an exception, the Indian Child Welfare Act is an attempt to preserve tribal identity, by giving the

19. *See, e.g.,* In re Parentage and Custody of A.F.J., 251 P.3d 276 (Wash. Ct. App. 2011), *republished at* 260 P.3d 889.

20. *See* ALI, *Principles of the Law of Family Dissolution: Analysis and Recommendations* § 2.08(1) (2002).

21. Indian Child Welfare Act, Pub. L. No. 95–608, 92 Stat. 3069 (codified as amended in scattered sections of 25 U.S.C.); 25 U.S.C.A. §§ 1911–1923 (West 2006).

Indian tribe exclusive jurisdiction over any Indian child.[22] In any state court proceeding regarding an Indian child for foster care placement or termination of parental rights, the Indian custodian of the child and the tribe shall have a right to intervene at any point. The goal is for the child to remain in the tribe and to not be placed outside of its boundaries or traditions.

With the exception of Indian tribes, states and courts are forbidden to make a custody determination based upon racial classifications. Indeed, it is also forbidden to "deny to any individual the opportunity to become an adoptive or foster parent, on the basis of the race, color, or national origin of the individual, or of the child."[23] In 1984, the Supreme Court decided unequivocally that the law cannot, directly or indirectly, give effect to racial and ethnic prejudices.[24] The issue remains as to whether race or ethnicity persists as a more subtle factor in making custody decisions. For example, a case in Tennessee involved Caucasian parents of a minor. When the couple divorced, the trial court awarded custody of the boy to the father even though the mother had been the child's primary custodian throughout the marriage. The mother appealed, asserting that the custody award was based on the fact that she had a close friendship with her employer, an African–American doctor. She denied having a sexual relationship with him, but admitted that often they saw each other outside of work. The trial judge denied that race had any impact on the custody decision. Instead, the court based its decision to award custody to the father on a comparison of two fit parents. The court held that the father was more fit than the mother, since it was wrong for anyone to have a relationship with his or her employer. The Tennessee Supreme Court affirmed, holding that the case was different from *Palmore*, and that a trial court should exercise broad discretion in making custody decisions.[25]

B. *Religion*

Religion is often used as a basis for custody determinations; religion is involved with visitation disputes too.[26] Overall, the

---

22. For emphasis on tribal identity, *see* Mississippi Band of Choctaw Indians v. Holyfield, 490 U.S. 30, 49 (1989); *see generally* Nat'l Indian Child Welfare Assoc., Indian Child Welfare Act (ICWA) *Compliance, available at* http://www.nicwa.org/Indian_Child_Welfare_Act.

23. Interethnic Adoption, 42 U.S.C. § 1996b(1)(A) (2006).

24. Palmore v. Sidoti, 466 U.S. 429 (1984); *see also* ALI, *Principles of the Law of Family Dissolution: Analysis and Recommendations* § 2.12(1)(a) (2002).

25. Parker v. Parker, 986 S.W.2d 557 (Tenn. 1999).

26. *See, e.g.*, Gerson v. Gerson, 57 A.D.3d 606 (N.Y. App. Div. 2008) (holding that visitation rights may be modified to accommodate parent's desire to

child's religious observance may be a factor in making a custody determination, as long as the religious observance was an important factor in the child's life. The religious observance cannot be a proven adverse factor in the child's life and development. Consistently, courts have held that a child's parent's religious beliefs and practices do not constitute grounds to deprive that parent of custody, unless there is a showing of actual harm to the health and welfare of the child caused by the practices. In one case, a trial judge awarded physical custody of a child to the Jehovah Witness mother, even though her religion barred her from the use of blood transfusions. The father argued that the mother's religion would jeopardize the child's health in the future. But the court held that before religion could be used as an adverse factor in making a custody decision, there must be a showing of actual harm to the health and welfare of the child, and that showing must be very persuasive.[27]

It is difficult for courts to avoiding a comparison of one parent's religious beliefs over the other parent, or avoiding conjecture as to what religious observance might do to the child, or to the child's relationship with the non-observant parent. Of course, the state must avoid First Amendment entanglement by evaluating the quality of religious observance, or as a corollary, by supervising the speech of either parent in reference to the religious observance. Courts will not enforce the religious preference of one parent upon the other by ordering that the child be raised in one religion or the other. And as protected free speech, each parent should have the opportunity to express his or her own religious views to the child, and to practice as he or she wishes.[28]

Courts will hold in contempt a parent who freely entered into a court-approved divorce agreement, and then violates a provision regarding religious observance. If the parent violates the terms of the agreement, and the agreement has been validly incorporated by the court, the parent may be held in contempt. In one case, a father had agreed in the divorce agreement to raise the children as Protestant, but then, when he had custody, advocated another faith to his children. The father waived his First Amendment rights by agreeing not to advocate any other form of religious belief. The

continue the religious observance of a child).

27. Harrison v. Tauheed, 235 P.3d 547 (Kan. Ct. App. 2010), *aff'd*, 256 P.3d 851 (Kan. 2011).

28. *See, e.g.*, D.R.S. v. L.E.K., 33 So.3d 428 (La. Ct. App. 2010), *review denied*, 34 So.3d 291 (La. 2010); Finnerty v. Clutter, 917 N.E.2d 154 (Ind. Ct. App. 2009), *review denied*, 929 N.E.2d 784 (Ind. 2010).

court held that he was not denied his rights when he was held in contempt for refusing to abide by the terms of the agreement.[29]

Society's religious pluralism suggests other issues may arise in reference to religion. One possibility is the enforcement of custody decrees based on religious observances that originate in other countries. In 2005, two Shiite Muslims, a man and a woman, who had married in an Islamic religious ceremony in Lebanon, eventually initiated a custody decree. After they had married in Lebanon, they returned to the United States. But their marriage began to dissolve so they decided to return to Lebanon and get a divorce in an Islamic court there. When they returned to Lebanon, the husband refused to get a divorce, but he did agree to a custody decree concerning their children. The decree was issued by an Islamic tribunal in Lebanon. Under Islamic law, the court ordered that the father had the right to custody of his two sons, one three and the other seven, and the mother returned to the United States without the children. But since no divorce was granted in Lebanon, the mother petitioned a Massachusetts court for a divorce and custody of the two children. The absent father was represented at the hearing by his attorney, where the father argued that the custody order issued in Lebanon settled the issue of custody. But the Massachusetts court disagreed, holding that the Islamic court's custody decree was not entitled to deference because it was not made in substantial conformity with Massachusetts law regarding the best interest of the children. The foreign court did not consider the best interest of the children, but only whether the father was a fit parent. Once the foreign court established the father's fitness, it awarded custody of the children to him based on his gender, and not in reference to the best interest of the children. Furthermore, Massachusetts, the court ruled, was still the home state of the children, even though they resided with the father in Lebanon. The court then went on to award physical and legal custody of the children to the mother, with liberal visitation rights to the father.[30]

C. Sexual Conduct

Overall, the sexual conduct of either parent should only be a factor in the determination of custody or visitation when it has an adverse effect on the child. Furthermore, similar to religious beliefs, the adverse effect upon the child must be actual and not conjectural. As previously quoted from the Uniform Marriage and Divorce Act § 402: "The court shall not consider conduct of a proposed

29. Rownak v. Rownak, 288 S.W.3d 672 (Ark. Ct. App. 2008).

30. Charara v. Yatim, 937 N.E.2d 490 (Mass. App. Ct. 2010).

custodian that does not affect his relationship to the child." Likewise, the American Law Institute's Principles of the Law of Family Dissolution § 2.12(1) prohibits a court from considering sexual orientation or sexual activity, unless it can be proven that the conduct adversely affects the child. These two pronouncements establish a test by which to measure the effect of sexual conduct on custody determinations. That is, the conduct must be proven to be an actual detriment to the child before it may be a factor in a petition to establish or to modify custody.

At least one court, following an award of custody to the mother of a child, permitted visitor restrictions on both parents, when either parent had custody of the child. The court ordered that neither parent could permit a person with whom the parent has a dating, or intimate sexual relationship, to remain in the parent's residence with the child present, between the hours of 10 pm and 6 am. The mother argued that the restriction was a ruse by which her former husband sought to control her life. The court responded by indicating that the restriction applied to both parents equally. In addition, the overriding concern was for the best interest of the child and the parental curfew met this objective.[31]

III. Visitation

The Uniform Marriage and Divorce Act stipulates that a parent not granted custody of a child is entitled to reasonable visitation rights, unless the court finds, after a hearing, that the visitation would endanger the child's physical, mental, moral, or emotional health. Consistently, judicial decrees and statutes based on the Uniform Act conclude that the best interest of the child is always served by having access to both parents after divorce. Even parents who have been adjudicated to have abused or neglected the child, are typically allowed supervised visitation with their child. But supervised visitation requires continued court supervision and opportunities for disagreements, parameters, and even further abuse. But these obstacles have not prevented courts from ordering supervised visitation, especially if there is a close connection between the child and the parent petitioning for visitation.

One case of supervised visitation involved a father who was incarcerated for twelve years for sexually molesting several boys. After he was convicted, his wife divorced him, but the man petitioned for visitation with their eighteen month-old daughter. The

---

31. Getschel–Melancon v. Melancon, No. 09–07–396, 2008 WL 4587639 (Tex. App. Oct. 16, 2008).

court noted that the infant had asked for her father. Based on their affection, the court ordered supervised visitation between the child and the father, who was in prison. He was allowed four visits a year, the child had to be accompanied by an adult (other than the mother), and the child and the escort must engage in counseling in connection with the visit. The father had to pay for the visits, for phone calls with the daughter, plus for the cost of counseling.[32]

Following the Supreme Court's decision in *Troxel v. Granville*,[33] the parental presumption was expressly applied to any dispute over visitation rights between a parent and a non-parent. At issue in *Troxel* was whether allowing a third party to compete for the best interest of a child on the same level as a parent, violated a parent's fundamental rights under the Fourteenth Amendment. When the Court held that there must be clear and convincing evidence of unfitness to rebut the parental presumption before the best interest of the child may be considered, the Court illustrated the constitutional underpinnings by citing to multiple prior decisions. Thus, if a parent objects to visitation by a non-parent, the parent's presumptive right to act in the best interest of the child must be rebutted prior to any best interest test. The parent has the presumptive right to say no to visitation by a non-parent.

By now, the *Troxel* decision has been the subject of many cases, commentaries, and statutory revisions. One case involved a man and a woman who had never married, but had a close relationship. When the woman gave birth to her husband's child, the other man was present. Two years later when her husband died, the woman allowed the other man to continue to see the child, as he had done continuously since the child's birth. But when the child turned six the mother ended her relationship with the man, preventing any further contact with the child, who was now six years-of-age. The man then petitioned the court to order visitation between him and the child, asserting that because the mother had fostered a close relationship between the man and the child, it would harm the child if the relationship ceased. The trial court held that the man had shown clear and convincing evidence to rebut the parental presumption, but that the best interest of the child would not be served by allowing visitation. The court reasoned that the visitation with the man would prompt the mother to inflict psychological harm on the child.

32. Culver v. Culver, 82 A.D.3d 1296 (N.Y. App. Div. 2011), *appeal dismissed*, 947 N.E.2d 1190 (N.Y. 2011).

33. 530 U.S. 57 (2000).

On appeal, the Connecticut Supreme Court ruled that once the non-parent had successfully rebutted the parental presumption, it was improper for the trial court to consider the mother's possible infliction of psychological harm in determining the child's best interest. To do so would allow any parent to prevent non-parent visitation simply by threatening to create a hostile environment. Instead, the court ruled that the trial court may order counseling to accommodate the visitation, or may rule that the parent is unfit.[34] Rejecting the mother's threats, the appellate court remanded so that the trial court could consider the child's best interest.

IV. Relocation

Families are now nationally and internationally mobile. A parent with physical custody of a child can easily move to a new location, which raises the issue of whether the court should prohibit the move as detrimental to the best interest of the child. Traditionally, orders of custody and visitation were designed to maximize the time each parent could continue to spend with the child post-divorce. Attempts at keeping the family intact were seen as in the best interest of the child. Indeed, if a custodial parent wished to move to a new location that would hinder the other parent's visitation rights, the custodial parent had to prove that there was a real advantage to be had in the other location that could not be had in the present location.[35] This was a difficult threshold; only exceptional circumstances could justify the move.

But in 1996, California and New York transformed the law. California ruled that a custodial parent had a "presumptive right" to move; New York courts adopted an approach that focused on what was in the best interest of the child. Many other states quickly followed the lead of these two states, and the American Law Institute adopted a position favoring a custodial parent's right to relocate. All courts specify that the purpose of the relocation must not be malicious. Instead, the courts generally accept relocation for career goals, education, or to be with a new spouse or partner in a new location.

Many states enacted statutes protecting a custodial parent's right to relocate, but the statutes did not always clarify the role and rights of the non-custodial parent. One case illustrates the conflict between the two parents with three minor children, and provides an explanation.[36] The mother, a bartender and waitress in New

---

34. DiGiovanna v. St. George, 12 A.3d 900 (Conn. 2011).

35. *See, e.g.*, Woodside v. Woodside, 949 N.E.2d 447 (Mass. App. Ct. 2011).

36. In re Heinrich and Curotto, 7 A.3d 1158 (N.H. 2010).

Hampshire, petitioned for custody of the three children when she and her husband divorced. She also requested the court to permit her to relocate to Florida with the children, since she could work with extended family there to operate a motel. The new job would provide her with health benefits and more flexible hours. The father opposed the move, arguing that it would diminish the time he could spend with his children because of the distance between New Hampshire and Florida. The New Hampshire statute governing relocation contains a two part test. First, the custodial parent seeking to move must show that the relocation is reasonable and for a legitimate purpose. Second, if the petitioning parent meets this burden, then the opposing parent must prove that relocation is not in the best interest of the children.

The New Hampshire Supreme Court ruled that the statute applied to initial custody determinations, and to custody petitions filed after the final decree of divorce and an award of custody. The unique feature of the statute is its requirement that, once the custodial parent has established a reasonable and legitimate reason for relocating, the other parent must bear the burden of rebutting the move by proving it would not be in the best interest of the children. Practically, this means that the parent objecting to relocation must prove that his or her relationship with the child is so strong, that relocation would have a serious detrimental effect upon the children. In this case, the court denied the request of the custodial mother to move to Florida with the children. The court admitted that the mother's economic, emotional, and educational benefits would be significant if she were able to relocate. But the quality of life that the children enjoyed with the father was so significant that the move to Florida would not be in the best interest of the children.

Examining the relationship of the child with the non-custodial parent is a reasonable part of the best interest test. Education, health care, friends, sports, and even cultural opportunities seem to pale in comparison to what courts have traditionally held to be most important: the continuing relationship between the child and both parents. Statistics indicate that states permit custodial parents to relocate, thereby jeopardizing visitation by the other parent. Motive is important, but the overriding concern of the judicial opinions, as well as the newly enacted statutes, is the best interest of the child. While many of these statutes are detailed, the trial court is often not required to analyze each part of the statute in ruling on a relocation petition.[37] But the trial court's determination is entitled to great weight, and will not be overturned absent a clear showing of abuse of discretion. Clearly, as demonstrated in the New Hampshire decision, the overriding factor in any relocation dispute is the relationship between the non-custodial parent and the children. The more substantial the relationship, the more adverse the reaction of the children if the relationship is suspended because of relocation. And any adverse reaction is not in the best interest of the children.

37. *See, e.g.*, Gathen v. Gathen, 66 So.3d 1 (La. 2011).

Chapter 10

Termination of Parental Rights

Historically, termination of parental rights severed all legal connections between a parent and a child, including custody, visitation, and inheritance. Today, because of statutory variations, a number of exceptions have arisen. For example, states sometimes allow for grandparent visitation after adoption of the child,[1] or allow a genetic parent to retain visitation or inheritance rights when a child is adopted by a stepparent, or finally, allow visitation by a genetic parent after the child is adopted in a form of "open" adoption. While some of these exceptions will be discussed further in Chapter 11, it is important to note their exceptional impact on termination proceedings.

A petition to terminate parental rights is governed by state laws and procedures. There are procedures by which a parent may voluntarily surrender a child, usually in connection with an adoption proceeding. Some petitions may originate through a non-parent with standing, but otherwise, termination typically occurs because the parent has committed a particularly heinous act that is injurious to the best interest of the child, or the parent has refused to substantially cooperate with reasonable state efforts to rectify a problem and reunify the family. In these proceedings, the termination of parental rights is classified as involuntary.

While petitions for termination begin at the state level, they must comply with Constitutional safeguards. For example, while a parent does not have a right to be represented by an attorney in a civil petition to terminate the parent's rights, the parent does have a Constitutional fundamental right to the custody of his or her child. The Due Process Clause of the Fourteenth Amendment safeguards a parent's fundamental right to custody, which includes the presumption of parental authority, fitness, and the right to discipline. Often, the best interest of the child is diminished by this fundamental right to parental authority. Increasingly, legislatures, courts, and commentators struggle to balance the rights of a child with the rights of a parent. These cases, which involve neglect,

---

1. *See, e.g.*, J.M.S. v. J.W., 20 A.3d 458 (N.J. Sup. Ct. App. Div. 2011) (remanding to trial court for consideration of grandparents petition for post-adoption visitation); Walchli v. Morris, 2011 Ark.App. 170 (Ark. Ct. App. 2011) (deny-

abuse, and abandonment of children, can be particularly devastating.

I. Constitutional Procedural Parameters

In 1982 the Supreme Court of the United States clarified parental termination parameters in *Santosky v. Kramer.*[2] The Court ruled that prior to an involuntary termination of parental rights, the state must support its allegations against the parent by at least clear and convincing evidence. The New York statute, which required only a fair preponderance of the evidence to terminate parental rights, was standard in a few states in addition to New York. The facts of *Santosky* are similar to other cases: The married parents had two children when state intervention first occurred, there was a two year-old Tina, and a one year-old John. The state removed the children from the custody of the parents because of complaints made by neighbors and by a local hospital. Tina had suffered a fractured femur, bruises on the upper arms, forehead, flanks, and spine. John was removed subsequently suffering malnutrition, bruises, cuts, blisters, and multiple pin pricks on his back. Later, based on the abuse of Tina and John, Jed was removed from the parents' custody when he was only three days old.[3]

Upon removal of the children, the state appointed an attorney to represent the parents while the children were in foster care. The state, according to procedural protocol, provided the court with a written plan to reunite the family, including counseling assistance to the parents, a nutritionist aide, a public health nurse, psychiatric assistance, and vocational counseling for the father. These services were considered reasonable in the context of the alleged abuse and neglect. Throughout the next four years, the children remained with the same foster parents, and the parents, during this same time, continuously disregarded most of the services offered by the state and only sporadically responded to other efforts. Then, after almost five years, the state initiated a petition to involuntarily terminate parental rights because the parents had made few efforts to take advantage of social services or even to visit their children.

The state's petition to terminate the rights of the parents was based on the state's statute, which permitted termination upon proof that, by the preponderance of the evidence, the parents were not cooperating with state reunification efforts. Here, despite significant state efforts to reunite the family, the parents' failure to

ing grandparents right of visitation after adoption).

2. 455 U.S. 745 (1982); *see also* Troxel v. Granville, 530 U.S. 57 (2000) (holding that parents have a fundamental liberty interest in the care, custody, and control of their children).

3. *Santosky* at 781, n.10.

cooperate for five years demonstrated sufficient preponderance of the evidence of parental unfitness and neglect. The trial court granted the state's petition.

On appeal, the appellate division approved New York's preponderance standard, holding that it properly balanced the child's rights with those of the natural parents. The parents then appealed to the Supreme Court of the United States, arguing that terminating their parental rights on such a low level of proof was a denial of due process. A majority of the Court ruled in favor of the parents, thereby safeguarding their parental rights. The Court's ruling balanced the private interests of the parents in the custody of their children against the risk of mistake or erroneous deprivation of custody. Because the parents' rights in their children were historical and fundamental, their children should not be taken from them without proof of parental unfitness or neglect by at least clear and convincing evidence. The Court then remanded the case for a determination of whether there was evidence of parental neglect which would meet the higher standard.

In invalidating the New York statute, the *Santosky* Court was divided five to four. In his dissent, Associate Justice Rehnquist, joined by three other members of the Court, argued that: (1) the process provided by the state was fair, (2) allowed each of the states to set its own family law standards, and (3) reflected a constitutionally permissible balance of the best interest of the children and the rights of the parents. The dissent explained:

> When, in the context of a permanent neglect termination proceeding, the interests of the child and the State in a stable, nurturing home-life are balanced against the interests of the parents in the rearing of their child, it cannot be said that either set of interests is so clearly paramount as to require that the risk of error be allocated to one side or the other.[4]

The ruling in *Santosky* modified the procedure in a few states and changed perceptions in all states. Following *Santosky*, all states had to prove parental unfitness by at least clear and convincing evidence. Many commentators lamented this, as it forced children to endure longer periods of time in placements that were not permanent, or to suffer from sporadic, although continuing, abuse and neglect; these same commentators favored the *Santosky* dissent.[5] But the Supreme Court's decision transformed the debate

---

4. *Id.* at 790–91.

5. *See, e.g.,* Raymond C. O'Brien, *An Analysis of Realistic Due Process Rights of Children Versus Parents*, 26 CONN. L.

REV. 1259 (1994); Andre P. Derdeyn & Walter J. Wadlington, *Adoption: The Rights of Parents Versus the Best Inter-*

over the best interest of children vis-a-vis the rights of parents into a reaffirmation of the rights of parents. In *Troxel*, eighteen years later, the Court addressed the issue of whether a parent may restrict visitation between his or her child and the child's grandparents, the majority reaffirmed the fundamental right of a parent to control his or her child. In addition to referencing many prior decisions, the Court described the parent's right over a child as perhaps the oldest of the fundamental liberty interests recognized by the Court.[6]

Once the Court ruled that parental rights were fundamental under the Due Process Clause, attention was focused on the following: (1) foster care, or alternative placements for children, as reasonable efforts are made to assist the parents to reunify the family; (2) the extent and exceptions to reasonable state efforts to assist parents; and (3) an increasing federal presence in the areas of child welfare, foster care, and efforts to promote adoptions. We will discuss these in turn.

A.   Foster Care

Our system of foster care has been variously praised and panned. Not too long ago, it was widely thought that the best general approach was to remove children from their homes quickly, upon a credible allegation, and then to provide the family with services in the hope of reunifying the families as quickly as possible. Reunification of the parent with the child was the primary goal. Eventually, when the complexities were better appreciated, reunification remained the goal, but now the process settled into years, or longer. During this time, children were often shifted to several different foster parents. When there were insufficient foster care homes, institutional care was arranged, but modern statutes express a preference for kinship foster care.[7] Kinship care allows a child to stay with an eligible relative, who may receive payment as a foster parent, but must meet the requirements of a foster parent and must comply with the demands of the child welfare agency or court.[8]

Federal funding of state foster care placements became significant with passage of the Adoption Assistance and Child Welfare Act of 1980. But with federal funding came greater federal oversight of

---

ests of Their Children, 16 J. AM. ACAD. CHILD PSYCHIATRY 238 (1977).

6. Troxel v. Granville, 530 U.S. 57 (2000).

7. *See, e.g.*, VA. CODE ANN. § 63.2–900.1 (West 2008).

8. *See* U.S. Dep't of Health & Human Serv., Admin. For Children & Families, Child Welfare Info. Gateway, Foster Care Statistics 2009, *available at*: http://www.childwelfare.gov.pubs/factsheets/foster.cfm#place.

foster care, a fact that is often criticized by child advocates and parental advocates alike.[9] After passage of the Act, federal law now requires that the state make reasonable efforts to rehabilitate the family before terminating parental rights. "Reasonable efforts" is a difficult standard to gauge. Most often, it means that a child will be placed in kinship care, foster care, or institutional care for extended periods of time while the parent is offered services. The federal requirement of reasonable efforts is only waived if such efforts are likely to be futile. The Act specifies that waivers occur when the parent refuses to substantially comply with state efforts, the parent has killed another child or the other parent, or the parent has done something particularly heinous to the child, such as incest or torture. Under these circumstances the state may forgo any reasonable efforts at rehabilitation, terminate the parent's rights, and place the child for adoption.

In some cases, the possibility of adoption is unavailable. Because of health conditions, mental issues, or age, a child may not have a feasible opportunity to be adopted. To meet the needs of these children, states have provided for long-term or permanent foster care.[10] To be eligible, the state court must find that diligent efforts have been made by the local agency to place the child with the child's natural parents and those efforts have failed. Also, the local agency must show diligent efforts have been made to place the child for adoption and these efforts have failed. Finally, the court must find that adoption is not a reasonable alternative for that particular child under the circumstances. The long-term placement is to last until such time as the child reaches the age of majority, at which point the child will be emancipated. The long-term foster parents are to receive the same payments and services as other foster parents, after they meet the same qualifications and comply with the same restrictions.

B. Reasonable Efforts

As illustrated in the *Santosky* decision, the state is required to provide parents with reasonable efforts to rehabilitate the family, all directed towards reunification. Most often these efforts consist of drug treatment programs, medical services, nutritionists, vocational counseling, classes on anger management, housing, or even a

9. *See, e.g.,* Elizabeth G. Patterson, *Unintended Consequences: Why Congress Should Tread Lightly When Entering the Field of Family Law,* GA. ST. U. L. REV. 397 (2008).

10. *See, e.g.,* VA. CODE ANN. § 63.2–908 (West 2008).

psychosexual evaluation.[11] Budget constraints will often determine what is reasonable too, as courts increasingly note that states can only provide services based on available staff and financial resources.[12] While the state provides these reasonable services, the child or children are classified as dependent children and are placed in foster care or similar placements, anticipating reunification. Eventually, if parents do not cooperate with the state's reasonable efforts, the state may initiate a proceeding to terminate parental rights, thereby allowing the child to be adopted. Throughout the process the state provides the parents and, as was done in the *Santosky* case, the children, with an attorney. But the attorney is not mandated. Rather, the attorney is simply part of the reasonable efforts the state must provide to accommodate the Constitution and the federal law requirements.

In 1981, the Supreme Court ruled that indigent parents in a civil termination proceeding were not always entitled to an attorney, but when the parent's interests were substantial and the state's interests were low, then due process may require the appointment of an attorney to represent the parents.[13] Certainly, there is no automatic right to an attorney as there would be in a criminal proceeding. The decision was rendered the year prior to *Santosky,* and may account for *Santosky's* ruling that the parents were entitled to a higher showing of clear and convincing evidence prior to termination. But this much is clear: If states are to provide reasonable services to parents, the presence of an attorney is one of the services that may lessen protracted delay. But, as is often stated by courts, there is always a balancing of the rights of the parent against the interest of the state in providing for an efficient and orderly administration of justice for all of the parties involved.[14] Nothing is guaranteed. Again, reasonable efforts are hard to gauge.

C. *Adoption and Safe Families act of 1997*[15]

Recall that in 1997 Congress revised the process by which federal support for indigent parents was paid. The Personal Responsibility and Work Opportunity Reconciliation Act eliminated a child support system that had been in existence for decades, and replaced it with Temporary Assistance to Needy Families. The new

11. *See* In re Dependency of D.C–M., 253 P.3d 112 (Wash. Ct. App. 2011).

12. In re Shirley B., 18 A.3d 40 (Md. 2011) (holding that the state's inability to provide better services due to limited state financial resources did not prohibit termination of parental rights).

13. Lassiter v. Department of Social Serv., 452 U.S. 18 (1981).

14. *See, e.g.*, In re Lukas K., 14 A.3d 990 (Conn. 2011).

15. Pub. L. 105–89, 111 Stat. 2115 (codified as amended in scattered sections of 2, 42 U.S.C.).

federal legislation challenged the states to establish paternity, reduce welfare dependency, and provide for stricter accountability. In a similar fashion, the enactment by Congress of the Adoption and Safe Families Act of 1997, revolutionized treatment of parents vis-a-vis their dependent children. The Act shifted focus to the children, rather than exclusively to the parents.

Santosky's requirement that the state provide clear and convincing evidence prior to involuntarily terminating parental rights, plus the reasonable efforts mandate of the Adoption Assistance and Child Welfare Act, precipitated consequences. One consequence was that the number of children in foster care placements increased dramatically. By 1998, there were 568,000 children in foster care placements; from 1980 to 1998, the number of children in foster care doubled.[16] This was an alarming increase in the number of children without permanent placements. In response to this rise in the number of children simply waiting for either reunification or adoption, Congress enacted the Adoption and Safe Families Act. The Act shifted the focus to dependent children, rather than parents, by placing a time limit on a parent's response to reasonable efforts offered by the state. The new legislation mandated that if a child spends fifteen out of twenty-two consecutive months in foster care placement, then the state was to initiate termination proceedings so that the child could be placed for adoption. If the child has been placed with relatives, or the state has concluded that termination is not warranted, then the provisions of the Act do not apply. Insignificant periods of time that the child may spend with the parent during these months prior to returning to state custody, do not count against the mandated time. In other words, if the child were to be returned to the custody of a parent for a brief time, only to have removal occur again, the time frame dictated by the Act does not start all over again.

Some commentators have criticized the Act as being too harsh on parents, giving them insufficient time to correct poor behavior patterns, and that the Act fails to recognize the difficulty in finding permanent homes for children. In addition, some argue that the Act is necessary only because the state does not do enough to assist parents experiencing difficulty when the child is still in the home.[17] But the fact remains that there is sharp contrast between the Act and the Adoption Assistance and Child Welfare Act of 1980. The latter emphasizes reunification of parent and child, while the

---

16. *See* Sandra Bass et al., *Children, Families, and Foster Care: Analysis and Recommendations*, 14 The Future of Children 5, 8 (2004).

17. *See, e.g.,* Richard Wexler, *Take the Child and Run: How ASFA and the Mentality Behind It Harm Children*, 13 UDC. L. Rev. 435 (2010).

former restricts the reasonable efforts provided to the parents and seeks to terminate parental rights in a fast and orderly fashion. The two acts illustrate the continuing tension between those advocating for the rights of the parent, and those advocating for the best interest of the child. State court decisions seem more adept at emphasizing the need for stability in the child's life,[18] but Constitutional safeguards remain a potent force in preserving the fundamental rights of parents.

II. Criteria for Termination

Not long ago, statutes might simply refer to "unfitness" as a general category to justify termination, but the evolution of Constitutional protections has made such general terms obsolete. Today, omnibus terminology has given way to fairly specific termination criteria that varies from state-to-state. As we have discussed previously, certain parental misdeeds require no reasonable efforts on the part of the state prior to termination of parental rights. To illustrate, the Adoption and Safe Families Act provides that termination may commence immediately if the parent is convicted of torture, sexual abuse, or the murder of the other parent. These are criminal offenses and require proof beyond a reasonable doubt. In addition, if the parent's rights to a sibling are terminated, then the parent's rights to custody of all the children may be terminated. [42 U.S.C. § 671(a)(15)(D) (2006)] But most often, it is the failure of the parent to respond to reasonable state efforts at rehabilitation that prompts termination of parental rights. The following is a list of factors that may occasion the removal of a child from parental custody and that, if not addressed by the parent, will result in termination of that parent's right.

A. *Abuse and Neglect*

The United States Department of Health and Human Services reports that during 2006, an estimated 905,000 children were determined to be victims of abuse or neglect: Approximately 60% suffered from neglect; 16% suffered from physical abuse; 9% suffered from sexual abuse; and 7% suffered from emotional maltreatment.[19] Every state has reporting statutes requiring specific people

---

18. *See, e.g.,* In re Adoption/Guardianship of Ta'niya C., 8 A.3d 745 (Md. 2010) (holding that the best interest of the child is the prevailing standard in termination of parental rights); Doe v. Roe, 690 S.E.2d 573 (S.C. 2010) (holding that the parent's rights could be terminated to provide stability for the child).

19. U.S. Dept. of Health & Human Serv., Admin. for Children & Families, *available at* http://www.acf.hhs.gov/programs/cb/pubs/cm06.

to report suspicions of child abuse.[20] Once reported, child protective services intervenes and, if there is a preponderance of the evidence that abuse has occurred, the child is classified as a dependent child and is removed from the custody of the suspected perpetrator. Then, if there is sufficient clear and convincing evidence of abuse submitted at a subsequent hearing, the child continues in state custody, while civil or criminal proceedings, or both, commence. If the custodian perpetrator cooperates with reasonable state efforts, then the child will be returned if conditions warrant. If not, or if the abuse or neglect is sufficiently severe, parental rights will be terminated and the child will be placed for adoption in a permanent home environment.

Difficulties arise when states seek to define statutory abuse or neglect. The Child Abuse Prevention and Treatment Act is a federal statute, offering definitions of sexual abuse, physical abuse, neglect, emotional abuse, and abandonment.[21] But often, the definitions are challenged in court proceedings as too vague under the Due Process Clause. Moreover, the definitions do not address the changing circumstances of abuse, or adequately protect parents who are poor or culturally different. The particular issue of the poverty of the parents is illustrated in the case of a single-parent who had three children and then gave birth to twins. Because she was very poor and had difficulty supporting the three children she already had, she decided that the twins should have a better life and therefore decided to place them for adoption. Using an adoption facilitator, the mother first placed the children with a California couple, but removed them after a ten day visit. She then placed the children with a British couple, but a British judge ruled the couple unfit. At this point, she decided she would keep the twins and raise them herself, but the Department of Family Services removed the children from her custody, alleging emotional abuse. At a hearing, a trial judge ruled that the mother had contributed severe and recurrent acts of emotional abuse of the twins by placing them with multiple prospective adopters. But the mother appealed, responding that the temporary placements were not abusive, that she only sought what was best for her children. The appellate court agreed with the mother, ruling that the mother had not exhibited a consistent pattern of abuse, nor did she appear unable to care for

---

20. Raymond C. O'Brien, *Clergy, Sex and the American Way*, 31 Pepp. L. Rev. 363, 430–435 (2004).

21. U.S. Dep't of Health and Human Serv., Admin. For Children & Families, Child Welfare Info. Gateway, Definitions of Child Abuse and Neglect: State Statutes, *available at*: http://www.childwelfare.gov/systemwide/laws_policies/statutes/define.pdf.

the twins in the future.[22] The decision established a pattern and a recognition of the plight of being poor and a parent.

In addition to cultural difference and disparate treatment of poorer parents, state statutory definitions of abuse must accommodate the right of parents to occasionally discipline their children. If circumstances warrant, many states permit a parent to raise the defense of parental discipline when responding to a charge of battery against his or her child. Most often, the parent has struck the child and is now charged with battery, or in other words, abuse. The discipline defense may be raised under a state statute, or under the common law.[23] But when allowing the defense, courts will look to the age of the child, the appropriateness of the discipline, and whether the parent's conduct was part of a pattern.[24]

So too, parents may assert a Free Exercise defense in response to allegations of child abuse or neglect. The defense often arises in connection with immunization of a child, medical treatment of a child, or when a reunification plan involves withdrawing a child from an environment, although religious, which poses a threat to the child's welfare. Many states permit a parent's religious beliefs to serve as a defense to neglect up to a reasonable point. Then, the well-being of the child takes precedence over the Free Exercise claim of the parent, and the court may order emergency consent so as to provide medical care for the child.[25]

Sadly, child sexual abuse has become more varied and seemingly, more pervasive. Most often, the perpetrator of the child sexual abuse is a parent or someone known to the parent, and most often the abuse takes place in the child's home. Because the abuse may range from sodomy and intercourse to indecent exposure and Internet lewdness, it is increasingly difficult to identify the abuse and remove the child from the custody of the offender. There are cases in which the parent's possession of pornography or sexual devices have occasioned the removal of a child from the home, the child welfare agency asserting that the materials or devices endan-

---

22. In re K.A.W., 133 S.W.3d 1 (Mo. 2004); *see also* New Jersey Div. of Youth and Family Serv. v. P.W.R., 11 A.3d 844 (N.J. 2011) (holding that the lack of heating in the home and poor medical care did not constitute neglect when parents faced financial difficulties).

23. *See, e.g.*, State v. Wade, 245 P.3d 1083 (Kan. Ct. App. 2010) (holding common law defense was appropriate as long as not forbidden by statute).

24. *See, e.g.*, Department of Children and Families v. C.H., 5 A.3d 163 (N.J.

Super. Ct. App. Div. 2010), *appeal denied*, 23 A.3d 412 (N.J. 2011) (rejecting parental discipline defense); Department of Children and Families v. K.A., 996 A.2d 1040 (N.J. Super. Ct. Ap. Div. 2010), *review granted*, 6 A.3d 442 (N.J. Oct. 14, 2010) (defining excessive corporal punishment).

25. *See, e.g.*, ARK. CODE ANN. § 20–9–604 (West 2009) (allowing consent whenever an emergency exists).

ger the welfare of the child. But courts appear to need something specific to warrant making the child a dependent. Conjecture based on the presence of pornography in the parent's possession is insufficient as a ground to justify removal of the child.[26] Also, in some cases, sexual exploitation of the child and the parental right to discipline may interact. In one case a father instructed his fourteen-year-old daughter to strip to her underwear and then the father struck her with his belt. The courts used a test of what was reasonable and age-sensitive to hold that the father's actions constituted battery. The father's assertion that he was simply disciplining his child did not immunize him from the offense of abuse.[27] And finally, associated with the complexity of proving sexual abuse allegations, children sometimes fabricate allegations, thereby adding another level of inquiry.[28] Even though studies suggest that the incidence of fabrication is very low, there are special rules concerning testimony given by children, and commentators have suggested ways by which to arrive at the truth of allegations.[29]

B. Abandonment

Abandonment, relinquishment, and surrender are sometimes mistakenly used interchangeably, but they are in fact very different. Surrender or relinquishment of a child takes place voluntarily, with the child's interest being of paramount concern. The term surrender refers to a special act or provision that is usually ancillary to an adoption statute, that which is necessary prior to adoption. For example, a parent may elect to voluntarily relinquish or surrender a child for adoption because of illness, incapacity, or financial difficulties, thus allowing another person or couple to petition for adoption of the child. The process is meant to provide for the best interest of the child. Abandonment, on the other hand, does not assume or require that the parents are choosing to act in the best interest of the child. In general, abandonment occurs whenever the parent's identity or whereabouts are unknown and the child has been left in a dangerous location, has suffered harm, or the parent has failed to support the child for a specified period of time. Many states include abandonment in the state's definition of neglect.

26. *See, e.g.,* Department of Human Serv. v. A.F., 259 P.3d 957 (Or. Ct. App. 2011).

27. *See, e.g.,* Hunter v. State, 950 N.E.2d 317 (Ind. Ct. App. 2011).

28. *See, e.g.,* Ducote v. State, 222 P.3d 785 (Wash. 2009).

29. *See, e.g.,* BETTE L. BOTTOMS ET AL. EDS., CHILDREN AS VICTIMS, WITNESSES, AND OFFENDERS: PSYCHOLOGICAL SCIENCE AND THE LAW (2009).

There is an interesting development in reference to abandonment, this is the rapid acceptance of what may be termed Safe Haven Statutes. In 1999, Texas enacted what the state legislature called The Baby Moses Law.[30] The statute was the first of an innovation that would be termed Safe Haven Statutes. Today, nearly every state has a version of these statutes, although the provisions of each vary considerably.[31] Overall, the statutes permit parents a short window of opportunity during which they may surrender their newborns to a specific person or facility, and do so with anonymity and impunity. The goal is to offer parents, presumptively very young parents, an alternative to abandoning the infant in an unacceptable location such as a trash bin or a public restroom.

Among the different state statutes, there are variations as to the following: (1) The age framework of the child, within which the child may be legally surrendered. Statutes that realistically focus on the original purpose of these laws typically limit their provisions to children less than a week old, some even less. However, a significant number of statutes use thirty days, or a few days less, in their definition of what constitutes infancy. Other states allow a physician to establish a reasonable age. One state, Nebraska, made the news when it enacted a statute without an age limit. The state was overwhelmed with parents seeking to abandon their adolescents, some parents coming from other states to do so. The Nebraska legislature amended its statute to apply to infants under the age of thirty days. (2) The locations where the child may be left vary in number and specificity. Most popular listings are hospital emergency rooms, police stations, and firehouses. (3) Legal immunity for the parent of the infant will attach as long as the infant shows no sign of abuse or neglect. A few states also allow for an indemnity to be paid to those facilities or persons that provide care and support for the child until the child can be placed elsewhere. (4) Some states specify a time period during which the parent may rescind the relinquishment and have the child returned. And (5) the statutes specify who must appear at the relinquishment of the infant. Generally, either parent may appear, but some states specify that only the mother may relinquish the infant, while some states allow an agent for the parents to relinquish the child. Generally, the anonymity of the parties is preserved.

---

30. Tex. Fam. Code § 262.302 (West 2008).

31. *See* Susan Ayres, Kairos *and Safe Havens: The Timing and Calamity of Unwanted Birth*, 15 Wm. & Mary J. Women & L. 227 (2009); Carol Sanger, *Infant Safe Haven Laws: Legislating in the Culture of Life*, 106 Colum. L. Rev. 753 (2006).

Not all commentators support the consequences of the Safe Haven Statutes.[32] Their concern is that often the father of the child may not be duly informed of the birth of the infant and thus lose the opportunity to establish paternity. The issue may be rectified in the manner consistent with state statutes offering a registry of paternity. These registries, modeled after the Uniform Parentage Act, allow notice to be provided to a man who suspects that he may have fathered a child. He will then have an opportunity to establish paternity.

C. Disability, Unwillingness, or Incapacity to Perform Parental Duties

Parents with mental, physical, or emotional disabilities may be subjected to the involuntary termination of their parental rights. These cases are particularly difficult, but the objective is to preserve the best interest of the children involved. Thus, if a parent is unable to meet the nutritional, educational, or disciplinary needs of a child and a court finds that this deficiency clearly and convincingly adversely affects the child, the parental rights of the parent may be terminated and the child placed for adoption. Because of the disability, issues may arise under the federal American with Disabilities Act ("ADA") too. Specifically, the provision of the Act provides: "no qualified individual with a disability shall, by reason of such disability, be excluded from participating in or be denied the benefit of the services, programs, or activities of a public entity."[33] The applicability of the Act may be very pertinent.

In one case a mentally disabled father had his parental rights terminated and then subsequently sought to appeal the court's holding on the ground that his disability should have been protected under the Americans with Disabilities Act. At the original termination trial, the attorney for the father never raised the issue of the applicability of the ADA, and on appeal, the appellate court ruled that the trial court had no independent duty to address the applicability of the federal statute. The court ruled that the attorney for the father could have raised the issue, along with an argument for any accommodations that could be made to assist the father.[34] But the parental rights of the mentally challenged father were nonetheless terminated.

32. *See, e.g.,* Jeffrey A. Parness & Theresa A. Clark Arado, *Safe Haven, Adoption and Birth Record Laws,* 36 CAP. U. L. REV. 207 (2007).

33. 42 U.S.C. § 12132 (2006).

34. In re Jeremiah S., 204 P.3d 769 (N.M. Ct. App. 2009).

D.   Incarceration

In and of itself, a parent's incarceration is not sufficient to warrant involuntary termination of parental rights, but often state statutes permit other factors to be considered that will then result in termination. In a West Virginia decision, the state removed a child from his parents' custody shortly after birth due to an imminent danger of abuse and neglect. Shortly after removal, the mother's rights to the child were terminated. When the child was five months old he was returned to the custody of his father, as the father had reasonably cooperated with state reunification efforts. Nonetheless, the father was arrested a short time later for selling firearms to an undercover agent in violation of a federal law barring possession of firearms by a convicted felon. The father was incarcerated and the child was then returned to state custody. At this time, the state petitioned to involuntarily terminate the father's parental rights. The child's foster parents sought to adopt the child, but the trial court denied the petition to terminate based solely on the father's incarceration. In addition, the trial court ruled, the state had not shown that the father could not remedy his neglect of the child after he was released from prison.

On appeal, the appellate court reversed, holding that the parental rights of the father may be terminated based on the state statute that provides for termination whenever there is no reasonable likelihood that conditions of neglect or abuse can be substantially corrected in the near future. Thus, even though conviction of a criminal offense is not a sufficient basis to terminate parental rights, the resulting imprisonment may unreasonably delay the permanent placement of the child, and the best interest of the child would be better served by terminating the incarcerated parent's rights. The court listed factors that should be considered, such as the nature of the offense committed, the terms of the confinement, the projected length of the incarceration, and the overall best interests of the child. The facts of this case indicated that the father, shortly after assuming custody of the child, made bad choices. Additionally, the father demonstrated no awareness of how he would be different when he would eventually be released from prison. Lastly, there was no strong emotional bond between the father and the child, since the child spent almost all of his life in the care of the foster parents.[35]

35. In re Cecil T., 717 S.E.2d 873 (W.Va. 2011).

Chapter 11

Adoption

I. Historical Underpinnings

Adoption terminates a pre-existing parent-child relationship, creating a legal status of parent and child between two persons without such a relationship previously. This is a unique status, different from foster care placement, or from equitable adoption, also known as adoption by estoppel. The parties are not stepparents and stepchild. We discussed foster care in connection with termination of parental rights, and we will discuss equitable adoption and stepparent adoption later in this chapter. Adoption is unique because it is a creation of statute, rather than common law. The laws of the various states establish the legal status of adoptive parents and these laws must be interpreted with the care and precision associated with any statutory interpretation. In some instances, federal statutes preempt state laws. For example, contrary state laws have been preempted in reference to race, ethnicity, or international application. Federal subsidies promote adoptions.

Although adoption has ancient roots, the modern version in the United States dates from the nineteenth century, and the twentieth century in England. Early developments in adoption law in Egypt, Babylon, and Rome, focused on matters of political succession, assuring continuation of family religious rites, or providing that a particular person could inherit. These ancient examples typically applied to adults, and benefitted the adopters far more than the persons being adopted. The evolution of this adult-benefitting format was manifested in some civil law countries. For example, the French Civil Code, during the nineteenth century, permitted adult adoptions, but the adopter had to be at least fifty years-old and have no legitimate child or descendant, and the adoptee must be an adult. The English, perhaps because they were more mindful of bloodlines, had no common law adoption, but did enact an adoption statute in 1926.

In the territories of Louisiana and Texas, early forms of adoption based on French or Spanish law might have been in use, but the first officially recognized adoption statute originated in Massachusetts in 1851, Texas in 1850, and Mississippi in 1846. The Civil Code of New York of 1865, the Field Code, was one of the earliest proposed statutory models, but it was never adopted. Nonetheless, the provisions of the Field Code were enacted in several western states. Unlike ancient adoptive practices, which sought to benefit the goals of the adopters, the objective of the modern statutes was to benefit the children, many of whom had been neglected by their genetic parents and were in need of permanent homes. This focus on the best interests of the minor child is widely regarded as indigenous to the United States. It remains the focus in present-day adoption law, now enacted in all of the states. Although infertility has increased among adults, adoption law has returned to fulfill the needs of an adult population seeking to have children.

II. Adoption of Minors

In 1953, the National Conference of Commissioners on Uniform State Laws promulgated a Uniform Adoption Act, and then a revised Uniform Adoption Act in 1969, and finally a new Uniform Adoption Act in 1999.[1] Few jurisdictions adopted the uniform legislation in its entirety, but the framework of the Act influenced every state. The Act was instrumental in establishing the rules of interstate adoption, agency adoption, evaluations, relinquishments, petitions, and stepparent adoptions. Perhaps most of all, the Act established the language of adoption.

A. Adoption Classifications

Adoption of minors is ordinarily classified according to either the method of placement, by licensed state agency or privately, or whether there is a prior kinship relationship between the parties, a relative placement. To have a valid adoption, there must be compliance with the state's adoption statute which, once validly completed, will result in a decree that is entitled to Full Faith and Credit in other states. The procedure of adoption usually initiates with a state agency investigation of the prospective adopter's home to determine suitability. The minor child is usually surrendered by the genetic parents, precipitating termination of parental rights and eventual adoption. Often, the surrender is to a state agency. Recently enacted Safe Haven Statutes permit surrender to a hospital, emergency room, or fire station, with a presumption that a parent who surrenders the child consents to termination of his or her parental rights. We have discussed these statutes previously in Chapter 9.

When a person, other than the genetic parent, secures the placement of the minor child, a situation arises that is often termed a "gray market." The other person may be a physician, social

---

1.   UNF. ADOPTION ACT, 9 U.L.A. Pt. IA 11 et seq. (1999).

worker, or an attorney. Several states have limited or precluded this practice because of concerns over the best interest of the child, the genetic parents, and the prospective adoptive parents.[2] Another option is an independent adoption. There, the genetic parents select the adopters themselves. Again, because of the possibility of an abuse of the process, some states limit independent adoptions, yet the practice has been advocated by some as desirable since it may lessen the time the child spends in foster care or in an abusive home.[3] In any adoption procedure, the process of obtaining adoption assistance is a corollary. Children whose adoptions were procured through a private agency may not be eligible for state adoption assistance subsidies because of failure to complete the proper funding requirements.[4]

B. Confidentiality

Although confidentiality in the adoption process is eroding through legislation and practice, many states still maintain strict procedures to isolate genetic parents from the children they surrendered and their adoptive parents. Admittedly, confidentiality is easier to maintain when the adoption took place through an agency; the agency takes custody of the child in connection with the termination of parental rights, and the agency does not have to notify the genetic parents of the subsequent adoption of the child. And the child cannot trace the identify of the genetic parents because after the adoption, the birth certificate is filed in a confidential location and a new one is issued and recorded. Rarely will a court permit the identity of a genetic parent to be disclosed. In a New York decision, a man's physician provided an affidavit to support the man's petition to obtain information regarding his parents' medical history. The physician thought the information would be helpful in diagnosing and treating the man and his children. But the man's petition for access was denied, with the court holding that granting access to the genetic parents' medical records, without establishing a particular medical condition, would undermine the confidentiality afforded by the state's Adoption Information Registry.[5]

2. *See generally* Kimberly D. Krawiec, *Altruism and Intermediation in the Market for Babies*, 66 WASH. & LEE L. REV. 203 (2009).

3. *See* Elizabeth J. Samuels, *Time to Decide? The Laws Governing Mothers' Consents to the Adoption of Their New-* *born Infants*, 72 TENN. L. REV. 509 (2005) (arguing against independent adoption).

4. *See, e.g.*, Laird v. Department of Public Welfare, 23 A.3d 1015 (Pa. 2011).

5. In re Timothy AA., 72 A.D.3d 1390 (N.Y. App. Div. 2010).

So, to better meet the future medical needs of a child being adopted, the most recent version of the Uniform Adoption Act requires a "person placing a minor" to furnish a written report to a prospective adopting parent containing:

> a current medical and psychological history of the minor, including an account of the minor's prenatal care, medical condition at birth, any drug or medication taken by the minor's mother during pregnancy, any subsequent medical, psychological, or psychiatric examination and diagnosis, and any physical, sexual, or emotional abuse suffered by the minor, and a record of any immunizations and health care received while in foster or other care ... [as well as information about] the medical and psychological history of the minor's genetic parents and relatives ... [6]

Not all states maintain such strict procedures. Some states permit access to adoption records by adoptive children after reaching the age of majority, usually over eighteen or twenty-one years-of-age. Sometimes permission is granted to relatives in connection with judicial proceedings, like the establishment of paternity. In spite of loosening confidentiality procedures, there are many media reports of persons seeking to "reconnect" with genetic parents. Usually, they are simply seeking to know more about their history. In this modern age, Facebook is one means by which persons seek contact.

Later in this chapter we will discuss open adoption and a state statute illustrating its parameters. As adoption often occurs when a child is older, having developed a connection with a genetic parent, open adoption statutes allow for the establishment of visitation between the genetic parents and the child post-termination of parental rights.

C. Liability of Adoption Agencies.

Courts have permitted civil suits against adoption agencies for negligence in the providing of information, failure to adequately discover and communicate defects or disabilities in the child to be adopted, and for actual fraud. One Pennsylvania decision involved a child who had been adopted in 1964. He continuously suffered from mental health issues, suicide attempts, drug abuse, and poor social interaction. He received treatment to cope with his problems, but the symptoms persisted. From 1980 through 1999, the adoptive

---

6.   UNIF. ADOPTION ACT, §§ 2–
106(a)(1)-(2), 9 U.L.A. Pt. 1A 11 et seq.
(1999).

parents sought access to the genetic mother's medical records so as to assist with treatment, and in 1999 the adoption agency gave the adoptive parents a letter from the genetic mother's psychiatrist that was in the file. The letter stated that the mother suffered from undifferentiated schizophrenia. Upon receipt of the letter, the couple filed a suit for "wrongful adoption." Specifically, the adoptive parents alleged that the agency negligently misrepresented the condition of the child and failed to disclose the mental history of the birth mother. The court ruled against the adoptive parents' petition, holding that the test of agency negligence is only what is foreseeable at the time of the placement. In 1964, when the child was adopted, schizophrenia was thought to be a product of environment, not something that was hereditary. Therefore, the agency was not liable because, at the time of the placement, the agency could not have foreseen that the mental condition of the child would result from the condition of the mother.[7]

In a related matter, adoptive parents have tried to "return" children that they consider defective. In one case from Arkansas, an adoptive couple returned a child that they had adopted to the child's abusive genetic parents. The adoptive parents were the grandparents of the child, the parents of the child's mother. Thus, the parties all knew one another. When they returned the child they claimed that they acted on the advice of the attorney for the genetic parents, even though they knew that they were placing the child in harm's way. The court ruled that the couple could not rely on the advice of the attorney in abandoning the child. Furthermore, the child was a dependent-neglected child because the adoptive parents had placed the child in harm's way.[8] Criminal and civil liability could result.

When courts permit an adoption to be abrogated, they require that the adopters demonstrate by clear and convincing evidence that the adoption occurred only through fraud or misrepresentation. Under these circumstances, the adopters would have to prove clearly and convincingly that the adoption agency procured the adoption through fraudulent conduct or misrepresentation of a material fact. While the court must be mindful of the best interest of the child or children, it must balance this against the harm committed by the agency against the adopters.[9] Thus, the court

7. Halper v. Jewish Family & Children's Service of Greater Philadelphia, 963 A.2d 1282 (Pa. 2009).

8. S.F. v. Arkansas Dep't Health and Human Serv., 274 S.W.3d 334 (Ark. Ct. App. 2008).

9. *See, e.g.,* In re Lisa Diane G., 537 A.2d 131 (R.I. 1988); CAL. FAM. CODE § 9100 (West 2004).

must decide whether to abrogate the adoption or to force the child upon the adopters.

D. Genetic Parents: Notice and Consent

When we discussed the rights of putative fathers and the establishment of registries of paternity in Chapter 7, we noted that, under the Uniform Parentage Act, Section 403, a man who registers with the state registry is entitled to notice of a pending adoption. Specifically, the provision requires that the registrant be given notice of a proceeding for adoption of, or termination of parental rights regarding, a child in a manner prescribed for service of process in a civil action. This process of registration resulted from a series of Supreme Court decisions holding that unmarried biological fathers have constitutional rights to their children, and that these rights must be protected through a notice mechanism. But the man must take the initiative in registering, and this may pose problems when some states have registries and some do not.[10]

It seems that notice to the putative father often can be sufficient, even if the notice is minimal, fraudulent, and eventually results in termination of his rights and the subsequent adoption of the child. In one Kansas decision, a man was sexually intimate with a woman. Later he became aware of the woman's pregnancy but did nothing to assist her financially or emotionally during the time. His lack of support, he asserted, stemmed from that fact that during the pregnancy, the woman told him that she planned on having an abortion during the fourth month of the pregnancy, which he asserts, signaled that he did not need to do anything for her or the baby. When the woman gave birth to the child, she lied about the identity of the father so he was not notified, and he claims that this fact should negate the adoption. Nonetheless, the court ruled that the man did not have the right to set aside the subsequent adoption of the child, and that the defective notice did not provide him with a valid argument under the Due Process Clause.[11] The court concluded that the facts of the case indicated he had sufficient notice to qualify as due process.

Notice to a parent is inextricably linked to consent. Once notified in accordance with constitutional parameters, the parent is expected to consent to the proposed termination and adoption. If not, then the parent is expected to petition for a hearing within a

10. *See generally,* Laurence C. Nolan, *Preventing Fatherlessness Through Adoption While Protecting the Parental Rights of Unwed Fathers: How Effective* *Are Paternity Registries?,* 4 WHITTIER J. CHILD & FAM. ADVOC. 289 (2005).

11. In the Adoption of A.A.T., 196 P.3d 1180 (Kan. 2008).

specified period of time. In a Utah case, a child was born to unmarried minor parents. The parents had a brief relationship prior to the birth of the child, but they had stopped seeing one another by the time the child was born. The father was notified of the child's subsequent birth, and he helped with some of the expenses involved with the newborn. Nonetheless, within sixteen days of the birth, the mother, with the assistance of her parents, surrendered the child for adoption, consenting to termination of her rights. Two months later, the father was informed of the adoption proceeding and the subsequent adoption. The father then petitioned the court to set aside the adoption as a violation of his due process and equal protection rights under the Constitution, all based on the fact that he did not consent. But the Supreme Court of Utah ruled against the father, holding that the father did not comply with the adoption code's requirements by which an unwed biological father obtains the right to consent prior to an adoption of a child.[12] The father had not filed a paternity action until more than three months after the mother had executed her consent to the adoption. In addition, even though he had helped with the infant's expenses, he never established a substantial relationship with the child. The court ruled that before a constitutionally protected due process interest may arise between a parent and a child, there must be more than a biological connection, there must be a substantial relationship. Thus, the father's petition was rejected on two grounds: First, the unwed father did not comply with the statute to secure the statutory right to consent to the adoption. Second, he did not have a substantial relationship with the child to secure a constitutional due process interest in his child that would have been adversely impacted by the termination and subsequent adoption of the child.

E. Who Can Adopt?

1. Racial and Religious Considerations

As discussed previously, the Indian Child Welfare Act of 1978, a federal statute, provides that whenever a Native American minor is involved in an adoption placement, "a preference shall be given, in the absence of good cause to the contrary, to a placement with (1) a member of the child's extended family; (2) other members of the Indian child's tribe; or (3) other Indian families."[13] The good cause exception to the application of the Act has been interpreted

---

12. In re Adoption of T.B., 232 P.3d 1026 (Utah 2010).

13. INDIAN CHILD WELFARE ACT, 25 U.S.C. §§ 1911, 1915 (2006).

to mean the following: (1) the request of the biological parent or the child, if of sufficient age; (2) the extraordinary physical or emotional needs of the child based on the testimony of experts; and (3) the unavailability of suitable Native American families for placement.[14] The placement of Native American children is the only exception to federal policy prohibiting placements based on race, color, or national origin of the individual adopters of the child [*see* the federal MULTIETHNIC PLACEMENT ACT]. But placements are often made based upon religion [*see* N.Y. Soc. Serv. Law § 373 (McKinney Supp. 2009)].

2.   Sexual Orientation

In 1977, Florida enacted a statute prohibiting adoption by practicing homosexuals. The state statute reflected the consensus of the legislature that adoption is not a right, but rather a statutory privilege. The legislature also opined that adoption is a public act, and when the state permits an adoption it is not permitting individuals the right to become parents, but rather, placing children with parents whom the state deems most capable of parenting adoptive children and providing them with a secure and stable home. The statute is unusual among the states, and it has been sustained at the federal level in spite of challenges based on due process, equal protection, and privacy.[15]

Florida state courts have repeatedly scrutinized the statute, noting that except for homosexual persons, there is no automatic exclusion of anyone from consideration for adoption. Homosexuals are singled out for disparaging treatment. In addition, state courts have noted that a homosexual is allowed to be a foster parent or a legal guardian for children, even though the same person cannot be an adoptive parent. Proponents of the ban rationalize the policy as one that provides children with better role models and less discrimination because they will be raised by heterosexual parents. But the ban against homosexuals does not compel parents to be married men and women. The state allows a child to be adopted by single parents.

In 2010, Florida's Third District Court of Appeals, basing its decision on the state's constitution, ruled that Florida's ban against adoption of children by homosexuals violated the equal protection

14. *See generally* In re Baby Boy C., 805 N.Y.S.2d 313 (N.Y. App. Div. 2005).

15. Lofton v. Secretary of the Dep't of Children and Family Serv., 358 F.3d 804 (11th Cir. 2004), *cert. denied*, 543 U.S. 1081 (2005).

of homosexuals.[16] The court ruled that there was no rational basis for the statute. The holding was narrow and specific to gay and lesbian persons. The ruling did not address allegations that the statute violated the rights of the children involved, specifically the right of children to permanency, pursuant to the federal Adoption and Safe Families Act of 1997.

The guarantee of Full Faith and Credit may assist same-sex couples in achieving a valid adoption in subsequent states. One case involved a child born in Louisiana in 2005, but then adopted by two unmarried Connecticut adult males in a New York family court. When the New York court issued its decree, the couple sent the decree to the Louisiana State Registrar so that a new birth certificate could be issued for the child, reflecting the change in parenthood. This procedure is common practice. But the Louisiana registrar refused to issue the new certificate, relying upon an opinion from the state attorney general that Louisiana did not have to recognize the adoption in another state. The attorney general argued that Full Faith and Credit of another state's decrees and judgements was not required because Louisiana had a state public policy of not allowing joint adoptions by unmarried persons.

When their petition was rejected, the same-sex parents petitioned for Full Faith and Credit of the New York adoption decree and for the birth certificate with both of their names. The couple argued that there was no public policy exception to Full Faith and Credit. But the United States Court of Appeals, Fifth Circuit, disagreed, holding that the adoption decree issued in New York was binding upon Louisiana under Full Faith and Credit. Nonetheless, Full Faith and Credit does not entitle the same-sex parents to a particular type of birth certificate. Louisiana's policy of not permitting any unmarried couples, whether adopting out-of-state or in-state, to obtain revised birth certificates with both parents' names on them is not a denial of Full Faith and Credit of the adoption itself.[17] The lengthy decision distinguishes between the decree and the mechanism of recognition in the subsequent forum.

F. Subsidized Adoptions

Subsidized adoption is an economic means by which minors may be removed from foster care placements and established in permanent homes. Subsidized adoption gained attention with the

---

16. Florida Dep't of Children & Families v. Adoption of X.X.G., 45 So.3d 79 (Fla. Dist. Ct. App. 2010); *see also* Rhonda Wasserman, *Are You Still My Mother? Interstate Recognition of Adop-*tions by Gays and Lesbians, 58 AM. U. L. REV. 1 (2008).

17. Adar v. Smith, 639 F.3d 146, 159–162 (5th Cir. 2011).

passage of the Adoption Assistance and Child Welfare Act of 1980, whereby subsidies were provided for placement of children who are hard to place. The Act provides that the state may contract with potential adopters to provide medical care for the child, plus a stipend similar to what a foster parent would receive. Thus, the distinguishing feature is that the adopters receive financial assistance from the federal government, payable through the states. In addition, the child cannot be moved by the state, as would be the case with a foster child. There are additional federal provisions to assist with adoption of children with special needs. Examples include tax credits offered to adopters, and there are general financial incentives offered to states to promote such adoptions.[18]

Virginia has a statutory procedure for subsidized adoption assistance.[19] The statute defines a special needs child as one with the following conditions: (1) physical, mental, or emotional conditions existing prior to adoption; (2) a predisposition to develop health issues leading to substantial risk of future disability; (3) individual circumstances related to age, racial or ethnic background, or a close relationship with one or more siblings. In addition to a subsidy, the adopters will receive any related fees or other expenses related to the adoption of the child, plus all expenses associated with legal costs. State assistance and subsidies will cease when the child with special needs reaches eighteen years-of-age, but if the child has handicaps that necessitate continuation of payments, then the payments may continue until the child reaches twenty-one years-of-age.

III. Adoption of Adults

When adoption was integrated into American law in the nineteenth century, its salient feature was its focus on the best interest of children involved. Thus, adoption of adults is a phenomenon in the law.[20] Nonetheless, if state statutes permit the adoption of adults, then it is available in that state and in others through the force of Full Faith and Credit. Some state statutes limit adult adoptions to situations where there is at least some informal relationship between the parties prior to the adoptee reaching majority. For example, stepparent adoption, which we discuss later in this chapter. Because both the adopter and the adoptee are

---

18. Protecting Incentives for the Adoption of Children with Special Needs Act of 2009, Pub. L. No. 111–20, 123 Stat. 1616 (2009).

19. *See* VA. CODE ANN. §§ 63.2–1300–1304 (2008).

20. *See* Walter Wadlington, *Adoption of Adults: A Family Law Anomaly*, 54 CORNELL L. REV. 566 (1969).

adults, the necessity of parental consent is eliminated, the adoptee is able to consent himself or herself. California permits adoption of unrelated adults, but limits the number to one each year, except when they are siblings of a previously adopted person or are disabled or physically handicapped.[21] New York courts will not permit the adoption of an adult if there is a sexual relationship between the adopter and the adoptee, since such a relationship is incompatible with the parent-child premise of adoption.[22] Persons of the same sex often sought to adopt their adult partners so as to provide status, but the enactment of same-sex marriage in New York state suggests that alternative means are available and the necessity to adopt will wane.

Often, adult adoption occurs in the context of inheritance. In a Nebraska decision, a woman and her brother were the beneficiaries of testamentary trusts created by their father. The trust provided that if the woman died without surviving issue, then her share of the trust would go to her brother's living issue. The woman was single and without issue herself, plus she and her brother were estranged. Therefore, in order to prevent the brother's children from inheriting her portion of the trust, she secretly adopted her fifty year-old male cousin in California. When the woman died, the cousin, as her adopted son, came forward to claim the inheritance under the terms of the trust. The surviving brother's issue challenged the adopted son's right to inherit as a child of the now deceased woman. They argued that the adopted cousin was not an issue as contemplated by the decedent in the trust provision.

The Nebraska trial court ruled in favor of the adopted son, holding that since the adoption was valid in California, it was valid in Nebraska. Furthermore, there was nothing in the language of the trust to prohibit the adopted son from taking the inheritance, which implied that the trust would need to have an express prohibition on inheritance by adopted persons. On appeal, the brother's issue argued that Nebraska did not have to recognize the California adoption since it violated Nebraska's public policy. But the Supreme Court of Nebraska affirmed the trial court, holding that there is no public policy exception to the Full Faith and Credit clause. Nebraska had to give Full Faith and Credit to the California judgement as long as there was proper jurisdiction.[23] The holding of the decision suggests that adult adoptions are valid everywhere by

21. *See* Cal. Fam. Code § 9303 (West 2004).

22. Matter of Adoption of Robert Paul P., 471 N.E.2d 424 (N.Y. 1984).

23. In re Trust Created by Nixon, 763 N.W.2d 404 (Neb. 2009); *see also*

Elrod v. Cowart, 672 S.E.2d 616 (Ga. 2009); Restatement (Third) of Property: Wills and Other Donative Transfers § 14.5 (2004).

force of the constitution if they are valid in the place where they occurred. Furthermore, unless the terms of a trust, or of a last will and testament provide otherwise, an adopted adult or child is an heir of the decedent, able to take under probate or nonprobate transfers, including trusts.

IV. Stepparent Adoption

As discussed in the first chapter of this book, family structure has changed in the United States. Increasingly, persons marry someone with a child and that new spouse then becomes a stepparent to the child. While many states statutorily mandate that the stepparent financially support the stepchild throughout the marriage, there is no legal parent-child relationship between the two. In order to create a legal relationship between the child and the stepparent, states, often relying on model acts, have enacted statutes permitting stepparent adoption to occur.[24] The effect of the stepparent adoption statute is that the child may now inherit from and through the stepparent since a legal bond has been created, and the child also may inherit from both of the genetic parents. The Uniform Probate Code provides that the genetic parent who is not married to the stepparent may not inherit from or through the child,[25] but the child may inherit from and through both genetic parents and from and through the stepparent, who is now considered a parent as a result of the adoption. Unless the stepchild is an adult and can provide consent, both genetic parents must consent to the stepparent adoption. But the consent does not terminate the parental rights of the genetic parents, a unique feature of stepparent adoption.

Stepparent adoption, as the term indicates, is restricted to persons who are married or have entered into a similar status. Thus, a person becomes a stepparent because he or she marries the genetic parent of a child. In those states that restrict marriage to persons of the opposite sex, stepparent adoption will not be available to same-sex couples unless they achieve the status through similar arrangements, such as civil unions or domestic partnerships. If stepparent adoption is not available because marriage or a similar arrangement is unavailable, the issue arises as to how a genetic parent may permit his or her child to be adopted by his or her partner without having his or her parental rights terminated in the adoption process. To illustrate, if two adult women are nonmar-

---

24. *See, e.g.,* Unif. Probate Code § 2–119(b) (2004); *see generally* Naomi Cahn, *Perfect Substitutes or the Real Thing?*, 52 Duke L. J. 1077 (2003).

25. Unif. Probate Code § 2–119(b)(2) (2004).

ital partners, but one has a child from a previous relationship, or the child is a product of assisted reproductive technology, how may the partner of the genetic parent achieve parental status? Some states permit adoption by a partner, but others will not permit the adoption without terminating the parental rights of the genetic parent.[26] The approaches among the states seem to reflect the different wording of the various state statutes. If the state permits same-sex marriage or a similar status, the solution is stepparent adoption. If not, the solution lies with any statute permitting adoption by a second parent without terminating parental rights of the genetic parent.

V.   Equitable Adoption

More than half of the states have implemented equitable adoption. Recall that adoption is a creature of statute, therefore, equitable adoption is not adoption in the strict sense of the term. Rather, it is a device to do equity; its application is very limited in scope, as it does not create a true parent-child relationship. Because it is a judicial doctrine, the theories upon which it rests vary. Most states consider the doctrine as a remedy to protect the interest of a person who was supposed to have been adopted as a child, but whose expected adoptive parents failed to do what they were supposed to do to complete the adoption.

In one case the elements of a successful application of equitable adoption are identified. The case, *Lankford v. Wright*,[27] lists the following elements as prerequisites to equitable adoption: (1) there must be some express or implied agreement between the genetic parents and the adopters that the latter will take the child; (2) there must be reliance upon the agreement; (3) the natural parents must actually surrender the incidents of custody to the adopters; (4) there must be some performance by the child within the home of the adopters; (5) there must be some performance by the adopters to indicate that they consider the child as their own; and (6) intestacy of the adopters occurs and the child seeks to inherit as a child of the adopters. In the *Lankford* decision, the majority of the Supreme Court of North Carolina held that equitable adoption had occurred between the adopters and a woman, who had been surrendered to them by her genetic parents almost fifty years earlier. Throughout the time the woman lived with the adopters

---

26. *See, e.g.,* Adoption of Tammy, 619 N.E.2d 315 (Mass. 1993) (permitting two unmarried women partners to adopt and retain parental rights); *but see,* In re Adoption of Luke, 640 N.W.2d 374 (Neb. 2002) (holding that child cannot be adopted by partner without genetic parent losing parental rights).

27. 489 S.E.2d 604 (N.C. 1997).

they were, for all intents and purposes, one family; she was their daughter and they were her parents. When the latter of the two "adopters" died, the issue was whether the woman would be able to inherit from the decedent's intestate estate.

There was a strong dissent to the decision, based on a common objection. That is, adoption is created by statute, and courts should not institute it through common law. But equitable adoption is not adoption in a strict sense. Rather, it is an equitable remedy of very limited scope. As is stated in the Uniform Probate Code, the doctrine is "an equitable remedy construed by courts to avoid what is perceived as an injustice arising from a strict application of the intestacy statutes."[28] Thus, the equitably adopted child would not be able to benefit under a trust establishing benefits to issue or descendants. Plus, doctrines such as anti-lapse do not apply. The child cannot inherit through the decedent parent, but only from an intestate parent. The scope of equitable adoption is very limited. In addition, courts require a high level of proof before application: Clear and convincing evidence of the elements previously listed is common.

VI. Open Adoption

Increasingly, various commentators have argued that genetic parents should be able to maintain some contact with the child that they have surrendered to adoptive parents.[29] Likewise, children surrendered for adoption have sought the identity of genetic parents; we have discussed this previously in connection with confidentiality. Such openness in the adoption process is a reversal of the traditional policy of maintaining strict confidentiality regarding the genetic parents.

With the advent of open adoptions, issues have arisen that include the enforceability of agreements between the genetic parents and the adoptive parents regarding such issues as visitation with the child. When we discussed the case of *Troxel v. Granville*, in connection with visitation in Chapter 9, we noted that the Supreme Court established the fundamental right of the parents to make decisions regarding the child's care, custody, and control. Any arrangement that infringes on the parent's fundamental rights may be viewed as unsupportable. Thus, if a genetic parent surrenders

28. RESTATEMENT (THIRD) OF PROPERTY: WILLS AND OTHER DONATIVE TRANSFERS § 2.5, cmt. k & Reporter's Note No. 7 (1999); *see also* ALI, *Principles of the Law of Family Dissolution: Analysis and Recommendations* §§ 2.03, 3.03 (2002).

29. *See* U.S. Dep't Health and Human Serv., Child Welfare Information Gateway, *Open Adoption*, (2003), *available at* http://www.childwelfare.gov/pubs/f_openadopt.cfm.

the child for termination of his or her parental rights, the rights commensurate with *Troxel* pass to the new adoptive parents. This is true in spite of any open adoption arrangement.

But states struggle with an approach that will allow open adoption. For example, New Mexico enacted a statute that permits the genetic parents to have contact with the child after the adoption, under a prearranged agreement with the adoptive parents. In addition, the adopters can agree to allow contact between the child and relatives of the genetic parents, most often grandparents or siblings.[30] The statute provides for the appointment of a guardian *ad litem* for the child, perhaps anticipating the need for a referee when visitation is part of the agreement, and there may be disputes between the adopters and designated persons in the future. Furthermore, the statute provides that the court retains jurisdiction in the event that future modification is required. But the statute does not lessen the consequences of the fact that the parental rights of the genetic parents have been terminated. It seems logical then, that future litigation will involve the effect of *Troxel* and the extent of a adopting parent's fundamental rights over his or her newly adopted child.

VII.   Intercountry Adoptions

Despite the large numbers of children in foster care who are or might be eligible for adoption in this country, many children are adopted from foreign countries.[31] Commentators criticize the practice as one that promotes baby-selling, colonialism, and even abuse. But advocates argue that intercountry adoption is humanitarian, and provides adopters with children who may match their own ethnicity, or provide them with an adoption that is more resistant to contest from biological parents, or the vagaries of state agencies.

Foreign adoptions are governed by state and federal laws concerning immigration, and of course laws regarding adoption in each of the individual states. The Full Faith and Credit Clause of the Constitution does not apply to foreign adoptions, only adoption judgements of the individual states of the Union. One of the significant international laws to affect these adoptions is the Hague Convention on the Protection of Children and Cooperation in

---

30. N.M. STAT. ANN. § 32A–5–35 (West 2006); *see also* TEX. FAM. CODE § 161.206(c) (West 2008) (permitting post-adoption visitation by grandparents).

31. Rose Kreider, ADOPTION FACTBOOK IV, *Foreign Born Adopted Children in the U.S.*, 138–139 (2000) (reporting that in 2000, 13% of adopted children in U.S. were foreign born).

Respect of Intercountry Adoption,[32] which has been enacted by the United States and ratified in 2007. The overriding concern of the Convention is to protect children from becoming victims of international adoption trafficking. In addition, the Convention establishes a system of cooperation among countries, thereby promoting the best interest of the children and enforcement of intercountry adoptions. Approximately seventy-five countries have implemented the Convention.

Among countries sending the most children to the United States for adoption were China, Guatemala, and India. Non–Convention countries sending children were Ethiopia, Kazakhstan, Liberia, Russia, South Korea, Ukraine, and Vietnam. From 2004 until 2007, China was the greatest source of intercountry adoptions; in 2008, the State Department issued more than 17,000 immigrant visas to children adopted from foreign countries.[33] The Children's Bureau of the U.S. Department of Health and Human Services has a chart comparing the differences between a Convention and a Non–Convention country. Important among the differences existent in Hague Convention countries is that primary providers must be accredited or approved by the Council on Accreditation (COA). Among the requirements specified are that for Hague Adoptions, prospective parents must be habitually resident in the United States, and the child must be habitually resident in a Hague country. If both parents of the adopted child are living, they may release the child for adoption if they are incapable of caring for the child. When only one parent is living, he or she need not show inability to provide care for the child. As in the United States, the Convention requires that the adoption be in the best interest of the child. Typically, the adoption takes place in the foreign country, and then the child is eligible to travel to the United States. If a foreign child is adopted by a citizen of the United States, the child automatically becomes a citizen of the United States. Then, once the child enters the United States, there must be another adoption procedure so that the adopters' state recognizes the foreign adoption.

The Convention cannot completely prevent the possibility of payments to parents; the possibility of payments becoming a motivating factor is a reality.[34] Nonetheless, an adoption within the

---

32. *See generally* Ann Laquer Estin, *Families Across Borders: The Hague Children's Convention and the Case for International Family Law in the Case for International Family Law in the United States*, 62 FLA. L. REV. 47 (2010).

33. *See* U.S. Dep't of State, Annual Report on Intercountry Adoptions (2009), *available at* http://adoption.state. gov/content/pdf/Adoption_Report_v9_SM.pdf.

34. *See generally* UNICEF's Position on Inter–Country Adoption, *available at* http://www.unicef.org/media/media_41918.html.

scope of the Convention shall take place only if the competent authorities of the receiving state are convinced that the prospective parents are fit, and that the child will be eligible to enter into the United States and remain there permanently. The fact that the Convention requires a Central Authority to supervise all facets of the adoption process adds a layer of protection to the process heretofore absent. This Central Authority has the ability to utilize ethnicity, something forbidden under domestic adoptions. And the fact that there must be a medical report concerning the child offers some assurance against future abrogation.

TABLE OF INTERNET CITATIONS

Adoption

http://www.childwelfare.gov/adoption/ [Resources on all aspects of domestic and intercountry adoption.]

http://statistics.adoption.com/ [Adoption statistics regarding trends, costs, filings, etc.]

http://www.childwelfare.gov/pubs/f_openadopt.cfm [Discussing the trend of open adoptions, in which the genetic parents are allowed to maintain contact with the child after adoption is finalized.]

http://adoption.state.gov/content/pdf/Adoption_Report_v9_SM.pdf [U.S. Department of State's 2009 Annual Report on Intercountry Adoptions.]

http://www.unicef.org/media/media_41918.html [UNICEF's general position on Intercountry Adoptions.]

Assisted Reproductive Technology

http://www.usccb.org/comm/Dignitaspersonae/Dignitas_Personae.pdf [Congregation for the Doctrine of the Faith, Instruction Dignitas Personae on Certain Bioethical Questions, 2008. Addressing ethical and moral concerns in cryopreservation procreation assistance.]

http://www.sart.org/ [Society for Assisted Reproductive Technologies is the primary organization of professionals associated with the practice of assisted reproductive technology in the U.S.]

http://www.cdc.gov/art/ [Center for Disease Control and Prevention resource center on assisted reproductive technology facts and statistics.]

Divorce

http://www.legalzoom.com/divorce-guide/state-divorce-procedures.html [Divorce procedures and requirements for each state.]

http://www.divorcehq.com/divorce-separation-agreements.shtml [Separation agreement examples and procedures.]

http://www.census.gov/hhes/socdemo/marriage/ [U.S. Census Bureau Marriage and Divorce statistics resource center.]

http://www.dealwithdivorce.com/effects-divorce/emotional-effects-divorce-children/30/ [Emotional and psychological effect of divorce on children.]

http://www.nycourts.gov/divorce/forms.shtml [Divorce resources from the New York State Court Unified System.]

Foster Care

http://www.childwelfare.gov/systemwide/statistics/childwelfare_foster.cfm [These resources provide state and national data on the number of children in the child welfare system, trends in foster care caseloads, and well-being outcomes.]

http://www.fosterparenting.com/foster-care/state-foster-parent-training-requirements.html [Foster care requirements in general, as each state has different rules, regulations and procedures or guidelines to follow.]

http://www.nacac.org/ [North American Council on Adoptable Children.]

Marital Status Alternatives and Cohabitation

http://www.cdc.gov/nchs/data/series/sr_23/sr23_028.pdf [Marriage and Cohabitation statistics in the United States 2002.]

http://news.change.org/stories/a-few-statistics-on-lgbt-issues [Same-sex marriage and cohabitation statistics and trends.]

Termination of Parental Rights

http://www.childwelfare.gov/pubs/factsheets/foster.cfm#place [Foster care statistics from 2009, discussing the federal foster care requirements.]

http://www.acf.hhs.gov/programs/cb/pubs/cm06 [Citing child abuse and neglect statistics from 2006 as reported by the U.S. Department of Health and Human Services.]

http://www.childwelfare.gov/systemwide/laws_policies/statutes/define.pdf [Listing the individual state statutory definitions of child abuse and neglect.]

TABLE OF CASES

References are to pages

INDEX

References are to Pages

---

†